بسم الله الرحمن الرحيم

FAMILY

From the Islamic and Psychological Points of View

FAMILY

FROM THE ISLAMIC AND PSYCHOLOGICAL POINTS OF VIEW

Muḥammad Reḍā Sālārīfar

Translated by

Mehdī Āzādī

British Library Cataloguing-in-Publication Data
A catalogue record for this book is available from the British Library.

ISBN: 978-1-911361-32-9 (pbk)

This English edition first published in 2016

Islam and West Research Center Ltd
3, Research Center, Golders Green
London NW11 8ED

Ordering Information:
Quantity sales. Special discounts are available on quantity purchases by corporations, associations, and others. For details, contact the distributor at the address below.

Shia Books Australia
www.shiabooks.com.au
info@shiabooks.com.au

ISBN 978-1-911361-32-9

Second Edition 2021

CONTENTS

Preface IX
Transliteration XI
Introduction 1
Chapter 1: The Islamic Outlook on Marriage 5
Introduction 7
1. The History of Discourse on the Family According to Islām 7
2. Definition of the Family 14
3. Stages of Development in the Family 17
4. The Developmental Stages of the Family 17
5. The Appropriate Time for Marriage 20
6. Advice for Selecting a Spouse 23
6. 1. Common Criteria for Choosing a Spouse 24
6. 2. Characteristics of an Appropriate Spouse According to Islām 27
6. 3. Priorities Within the Various Criteria 28
6. 4. Various Objectives and Different Types of Marriage 33
Chapter 2: The Psychological Effects of Marriage 43
1. Satisfying Sexual Desire 45
2. Peace of Mind 49
3. Growth and Development of the Personality 52
4. Preparing the Ground for Bringing Up a Child 53
5. Expanding Social Relationships Through Blood Ties 55
5.1. The Importance of Family Relations 55
5.2. Types of Family Relations 57
5.3. Family Relations Following the Marriage 57
5.4. The Effects of Family Relations 59
5.5. The Effects of Cutting off Family Ties 61
5.6. Levels of Family Relations in Islām 62
5.7. Problems in Family Relations 63

Chapter 3: The Pillars of the Family 73
1. The Mutual Responsibilities of Husband and Wife 75
1.1. Primary Compatibility 75
1.2. Continuity of Optimum Relations 76
2. Responsibilities of the Parents 78
3. Responsibilities of Children 81
3.1. Duties of Children Towards the Parents 82
3.2. Duties of Children Towards Each Other 85
4. Hierarchy in the Family 86
5. Boundaries within the Family 89
5.1. Boundaries within the Family According to Structuralism 90
A. The Concept of Boundaries within the Family 90
B. Boundary Problems 91
C. Making Boundaries in Treatment 91
5.2. Boundaries in the Family According to Islām 91
A. Boundaries within the Family 92
B. Boundaries of the Family and Society 94
C. Boundaries in Sexual Relationships 94
D. The Religious Dress Code and the Limits of Relationships Between Men and Women 96
Chapter 4: Guidelines for the Efficiency and Proper Development of the Family 105
1. The Role of Religious Insight in the Family 107
1.1. Belief in God 107
1.2. The Belief in the Divine Mission and Imamate 109
1.3. Belief in the Afterlife 110
2. Moral Advice for Further Efficiency within the Family 112
2.1. Honesty 112
2.2. Optimism 113
2.3. Contentment 114
2.4. Patience 115
2.5. Generosity 116
3. Behavioural Teachings of Islām for Desirable Family Efficiency 117
3.1. Verbal Communication 117
3.2. Nonverbal Communication 118
3.3. The Home Environment 119
3.4. Running Household Affairs 121
3.5. Worshipping in the Family 122

Chapter 5: The Teachings of Islām and Family Problems 131
1. Factors Affecting Family Conflicts 133
1.1. Psychological Factors 134
1.2. Social and Cultural Factors 136
1.3. Economic Factors 137
1.4. Physical Factors 138
1.5. Religious Factors 139
2. Ways to Prevent Family Disputes in the Teachings of Islām 141
2.1. Attention to the Selection of an Appropriate Marriage Partner 141
2.2. Training the Spouses 142
2.3. Religious Education 143
2.4. Observing Boundaries in the Family 143
2.5. Consultation and Agreement with Others in the Family 144
3. Ways to Settle Family Disputes According to the Teachings of Islām 146
3.1. Accepting the Obligations of Family Hierarchy 146
3.2. Solving Emotional and Sexual Problems 147
The Qur'án and the Settlement of Family Disputes 147
3.3. Consultation and Arbitration 150
3.4. Separation of the Husband and Wife 152
Chapter 6: The Family System in Islām 161
1. The Psychological Effects of the Economic Laws of Islām … 163
1.1. The Marriage Portion or Dowry 163
1.2. Living Costs 166
1.3. Inheritance 167
2. Model Families in Islām 168
2.1. Facing the Marriage 168
2.2. The Prophet's Treatment of His Wives 169
2.3.The Prophet's Attitude Towards Children 170
2.4. The Way Imam 'Alī and Ḥaḍrat Fátima Lived 171
2.5. The Family Practice of the Other Imams 173
3. The General Outline of the Family System in Islām 173
3.1. The Comprehensiveness of Islām's View of the Family 174
3.2. The Most Important Health Strategies and the Appropriate Functioning of the Family in Islām 175
3.3. A Final Word 178
Bibliography 187
Index 203

PREFACE

Considering necessity of preparing appropriate Islamic texts in English for the modern world and aiming at satisfying that need, Al-Mustafa International Research Institute (M.I.R.I.) decided to establish "Islam and West Research Centre" in 2009. This centre has accomplished that duty in the best way by producing, translating, and reprinting tens of such appropriate texts.

The present book entitled *family from the islamic and psychological points of view* , which is published in Farsi by the Organization for Researching and Composing University textbooks in the Humanities (S.A.M.T) and Research Institute of the Ḥawzah and University (R.I.H.U), , is among works translated and published by Islam and West Research Centre.

This book is a response to the widespread need for references and textbooks reflecting the Islamic viewpoint, in both the various disciplines of the humanities in universities and the specialist faculties of scientific and research centres. It is a committed answer to this need, that can be used by these institutions to approach their common goals and, in addition to improve both the quality and quantity of educational references, avoid repeated work.

We hope that this book should form a link showing the way for those who seek advancement.

Islam and West Research Center (I.W.R.C.)

TRANSLITERATION

Arabic characters	Roman Equivalent	Arabic characters	Roman Equivalent
ء	ʾ	ى	y
ب	b	ة	ah ; at (construct state)
ت	t		
ث	th		
ج	j		
ح	ḥ	**Long Vowels**	
خ	kh	آ ; ى	ā
د	d	ـُو	ū
ذ	dh	ـِي	ī
ر	r		
ز	z	**Short Vowels**	
س	s	ـَ	a
ش	sh	ـُ	u
ص	s	ـِ	i
ض	ḍ		
ط	t	**Diphthongs**	
ظ	z	ـَو	aw
ع	ʿ	ـَي	ai ; ay
غ	gh		
ف	f		
ق	q	**Persian letters added to the Arabic alphabet**	
ك	k		
ل	l		
م	m	پ	p
ن	n	چ	ch
ه	h	ژ	zh
و	w ; v	گ	g

INTRODUCTION

Family is one of the first systems in the human community which, despite all other developments, has remained the same and preserved its essential significance. It is the most appropriate system for fulfilling the material, psychological and spiritual needs of man and the best arena for providing psychological peace and security for its members, bringing up the new generation, and fulfilling the emotional needs. Nevertheless, in the contemporary era, the family system has suffered basic problems and met with basic challenges that sometimes even questioned its integrity. Due to the social, industrial and scientific developments, in most societies, including Iran, numerous problems have been created for the family. Family disputes, divorce, guardianless children, adolescent and juvenile delinquency all indicate essential problems in our families. Traditions, morals and methods that strengthen the family have been somehow shaken, and the abandonment of national and religious identities to adopt materialistic values with no morality threatens many of our people.

All of these problems indicate that families require a great deal of educational and psychological advice in order to tackle the complexities of modern life. Nowadays, bringing up children and establishing appropriate spousal relationships are not such easy tasks as they were a few decades ago. Factors affecting the family are so numerous that, in order to handle the damaging factors, we need to train and educate families at the national level. The interesting point is that we have a notable and effective cultural and scientific history of dealing with family problems. Our most important religious texts, i.e. the Qur'ān, the words of the Prophet and his household (Ahl al-Bayt) are full of effective advice for even the smallest details of family life. The sum of Islamic teachings concerning the family offers us a structure for all the material, psychological and spiritual needs of the family.

In addition to the structure of the family – its internal and external boundaries and levels – the meaning of the formation of the family can also be inferred from the Islamic texts. Islamic teachings have much binding moral advice regarding the nature of the relationships between family members, their mutual rights and responsibilities. The words and family practice of the Prophet and his household illustrate many of the fine points of behavioural traits that, although seemingly minor, play an essential role in consolidating the foundations of the family. In this book, we began the discussions of the family by defining the family, marriage and its preliminaries – such as what to look for in a spouse – and then deal with the psychological effects of marriage and relationships within the family, with an explanation of the relevant Islamic viewpoints.

Various aspects of marriage and family relationships and their effects are examined. Chapter 3 deals with the foundations of the family and the responsibilities of the husband and wife, parents and children. Chapter 4 looks at the role of religious beliefs, ethics and behaviour in Islām. Chapter 5 deals with factors in family problems and the solutions Islām offers for preventing and solving them. Chapter 6 deals with the family economy from Islamic and psychological point of view. Finally, family models in Islām are outlined. Since most studies of this kind approach these topics from either an Islamic or psychological viewpoint, in the various discussions presented here we have considered both points of view. While humbly admitting any shortcomings on the part of the author, it is hoped that this study will help clarify some of the psychological and religious problems relating to the family. While praying for the assistance of the Pure Family, it is my fervent hope that families will flourish spiritually and morally. I welcome criticism and suggestions from researchers and specialists in family matters, especially family therapists, in order to be able to eliminate any deficiencies.

Finally, I would like to express my appreciation for their contributions to the following: Professor Sayyid Muḥammad Gharavī, head of the

Psychology Group at R.I.H.U, who supervised the discussions in this study, Dr. Muḥammad Kāzim 'Ātif Wahīd for his guidance throughout the project, Dr. Bihishtī, Dr. Mazāhiri and Dr. Fatḥī Āshtiānī for their beneficial views.

The authorities at R.I.H.U, especially professor Dr. 'Alī Reḍā A'rāfī, whose generous support provided me with this research opportunity.

Muḥammad Reḍā Sālārīfar

CHAPTER 1

THE ISLAMIC OUTLOOK ON MARRIAGE

INTRODUCTION

The family is a human institution of fundamental importance in society. The effect of the family on the growth, balance and well-being of individuals and society is so great that it cannot be denied. Therefore, all philosophers and specialists in the humanities since the beginning of written history have offered guidance regarding the family. The divinely revealed religions have also provided important teachings in this regard, because of the important role of the family in ethics, spirituality and Islām, the last revealed religion, contains useful edicts and teachings regarding various aspects of family life. Islām presents marriage and the family as the most loved[1] and the dearest[2] of institutions before God. According to a Ḥadīth of the Prophet Muḥammad:

> "The gates of Heaven are opened when a marriage contract is concluded, and when a child looks at his parents face to face."[3]

In this introduction, we will examine the history of Islamic discourse on the family.

1. The History of Discourse on the Family According to Islām

According to Islamic texts, since the beginning of the existence of mankind, God has chosen prophets from among the people to steadily guide them in conduct appropriate for life within society, including that of the formation of the family. Since the family has a substantial effect on the entire life of the individual and all aspects of society, all religions have given it special attention. As the final religion, a major part of the laws and guidance of Islām is allocated to the family. Particular norms for family life are defined, which have affected many of the models relating to marriage and the family in a major part of the world, thus establishing an ideal basic standard for the family.[4] The Prophet Muḥammad and the religious leaders have paid attention to family issues and guided individuals in respect of family relationships, even in very private marital matters. They directed the people and solved their problems with regard to selecting a spouse, the quality of family relations, the treatment of children and the different kinds of affective relationships within the family. This book examines the teachings of Islām in respect of the family. The main texts of Islām consist of the Qur'ān and the words of the Prophet and his household (Ahl al-Bayt)[5] (*hadiths*). The accuracy and validity of the Qur'ān has been proven by its successive transmission among Muslims throughout the centuries. The words of the Prophet and his household have been retained in various narratives, including *Biḥār al-Anwār*, *Wasā'il al-Shī'a* and other reliable sources. At the beginning of the discussion, it is therefore appropriate to examine the history of this topic from the Islamic viewpoint.

Muslims scholars since the early days of Islām have paid attention to family issues and emphasised the mutual rights and duties of family members. Here we will mention some of the prominent theories of the past centuries, as well as some of the ideas of contemporary experts on the family, in order to clarify the Islamic perspective on the family throughout the course of history.

1.1. Ibn Sīnā (Avicenna): This great Muslim philosopher and scientist of the fourth and fifth centuries AH examined the importance of the family and its foundations, and the relationships between the husband and wife and their children. He defines the purpose of the formation of the family as economically and socially motivated, as well as a means for love, peace and the fulfilment of sexual needs. He considered the wife to be the husband's economic partner and trustee, his colleague and companion in running the household, and a support of his peace of mind. Ibn Sīnā believed that marriage must be governed by certain principles in order to be perfect.

Firstly, people should be encouraged to marry in order to guarantee the continuation of humanity.

The marriage ceremony should be performed in public so that the familial relationships are made clear. The marriageable age is subject to a certain degree of physical and mental maturity, so that the two partners are able to manage a family. Ibn Sīnā mentions desirable characteristics in the woman, which are mainly taken from the main texts of Islām. Some of these characteristics are: reason, perspicacity, modesty, religiosity, kindness, the ability to give birth to children, deference to and trust in the husband, dignity, respect and the capacity to bring contentment to the spouse.

According to Ibn Sīnā, the man should consider three principles regarding the wife and the administration of the family:

A. Mutual Respect: This is the providential basis of the family; it remedies defects and weaknesses, and without it the relationship between husband and wife does not have a sound basis. The respect of the husband for the wife involves remaining sincere, protecting his faith and high standards, and fulfilling his promises. If a man does not enjoy a certain degree of deference and respect from his wife, she will tend to belittle him, have no regard for him, and try to manage and provide for the family without him. Ibn Sīnā warns against this, since he believed that a woman should not be principally responsible for managing the family.

B. Reverence: The husband should hold the wife in high regard and revere her. When the wife sees how much the husband thinks of her, she will reciprocate by trying to protect this, and this will result in mutual respect and reverence. According to Ibn Sīnā, this is the right way to behave with a woman, while compulsion and threats lead nowhere.

C. Employment: The husband should ensure that his wife has plenty to do around the house and with the raising of children, so that she does not have the leisure to do things that would damage a healthy relationship.[6]

While greatly emphasising love in the family and the continuation of the familial bond, Ibn Sīnā allows for divorce in exceptional circumstances and according to specific circumstances in agreement with the Sharīʿa. In his opinion, attempts should be made to help reconcile differences between the couple, and it is only when there is no hope of marital compatibility that one should consent to separation. Moreover, the right of divorce should be vested in the man rather than in the woman, or, in a case where the man is incompetent, in a judge, because this has very important repercussions on the family. Ibn Sīnā places the responsibility for children mainly with the parents, and has defined certain duties in accordance with their stage of development. He states that one of the basic purposes of marriage is to bring up children who are worthy to enter society.[7]

1.2. Ghazālī: This 5th century AH scholar presents moral discussions in which he describes the following protocols for family life:

1: The marriage should be celebrated with festivities.
2: The man should treat his wife well, so as not to upset her, and even her harsh words and errors should be tolerated.
3: He should have a sense of humour and be kind to his wife, seeking mutual understanding.
4: However, he should moderate his humour and kindness in order to preserve a deferential atmosphere and his own authority.
5: He should observe a path of self-restraint to protect his honour.
6: He should not be too restrictive in providing living expenses, whilst at the same time avoiding extravagant spending. He should eat with the family and never eat alone.
7: He should not fail to provide sufficient opportunities for the wife to learn about the religion.
8: If he has more than one wife, he should treat each of them justly.
9: If the wife is disobedience, he should treat her gently and tenderly.
10: In sexual matters, the pleasure of both parties should be taken into consideration. This is actually the husband's duty towards the wife. The wife has more important duties, such as always keeping herself clean so as to be a good companion. She should not boast of her beauty in front of her husband. She should seek his happiness and avoid unduly getting angry and finding faults. She should be economical with the husband's properties and preserve his well-being, and not reveal any marital differences to others.[8]

1.3. Nasīr al-Dīn Tūsī: A 7th century AH scholar, he considered respect, reverence and mutual participation in activities as necessary ingredients regarding the husband's providence and treatment of the wife. As for revering and respecting the wife, he says:

> "The husband should care about the economic circumstances and appearance of the wife, and how they may be improved. He provide proper clothing for her, consult her on family issues, give her freedom in matters of home management, whilst preventing her from taking a dominant role. He should be on good terms with her relatives, and if he sees merit and competence in her, avoid preferring other women to her, because a woman's jealousy disturbs matters at home, and results in a lack of cooperation, hence disruption; for the husband in the home is like the heart in the body, and a heart cannot support two bodies, which is why a man cannot manage two homes."

According to Tūsī, the husband should avoid getting involved in home management. In order to satisfy the husband, the wife should always observe chastity, respect him, be kind to him, treat him well, and cooperate in sexual matters. She should also avoid scolding him. As regards the husband and wife relationship, Tūsī says:

> "The wife is like his mother and friend. She is like the husband's mother in that he wishes for her presence at home, since her absence is difficult for him. She is like his friend in that she should be contented and not expect too much in life. Therefore, she should excuse him for any shortcomings, and bring comfort to his life."[9]

1.4. Fayḍ al-Kāshānī : In his works, this scholar of the 11th century AH pays special attention to the psychological aspects of marriage and family life, while examining the peace that results from the husband and wife relationship. In his opinion, without appropriate relationships in family life, it would be hard to deal with the difficulties and boredom of daily life. He quotes the Divine Leaders by saying that someone who has fled from the family is like a slave whose prayers and fasting will not be accepted unless and until he returns. Moreover, an individual who fails to properly fulfil his family duties is like an escaped slave, even if present among the family. Fayḍ declares one of the parental duties towards children as being one's behaviour towards the wife and in family life. He mentions as an example his fatherly advice to his daughter upon her marriage for establishing a balanced spiritual life:

> "My daughter, from the nest in which you grew up, you are going to a place you do not know very well, in order to be with a companion whom you are not used to being with. Be humble towards him, so that he will make you proud. Be a cradle to him, so that you may rely on him. Obey him, so that he will obey you. Do not provoke his anger and do no avoid him. If he approaches you, you should approach him as well. If he avoids you, you should avoid him as well."[10]

1.5. 'Allāma Tabātabā'ī: In *Tafsīr al-Mīzān*, while examining the verses relating to issues on family life, he explained that the creation of Man was accomplished in such a way that the husband and wife physically complement each other, while each on their own is incomplete and has need of the other. This need results in the man and the woman moving towards each other and achieving peace. In his opinion, this is one of the greatest and most obvious blessings of nature, because it is the foundation of the human community and is the reason why there is cooperation between individuals. As for the friendship and kindness between husband and wife, he says:

> "Friendship is a love whose effect is manifested in one's behaviour and kindness, and is a psychological effect that happens when one sees another's need or blemish and is provoked to help them. The small social group of the family is the most obvious manifestation of friendship and kindness, because the husband and wife always accompany each other and express feelings towards each other, as does the woman especially towards the smaller children. This love and friendship motivates the parents to work for the protection, sustenance and upbringing of the children."[11]

As for the hierarchy within the family, following the Qur'ānic verse: *Men are guardians of women* (4:34), he says that the man is the protector of the family, and he explains this by mentioning certain aspects of social life and the natural attributes of the man and the woman. The need for the man's strength and the woman's softness and receptivity is something that all people more or less believe, and this is sometimes reflected in the various languages of the world by calling a non-submissive person "man-like" and a soft-natured person "effeminate." Islām has accepted this natural law in its legislation and precepts, and made strength the responsibility of the man.

Because of normally a man's physical strength and the woman's affective capacities and tender nature, the man has been given the role of guardian. Another reason for this responsibility is the administration of the economic affairs of the family, which is to be undertaken by the man as provider. The man is the woman's protector in marital affairs, which places him in control and accountable, while the woman should comply with her husband in such matters and other related issues. This does not mean that he should either deprive her of her rights to property, her independence in individual and social concerns, or the protection of her assets.

In other words, since he is the provider, she should cooperate with him as a complementary partner, which includes matters of a sexual nature.[12]

1.6. Muṭahharī: A great deal of importance is given in the works of Muṭahharī to marriage, including the elucidation of Islamic edicts in respect of the needs of contemporary man. According to him, Islām greatly insists that the family environment should be fully conducive to the mutual contentment of the husband and wife. The man or woman who fails in this is clearly reproached. According to Muṭahharī, of all the revealed religions, Islām pays the most attention to the sexual element of family life, and illustrates its sacred aspect. In the emotional dimension, the family environment is the place where the deepest feelings emerge, and is the source of other emotional relationships within society. An interesting facet of Muṭahharī's viewpoint is its similarity to the systems theory,[13] in which the individual is at the service of the system, and the relationships between the components should be so that the entire family as a unit can achieve its intended objectives. According to him, marriage is the first step that man takes from the love of self to the love of the other. Before marriage, there was only a single ego for which everything was done. The first phase is that in which this ego is broken, and another being is juxtaposed to it, becomes meaningful for it, does things for it and serves it, rather than it fending for itself. Then, when the two become parents, the "(s)he" becomes "they" and the ego is often overlooked.[14]

In his opinion, the marital relationship is composed of various aspects which create an environment where the future generation is accepted and their happiness is provided for. The capable hands of creation have ensured a strong love between the husband and wife on the one hand, and between the parents and the child on the other, in order for the future generation to emerge, be nurtured and to endure. Communal human kindliness grows within the family. The natural innate warmth of the parents encourages the child's soul to be mild and responsive. When we recognise the affection between two people, we may extend it to say that the individuals in a nation are like brothers and sisters to each other. According to a Qur'ānic analogy, the pure affections of devout people are like brotherly affections: *The believers are naught else than brothers.*[15] Brotherly affection is not created only by blood relations. The main point is that two brothers grow up in a family in the same centre of love, and this brotherly affection is the source of affection within society.[16] In general, certain points can be drawn from this regarding the psychology of the family. The discussion of the family hierarchy and the higher authority of the man are agreed upon by all these scholars, and the duties and boundaries of the family members are described to a certain extent. Factors that cause malfunction within the family are discussed, and preventive measures taken into account. The psychological states of both the husband and the wife and those that consolidate relationships within the family are taken into consideration.

2. Definition of the Family

The family is a small intermediary group situated between the individual and society. Scholars have provided various definitions of the family, each of which considers one aspect of the family. Therefore, it would perhaps be appropriate to define the basic features of the family as follows:

A. It is based on marriage, and is a foundational social institution.

B. Blood relations or documented relations (in the adoption of children) can be found therein.

C. There is usually a shared location.

D. It usually assumes various personal, physical, economic and educational functions, and so forth.

The family is like a mirror that reflects all the main elements of society, as well as social disorders. At the same time, it is strongly affected by society. One might say that: "A healthy society is possible only with healthy families."[17] The teachings of Islām also emphasise these characteristics in the family. According to these teachings, the family is a collection of people related by marriage or by blood (parents, children and siblings). These individuals have social, legal, educational, behavioural, economic and religious responsibilities towards each other, depending on the specific relationship. Accordingly, the family consists of the nuclear and extended family. Nevertheless, considering the degree of responsibility and the economic, social and behavioural rights of family members in view of each other, the Islamic family consists of three levels:

-1: The husband, the wife and their children;

-2: The husband, the wife, and their parents (the grandparents of the children in the first level);

-3: The husband, the wife, the grandparents and the siblings of the grandparents (uncles and aunts of the children in the first level).

This prioritisation is based on the responsibilities of the wife and the husband to each other, parents towards the children, the children towards their grandparents, the siblings of the mother and the father, the economic rules of Islām, such as alimony, inheritance and religious tax, and common laws such as the guardianship of the paternal grandfather and the blood money of paternal kinsmen. Most verses of the Qur'ān that relate to the members of the family are to do with the first level,[18] with fewer verses concerning the second level,[19] and still fewer – such as those relating to inheritance – mention the third level.[20] Figure 1 shows the three levels of the family, and illustrates how person A belongs to six family groups: two first-level families, two second-level families, and two third-level families.

- First-level family: the husband, the wife and their children, and the husband's brother, sister, father and mother.
- Second-level family: the husband, the wife, their children, and the grandparents.
- Third-level family: the husband, the wife, their children, the children's grandparents, and the children's aunts, uncles and cousins.

Figure 1: Types of family in Islām

by using the relations chart in *An Introduction to Sociology of the Family*, p. 191.

Husband

wife

Relation by marriage

Relation by blood

1st-level relatives

2nd-level relatives

3rd-level relatives

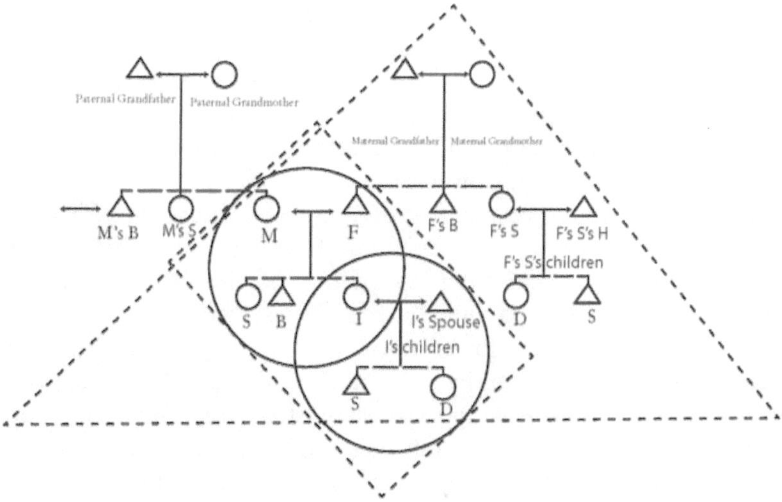

F: Father; M: Mother; B: Brother: S: Sister: H: Husband: W: Wife: D: Daughter; I: Individual

This definition of the family is based on the responsibilities of various individuals regarding other members of the immediate family and the extended family group, and shows the various functions concerning marriage and the formation of the family according to the teachings of Islām, which define a strategy for happiness in this world and the next, and provide for the well-being of people – which includes the formation of the family. Within this strategy, man's natural needs and all social conditions throughout history are taken into consideration. Therefore, social changes, especially those contemporary developments which have drastically affected the family and occasionally prepared the ground for moving further away from the objectives of the formation of the family, should not invalidate a proper definition of the family or cause us to be unable to realise the objectives of the family. One should therefore work within social change towards the formation and continuation of the family, in order to guarantee the happiness and well-being of the people. One can take steps in this regard in those societies with an Islamic culture. Strengthening family relationships is one of the guidelines for helping families to realise these objectives. The nature of the relationships with relatives in the second- and third-level family is examined more in Chapter 2. In the other chapters, discussions concerning first-level relatives are presented, although in certain cases issues that concern second- and third-level relatives are also considered.

In addition, in a similar way to the systems theory, the family is considered as a social unit that is more than the sum of its parts. Evidence for this is the responsibility of individuals within the family regarding economics and education. In the Qur'ān, attention is paid to the otherworldly happiness of both the individual and the family, for God asks people to save not only themselves, but also their families from the pain of Hell.[21] In addition, God addresses the Prophet and tells him to call his family to prayer.[22] Verses pointing out the effect of the children's behaviour on the spiritual development of the parents[23] further stress the strong interdependence of the family members in matters of this world and the afterlife. The sensitivity of the prophets towards their families and concern for their guidance[24] is further evidence of the interdependence of each member of the family. The strength of these relationships was such that sometimes the prophets prayed that members of their families might be saved, and since these individuals insisted on a wrong path, God reprimanded the prophets for praying for them.[25]

3. Stages of Development in the Family

Psychologists have defined various developmental stages in social groups, ranging from their formation to their expiration.[26] The family also passes through several stages during the passage of time, and every family can be said to be in one or another of these stages. The family is not a static social unit, but a process of constant change. The entry of individuals into the family or their exit from it causes changes within the family. If we consider change as normal in human life, we should understand that the family is very flexible, in constant fluctuation, or more or less in a state of imbalance. As with all living organisms, the family inclines towards its continued existence, and changes are sometimes made for its survival and to maintain a balance. In the development of the family, four stages are generally considered (the 2-person unit of husband and wife, the family with small children, the family with schoolchildren or adolescent children, and the family with grown-up children);[27] but there are sometimes up to nine stages, as follows:

1. The selection of a spouse and the engagement;
2. Couples without children;
3. Families with children under 30 months;
4. Families with pre-school children (2.5-6 years old);
5. Families with schoolchildren (6-13 years old);
6. Families with adolescent children (13-20 years old);
7. Families whose young children have separated from them;
8. Middle-aged parents;
9. Family members in old age.[28]

Duval believes there are eight developmental stages in the family, but the stage of selecting a spouse, although before marriage, should be considered important.[29] Although a general model for the development of the family has been presented above, one should recognise that each family has its own benefits, coordination, rhythm and experiences, or lack thereof, which should be taken into consideration in allowing for a general referential framework of family development.

4. The Developmental Stages of the Family

Marriage is an important turning-point and the beginning of a family and, from various individual, biological and social points of view, is the most common formal ceremony. It is directed towards a stable goal. The process consists of the interaction of a man and a woman who have fulfilled certain legal conditions. Marriage creates a balance between society and nature that is essentially sacred. It enjoys a unique integrity compared to other human relationships, in the sense that it includes the biological, economic, emotional, psychological and social dimensions of life.[30]

The teachings of Islām emphasise the above aspects of marriage, although some are considered more important than others. Islām considers marriage as a contract with special conditions.[31] Compared with other religions, Islām generally has more conditions for marriage, although it recognises marriage in other cultures according to their own conditions.[32] The next stage is the consolidation of this contract. The Qur'ān considers marriage a "strong foundation,"[33] and phrases uttered by both parties in the wording of the marriage ceremony, which each party accept, indicate this solid bond.[34] Some of the phrases are taken from the Qur'ān, and they form the basis of the pledge that the husband and wife should continue their lives together in a good and appropriate manner, and that should they wish to separate, they should do so with a kindly attitude.[35] At the same time, the Qur'ān speaks of the marital bond as the most solid social contract that can be established for enduring friendship and mutual kindness between a man and a woman.[36] This friendship is the strongest of such experiences, for which one trusts the other and leaves parents, brothers and sisters, and indeed one's entire family of birth, to live with someone who is unrelated by blood, and to be with them in good times as well as bad. A sign of God in the creation of man is the psychological attraction men and women have for each other, for which they would agree to leave their kin in order to be with a stranger, give each other peace, and establish a profound relationship. It is apparent that a man and a woman would only consent to marriage if they were convinced of the depth of their relationship and the goodness of a life in common. This intrinsic agreement is above and beyond sexual satisfaction, and the mutual trust of the man and the woman exceeds that of any other human relationship. It is such things that make marriage a solid contract.[37]

Another psychological effect of marriage, which is to a certain extent related to this type of contract, is the interaction between the husband and wife, which can perhaps be considered the deepest and strongest interaction within social relationships. Certain phrases in Islamic texts mention this. It has been said that in marriage the man loses authority to the woman, and should beware of to whom he is giving authority.[38] In addition, it has been said that upon marriage one should know to whom one allies oneself as a partner in property and as one's confidant in religion and secrets.[39] As for women, it has conversely been said that they will be put entirely under the man's authority.[40] Both expressions indicate a deep mutual relationship between the man and the woman. Accordingly, each partner will be strongly affected by the other in behaviour, thought and attitude. As this is a requirement of marriage, Islamic teachings contain advice in which a special emphasis is placed on the selection of the spouse, including aspects such as beliefs and behaviour that indicate that the individual is on the right path.

Other points are the spiritual aspect of marriage and its sacredness in Islām. It can generally be said that the sanctity of marriage is rooted in religion.[41] Many human communities hold the marriage ceremony in their places of worship. For example, Christians do not think of marriage as a worldly matter, because marriage symbolises God's love of man. They hold the ceremony in a church, just as other religions perform the marriage ceremony in their places of worship.[42] Expressions in Islamic texts, whether in the Qur'ān or the words of the divine religious leaders, emphasise the sanctity of marriage in a variety of ways. Some examples are: "Most people in hell are those who did not marry;"[43] "The one who marries has completed a half of the faith;"[44] "One of the times when blessings come down from God is the time of holding a marriage ceremony."[45] Moreover, many functions of the family are deemed acts of worship in Islām, a few of which, in certain circumstances, are said generally to be more accepted to God than some of the more obvious acts of worship.[46] All these matters referring to the sanctity and spirituality of marriage encourage the individual to consider the responsibilities within the family and proper behaviour as religious duties, thus situating the affairs of life in the world on a spiritual and otherworldly plane. If we observe that in the teachings of Islām it is recommended to pray and place one's trust in God when choosing a spouse and at the time of marriage,[47] it is because they are intended to establish the link between marriage and spirituality and sanctify it, so as to prepare the ground for human growth and perfection.

Another point considered in Islām is that of the formalities when getting married. The ceremonies are so important that, according to the divine religious leaders, the only difference between marriage and illegitimate relationships is the holding of special ceremonies and the happiness involved.[48] Yet the teachings of Islām mention things that should be excluded from the marriage ceremony,[49] but this is in fact to promote a happy and celebratory atmosphere. Joyful singing is allowed in some marriage ceremonies within certain limits.[50] The marriage ceremony prepares the couple psychologically for the beginning of a new common life, and helps to make marriage an important matter, and takes place in a context where one is assisted by many others, rather than being a simple matter that could easily be disturbed or treated with indifference. The joyful presence of others at the ceremony strengthens the couple's commitment and positive feelings. Therefore, the beginning of the new life is accompanied by ceremony and encouragement, and sets an example for other people to follow.

5. The Appropriate Time for Marriage

Throughout the world there is no upper time limit for getting married, but most people get married when young. Nowadays, the average age for getting married in industrial societies is older, due to an increase in the number of nuclear families and economic difficulties. According to statistics, the average age of a first marriage in Iran follows a similar trend, a difference being that it is more obvious in the case of women. According to the 1996 census, the average marrying age of men was 25.6 years, with a 2-year increase compared with 1986, and 22.4 years for women, with a 2.6-year increase.[51] An increase in the average age of marriage would have particular consequences in Iran, since any relationship between men and women, including sexual relationships, have certain rules as required by Islām. In other cultures, more freedom in sexual relationships automatically removes some of the consequences of delayed marriage. Young people who wish to marry, but whose circumstances prevent it, should firmly control their behaviour for a relatively long period of time, in order to avoid illegitimate sexual relationships. There are indeed various intermediary phases involved. Inhibiting sexual desire could lead to psychological problems, complexes and possibly depression. On the other hand, a sexual relationship in violation of the Sharīʿa can result in feelings of guilt which have their own psychological consequences, such as a short temper, an inferiority complex or retreating from society.[52] As these issues damage the mental health of individuals and society as a whole, in addition to the fact that adherence to Islamic values is considered an integral part of our culture, it is appropriate for us to examine first of all what is a good time to marry in order to guarantee mental health, and then to consider the obstacles. This is to hopefully ensure the mental health of both the individual and society, whilst preserving Islamic values. It is evident that, if an acceptable age for marriage is decided upon, then all social institutions, including the family, education, government and various other organisations, would be able to provide the suitable conditions for that age group to marry.

Islām recommend marriage at the stage of teenage,[53] obviously, the fulfilment of various roles in such a marriage is subject to physical and social maturity.[54] By examining the objectives and functions of marriage according to Islām, one might consider age of teenage as the appropriate age for marriage, as indeed the Imams have advised,[55] since one of the basic objectives in marriage is the fulfilment of sexual desire, and the emergence and increase of these needs would indicate the practicality of early marriage. Sexual desire develops in adolescence and gradually grows stronger, and marriage is the legitimate answer to this. On the other hand, the suppression of sexual desire and a life of seclusion is not accepted in Islām.[56] The Imams strongly reprimand those who refuse to marry.[57]

Another purpose of marriage is stability, peace and mutual friendship, and marriage is perhaps the only way for a man and a woman to achieve this.[58] Also, such things are needed in teenage more than at any other time, because it is then that friendships and strong affective relationships are formed. In addition, this period involves many psychological and social crises.[59] Without marriage, the individual is deprived of a desirable affective relationship, and will not benefit from the appropriate support of someone as close to them as a wife or husband. The divine religious leaders have referred to the undesirable consequences of delayed marriage. For example, delay in marriage, especially in the case of girls, has been likened to failing to pick ripe fruit from a tree, which decays in the sunlight and wind.[60] In other words, postponing marriage from a young age, in which the affective sexual desires are active and there are high spirits and sufficient energy, will in time have unfavourable results that damage the character. For instance, if sexual urges are very strong and cannot be expressed, they have to be either suppressed or fulfilled in a way contrary to the norms of society, in the latter case causing guilt and damaged self-esteem.

Among the other objectives of marriage that have been emphasised in Islām is the protection of the decency and morality of the individual and society.[61] As young people usually face serious problems in controlling their sexual desires, and often fail to do so, they are more likely to indulge in immoral behaviour outside the limits of the Sharīʿa, whereas marriage at this age is the most appropriate way to prevent this, and thus protect individual morality and that of society.[62] The teachings of Islām consider marriage necessary for those with strong sexual needs,[63] but also express the undesirable consequences of failing to prepare for marriage.[64] In this regard, the Imams have said that failure to do so pave the way to sin and corruption on the earth.[65] Reproduction and the raising of children, which are among the main goals of marriage in Islām, is not harmful for women of a certain age, but later in life the health of the mother and child might be jeopardised. If the age pyramid of a given society[66] approaches old age, the age structure of pregnant women will also be older. The peak age group of pregnant women in Iran for the years 1973 to 1976 was 20-22 years, which increased to 25-29 years in 1986. This illustrates changes in the pregnancy model in Iran, and increases the possibility of problems related to pregnancy in older women,[67] which include the duration of pregnancy and the likelihood of disabilities in children.[68] Therefore, a more advanced age is less suitable for the purposes of reproduction.

As already mentioned, marriage at a younger age is better regarding mental health and spiritual and religious development. Indeed, one cannot categorically state an ideal age for marriage, although according to more than 90% of the participants in surveys in Iran considered 20-25 years as the ideal age for females to marry, and less than 5% chose 26 years or older. An even smaller percentage considered over 30 years as ideal. Most respondents considered 21-25 years as ideal for males. In fact, young people consider over 25 to be better, because of the possibility of a higher income.[69] However, it is necessary for all young people and social institutions to work towards removing any obstacles to marriage, since the beginning of a shared married life in one's youth is accompanied by a variety of problems that marriage at a later age does not have. Even so, young people should prefer the psychological and social advantages of marrying at a young age, and not expect everything in life to be perfect. For example, marrying as a university student should be made more straightforward, with lower expectations, so that each partner can be happier.

The biggest obstacles for young people facing marriage are to do with money, jobs and housing. Although one should not ignore any responsibilities to other people and institutions, the individuals themselves, despite economic hardship, should not delay marriage if they strongly desire it,[70] because it explicitly states in the Qur'ān that God has promised His generosity to the husband and wife in need.[71] The divine leaders of religion have also said that marriage will improve one's sustenance.[72] It is evident that social interaction after marriage becomes more extensive, and encouragement and help from the parents of both spouses prepares the ground for the new family to develop.

6. Advice for Selecting a Spouse

An important juncture in life is when one selects a spouse, the consequences of which will remain for the rest of one's life. Things to consider are the criteria for selecting a spouse, taking into account the views of the parents whilst maintaining one's independence in making decisions. One must be prepared and ensure that there is sufficient maturity for marriage. Strong sexual desire is a characteristic of adolescence, and has been described as a kind of "leap forward."[73] It is an important duty at this time to control sexual desire and prepare for marriage. In this connection, the Qur'ān advises those who cannot marry to remain chaste, so that God will ensure that they do not lack His generosity.[74] In this way, the teachings of Islām advocate certain ways to control sexual desire, such as fasting, as well as other activities,[75] like physical exercise, I in order to strengthen one's will.[76] Reviewing the passages in the religious texts concerning the otherworldly blessings and virtue of those who control their desires in youth can strengthen one's resolve.[77] For example, it has been said that the one who is chaste and has avoided sexual corruption is almost like an angel, and attains spiritual infallibility.[78] At the same time, as mentioned earlier, there is emphatic advice that those with strong sexual desires should marry as soon as they can. This is expressed in statements such as: "Whoever marries has protected half of the faith,"[79] and "Two units of prayer by the one who is married is better than seventy units of prayer units of the one who is not."[80]

There is a great deal of psychological pressure prior to marriage. Fear and anxiety over money difficulties and the characteristics of the future spouse are just two examples. Trust in God and His promises, and other recommendations, such as making two units of prayer to ask for a good spouse and a good marriage,[81] can help the individual face the psychological pressures of this time. The selection of a spouse is possibly one of the biggest pressures and is a kind of crisis, for one should determine the necessary criteria of an ideal spouse and match these with one's choice of partner before making a final decision. Sexual motivations and attraction, psychological and ideological criteria, and the views expressed by parents and other people exert strong influences, but Islamic teachings contain practical advice for solving these problems. Before examining the views of Islām, we will consider the customary criteria for selecting a spouse, as generally accepted in most societies.

6. 1 Common Criteria for Choosing a Spouse

In the past, it was much less common for the couple who were to get married to themselves make the choice of who to marry, and the decision was usually left to the parents and older members of the family. This may have been because marriage was often at a young age, especially in the case of girls, and also because the couple might remain dependent upon the wider family for some years to come. At the present time, especially more recently in Iran, the wishes of the couple have become the main factor in taking what is considered a very important step in life, and there is more freedom for the boy and the girl to make their own choices. Nevertheless, the partner should be selected according to very precise and complex rules, with the parents meanwhile playing an important role. The boy and the girl should make their decision giving due consideration to their mutual affection and knowledge of each other. By examining the criteria for selecting a spouse, we will point out the emotional and rational challenges that young people face in this respect when making a decision.[82]

We come across five general criteria: physical, psychological, economic, social and familial. As for the first physical criterion, the physical health of the partner should be considered, as well as any age difference, which itself has become a research topic in the sociology of the family.[83] Physical beauty is also involved. Despite wise counsel in most cultures on the importance of inner qualities, most individuals react to the general physical appearance and the beauty of the face. Studies show that men are influenced more by physical beauty than women.[84] Fertility is another physical characteristic, and in the past was taken more into consideration in the case of women, although nowadays that of men is included. Mixed-race marriage has become a subject of controversy, and some believe that it is instinctive to marry someone of the same race. However that may be, one cannot deny the existence of such a tendency.[85]

The second criterion is to do with psychological characteristics. Compatible levels of intelligence has been given as a prerequisite for a satisfactory married life. Research on the relationship between intelligence and family happiness shows that if one partner considers the other less intelligent, there is less marital satisfaction,[86] and the level of education is now accepted as a factor in the choice of a spouse. A similarity of attitudes is another important psychological factor when couples first meet and are attracted to each other.[87] Some of this has to do with the affective disposition and the individual personality; for example, the man's ability to take control of situations and, conversely, the woman's compliance.

Moral and behavioural traits are also at work in the process of choice. Suitable personal characteristics are sometimes emphasised to the extent that they are considered necessary. According to surveys in Iran, more than half the people consider characteristics such as good manners, nobility of soul, honesty and generosity among the most important attributes of a good marital partner.[88] Since one's general behaviour is very important, and particular attributes can be traced in the personality, all this should be considered amongst the various psychological criteria.

The third criterion concerns money. Things to be considered before marriage are, in the case of the man, the ability to maintain a family, employment, income and savings, and, in the case of the woman, good money management, the capacity to have a job and income, and the ability to run and maintain the household.[89]

The fourth criterion is to do with social matters. These include cultural background, social class, ethnicity, nationality and religion, including the religious denomination. Throughout the world, religious belief is one of the most important factors to take into consideration when selecting a spouse, so much so that more than 98% of marriages among Jews, 93% among Catholics and more than 74% among Protestants are within the same denomination. Being in a similar social class is also important, although in recent years marriages that cross social boundaries have increased.[90]

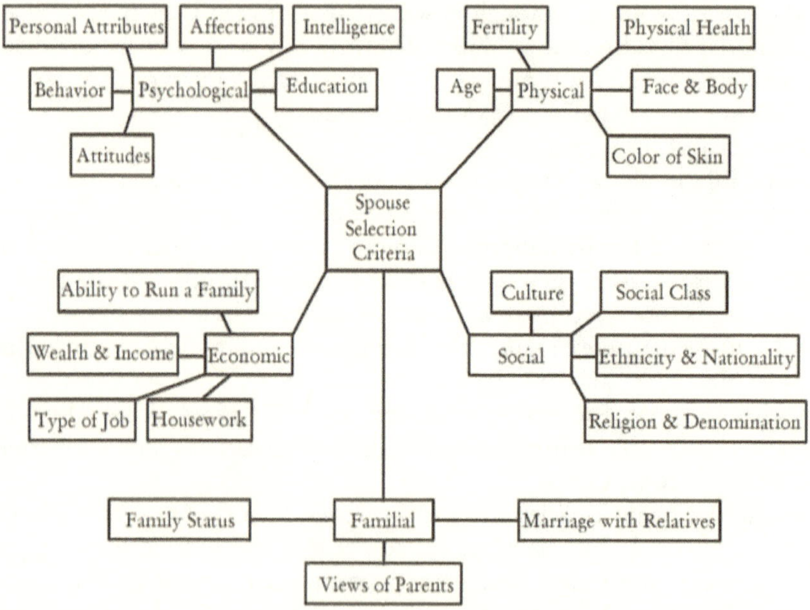

Figure 2: Spouse Selection Criteria

Regardless of the other criteria for selecting an appropriate spouse, choosing a similar type is generally accepted throughout the world as a universal rule. This includes a similar living environment, racial and cultural background, social class, personal and psychological characteristics, religion and age.[91] For a psychological explanation of this rule, it could be said that in the first place, similar types attract each other, and this encourages positive affections.A general connection between similarity and attraction has been proven by extensive studies of various age groups, and different socio-economic groups and cultures. In addition, greater similarities mean greater compatibility. The more two individuals harmonise, the more they will be interested in each other, and if a disagreement emerges, they will try to adjust their psychological positions to reach agreement.[92] Research shows that similarity favours the consolidation and continuity of ties. On the other hand, dissimilarities are demonstrated to be causes of marital strife, and studies on family satisfaction reflect the same conclusion.[93]

6. 2. Characteristics of an Appropriate Spouse According to Islām

The teachings of Islām emphasise the following positive characteristics:

1. Physical characteristics such as good health, fertility,[94] purity[95] and beauty. Scholars have mentioned the beauty of the face,[96] the body[97] and the hair.[98] However, Islām does not consider race or the colour of the skin as important factors.[99]

2. Psychological attributes such as a good personality, sufficient intelligence,[100] appropriate behaviour (such as modesty) towards the spouse,[101] a soft and forgiving approach,[102] trustworthiness,[103] gratitude,[104] love and kindness towards both the partner and children,[105] cooperation in sexual acts,[106] and patience in the face of difficulties.[107]

3. Good financial management of the household and family,[108] personal expenses,[109] and mutual assistance if there are problems.[110]

4. Belief in God and the afterlife,[111] and the reliance on God when faced with the problems of life. Some affective and behavioural manifestations of religiosity are patience,[112] piety, the avoidance of sin,[113] chastity, observance of the religious dress code,[114] and loving and following the divine religious leaders.[115]

5. Social and cultural backgrounds those are usually comparable. Some narrations advise against marrying people from certain regions or tribes,[116] and therefore can be considered as emphasising the cultural similarity of the husband and wife. Perhaps a better explanation is that they refer to the cultural conditions of the regions or people concerned, which might foster inappropriate behaviour.[117] However, according to Islamic teachings, merely living in a particular region or belonging to a specific ethnicity or nationality indicates neither superiority nor inferiority.

6. In amongst the different criteria, the choice of a relative as one's spouse has been mentioned,[118] although some religious narrations mention the possible defects in children born of such marriages.[119] Islamic teachings very much emphasise proper family conditions, and consider the influence of the families of the husband and the wife on the

children to be an important element in their upbringing.[120] Marriage to someone with suitable characteristics but whose family is clearly unsuitable has been prohibited.[121] The effect of the family on a child, whether in terms of heredity or upbringing, strongly affects the development of the child's personality.[122] Therefore, although an individual may overcome certain bad aspects in their family background by their own will and persistence, since other individuals may be influenced by these aspects as well, the divine leaders of the religion seriously recommend that the individual's family status should be scrutinised. Moreover, the way one is treated by one's future in laws can be an indication of how one would be treated by the spouse.[123]

In addition to the above Piety is also important, and has a clear effect on family life and a good relationship, even if there are other differences between the husband and wife.[124]

Following on from the matter of religious belief is the degree of faith, as well as moral characteristics, concerning which it has been said that if Imām 'Alī had been absent, there would have been no equal among the people to marry Fātima Zahrā. It has likewise been reported that certain other devout people have had counterparts of the same degree.[125] Therefore, the mere fact of having faith does not make two people equal, since the level of faith and morality should also be taken into consideration. The explicit mention in the Qur'ān of pure and free individuals who belong with each other[126] is another indication of the need for similarity in piety, the avoidance of sin and religiosity.[127] In a survey of students, mutual understanding and similar religious beliefs were considered important characteristics of the ideal spouse.[128]

6. 3. Priorities Within the Various Criteria

After clarifying the criteria for choosing a spouse, one should examine their relative importance and their degrees of priority. We should consider the person's qualifications and what is expected of him. It makes the decision-making problematic if someone is lacking to a certain extent in suitable characteristics. In this discussion, we will deal with two theoretical and applied processes for the selection of a spouse.

According to Islām, the most important thing is proper religious beliefs, and an appropriate level of them at that. This can indeed be considered a necessary and decisive factor that applies at all times and in all places, without which he is disqualified regardless of whether he has the other attributes. Various verses in the Qur'ān[129] and the words of the divine religious leaders[130] affirm the absoluteness of this condition:

> *And do not marry polytheist women until they believe. And a believing slave woman is better than a polytheist, even though she might please you. And do not marry polytheist men [to your women]. And a believing slave is better than a polytheist, even though he might please you. Those invited [you] to the Fire.*[131]

According to this verse, marrying an unbeliever will prevent happiness in the afterlife, and therefore should not take place. The important point in this verse is that, even if the marriage is to a believer of the lowest social class of the time, i.e. the slaves, who had no property and were themselves the property of another, such a marriage would be better than to marry a free person with no solid faith or religious belief. Imām Bāqir has said: "A Muslim said that a Muslim should not marry a non-Muslim." He was referring to the Qur'ānic verse: *And hold not to marriage bonds with disbelieving women.*[132] Following on from this, experts in the Islamic sciences also consider religious faith a necessary condition in a spouse.[133]

This primary attitude of faith and religious belief either directly or indirectly affects all aspects of the personality, one's goal in life, one's social, cultural and economic outlooks, and one's views regarding marriage, education and employment, and even less important issues such as recreation, interests, and other behaviours.[134] Therefore, the teachings of Islām put the most emphasis on the criterion of faith.

The second necessary characteristic of a good spouse is a good temperament, which here means behaving properly in one's interactions in life, and one's compatibility with and tolerance of others.[135] The basis of married life is compatibility, mutual understanding and cooperation, which only a good temperament can provide.[136] Therefore, a good temperament is a necessary condition and deciding factor in a good spouse. Hence, if an individual does not have a good temperament, he fails to fulfil the necessary conditions. Therefore, the divine religious leaders have explicitly prohibited marriage to bad-tempered individuals.[137] One should consider here that, if one discovers after marriage that one's partner is bad-tempered, the way to tackle the issue is different from when initially looking for a spouse. In these circumstances, if a bad temperament results in severe incompatibility between the husband and wife, it is inappropriate to continue with the marriage.[138] However, if the bad temperament is of a lesser degree, then under certain conditions patience, tolerance and continuing family life is the best answer. Narrations that refer to the spiritual rewards of patience and the tolerance of a bad temperament relate to such circumstances.[139] Otherwise, if it is clear from the beginning that someone is bad-tempered, then marriage to them is inadvisable, since an important condition is absent. Another point to remember is that a good temperament is a support of faith,[140] and therefore bad manners are an indication of weak faith.[141] Good manners in the family are a criterion of religiosity that leads to perfection.[142] Therefore, a bad temper renders a person defective in this respect.

The third attribute of a good spouse is a pious attitude.[143] Such sins as adultery[144] and drinking alcohol[145] are disavowed, as well as sins that are not committed openly in public.[146] This criterion is considered absolute. If it is discovered that a person lacks such piety, then their selection is out of the question. Physical and mental health is also among the conditions of a good spouse. Therefore, if an individual suffers from an incurable physical or mental illness, then that person is unable to fulfil the functions and purposes of marriage. Hence, Islamic jurisprudents in certain cases mention physical or mental defects as a reason for cancelling a marriage.[147]

The other criteria are considered relative to the four attributes just mentioned, in the sense that they should be considered according to their weakness or strength in relation to them. It should be remembered that sometimes, after ensuring that the individual has the desirable degrees of faith, piety and good manners, a rejection of the marriage proposal can result in individual and social problems, for certain customary and rational reasons. Therefore, the divine religious leaders have said that if one proposes marriage to someone whose temperament and religiosity one admires, then one should marry them, for otherwise corruption will prevail on earth.[148]

Beauty of appearance and attractiveness is an important factor for the lasting bond of marriage. Mutual attraction and the fulfilment of sexual desires are based on the beauty that each partner perceives in the other. The magnetism of beauty is something natural and is mentioned in Islamic texts: "God is beautiful and He loves beauty",[149] and "Seek goodness with the fair of face, because their actions and conduct are more suited to goodness."[150]

If there is no desire for or interest in marriage, this will already be a cause of discontent within the family. Therefore, interest on the part of the person who is to get married is very important, and even takes precedence over the wishes and opinions of the parents.[151] The emphasis placed by the divine religious leaders on this psychological aspect, i.e. an affective attraction to the other party[152] before marriage, is in order to fulfil the important goals of marriage, such as friendship and strong mutual affection[153] between the man and the woman, and giving each other psychological support.[154] Thus, beauty and an attractive appearance is a major element of the love of the two parties for each other, and a decisive factor in marriage. Therefore, according to the teachings of Islām, one should be pleased when one looks at the person one wishes to marry. This is not only permitted,[155] but emphasised,[156] since it sets the scene for continuing emotional bonds between the man and the woman.[157] Another point to consider is that both parties should not only appear attractive to each other, but also to all family members from both sides. In other words, two individuals may be physically attracted to each other, but a third party might not perceive beauty in them.

Nevertheless, although beauty is important in Islām, criteria such as religiosity and fertility take precedence over it. Consequently, even though a person may be beautiful, if they are infertile, they do not fully qualify.[158] Moreover, if someone marries only for beauty, they may be deprived of a partner having other characteristics, such as religiosity.[159] Fertility is important for a marriage, and makes up for any deficiency in beauty,[160] whereas the converse does not apply.[161] The mere consideration of wealth may also deprive the person of the other aspects, but if marriage is based on religiosity, then beauty and wealth will be provided by God.[162] Since reproduction and the raising of children is fundamental to marriage, as well a central psychological need in humans is attachment to and relation with children,[163] fertility is an important characteristic of an ideal spouse. In rare cases one might discover infertility before marriage. Similarities between the husband and wife, despite being very important, are relative criteria, in the sense that there are various levels, and they should be considered in relation to other aspects. As already mentioned, "equality" is comparable with the concept of the "similar-spouse marriage" in the sociology of the family, and the similar-spouse marriage has various aspects which have been mentioned. Therefore, the similarity of the two individuals should be considered when summing up all the other criteria. One person may score higher than the other in certain aspects, and vice versa. According to the divine religious leaders:

> "One's counterpart is one who is at the same social level, is chaste, and life with them is accompanied with comfort."[164]

Elsewhere, Imām Jawād said in response to a letter:

> "Do not reflect much on finding a counterpart. If you are satisfied with the temperament and religiosity of those who propose marriage, marry your daughters to them. Otherwise, corruption will prevail on the earth."[165]

And Imām Reḍā has said:

> "If we wanted to marry our family members to those who are our exact counterparts, they would remain unmarried."[166]

Each of these three narrations makes it clear that having a counterpart in marriage is a relative matter, and may be overridden in certain circumstances.

Consequently, one is ill-advised to give up the idea of marriage – an important tradition of the divine prophets – simply because an exact counterpart cannot be found, since other standards, such as faith, a good temperament, mental and physical health are good qualifications. An interesting point is that the spouses of the Prophet Muḥammad and many of the wives of the Imams were not their precise counterparts, but this did not stop them from marrying.[167] In general, according to the teachings of Islām and various verses in the Qur'ān,[168] the principle of marrying someone of good faith and temperament prevails over other factors.[169]

The similarity of the man and the woman in cultural, social and economic aspects helps their compatibility, but cannot be considered a necessary requirement of an suitable spouse. According to certain verses of the Qur'ān[170] and the guidelines and practice of the divine religious leaders,[171] it is not acceptable to consider these criteria only. As opposed to any consideration of ethnicity and wealth in marriage[172] Imām Sajjād said:

> "God uses Islām to raise the low upwards, to perfect the imperfect, and to give dignity to those who are low in society."

A Muslim is not "low," for it describes those of the pre-Islamic ignorance.[173] The Prophet married a poor black man to a very wealthy Quraishi woman, and said:

> "I did this to facilitate marriage. Make the practice of the Prophet your tradition, and know that the highest of you before God is the most pious of you."[174]

In addition, other similarities include psychological elements such as intelligence, emotion, education and attitude. As already mentioned, these will greatly affect the consolidation of the bond between the two people and its continuation. Wide differences in levels of intelligence results in differing behaviour, reasoning and even beliefs, and are likely to cause problems in the family.[175]

6. 4. Various Objectives and Different Types of Marriage

The points mentioned thus far are based on the sacred worldview and teachings of Islām. Therefore, the qualifications of an ideal spouse are considered in line with the fulfilment of Islamic objectives, whereas a materialistic person, or someone with weak religious convictions, might consider material criteria such as physical attraction and wealth as primary factors.

At the same time, the objectives of marriage that have been mentioned relate to most marriages, especially the first and what is usually the only marriage. A small number of marriages may take place for other reasons. For example, someone who has lost a spouse and has several children might not consider fertility important in a subsequent marriage. Moreover, in marriages with short-term goals, only certain absolutely necessary criteria are considered.

Conflict between the criteria and the decision-making: In the process of selecting a spouse, after understanding the necessary criteria, it is difficult for most people to apply them to the person in question. Residing close by one another, or knowledge of each other's education or employment, will greatly add to the impressions of each person. Nevertheless, marriage between people from different backgrounds has increased. This, along with other developments in matters of choice, is an effect of scientific and IT progress in the contemporary era. This has made it more difficult for two people to know each other's characteristics. In these circumstances, the first step is to know how to discover such necessary conditions as strength of faith, piety, good temperament, and physical and mental health. Obviously, at this stage, the known psychological and physical characteristics of the man and the woman are what make them attractive to each other, otherwise they would not pursue the matter further. A likeness of type is most important, and if there is a clash, then other psychological aspects need to be considered, such as behaviour in the family, opinions on bringing up children, and changes of mood. Considering these priorities, it seems that conflicts mostly emerge due to an inadequate knowledge of the other person. However, if things turn out badly, one can disregard one's passing affection and look for someone more suitable. One should be more cautious about rejecting a qualified person who lacks certain less important characteristics, since such a selection should not result in any problems in marital life. As already mentioned, according to the guidelines of the divine religious leaders, the rejection of such a person may have undesirable individual and social consequences. Therefore, two important principles should be observed in the process:

The first is studying the necessary conditions and the other characteristics of an appropriate spouse, including those which might disrupt an ideal marital life.

The second is acquiring sufficient information about the person offering themselves for marriage. In this respect, information is obtained about crucial elements of the individual's personality by observing where they study, work and live, and inquiring about their family. In addition, the two persons involved should meet a few times to talk to each other and get to know each other's nonverbal behaviour. Apparently, the more attention they give to these two principles, the easier the choice will become. It is also an important duty of the parents and close relatives to help a young person when choosing a spouse and starting family life. The Qur'ān addresses Muslims in general, advising single men and women, especially those of lower incomes, to get married.[176] In addition to economic help and guidance in the selection process, the parents should also take into consideration the freedom and independence of the young person involved. The help of others[177] in terms of introductions and mediation is highly valued in Islām, so much so that it has been called the highest of intercessions.[178] Help from others can take the form of financial support, loans, gifts, and emotional support, such as helping to eliminate doubts and offering guidance for marriage and family issues.

Notes

1. Al-Ḥurr al-'Āmilī, Muḥammad ibn Ḥasan, *Wasā'il Shī'a*, vol. 14, p. 3.
2. Majlisī, Muḥammad-Bāqir, *Biḥār al-Anwār*, vol. 100, p. 222.
3. Ibid., p. 221.
4. Jamāl, Ibrāhīm-Muḥammad, *Ta'addud al-Zawjāt fī al-Islām*, p. 39.
5. The Prophet, his daughter Fatima, and the first twelve Imams.
6. Ibn Sīnā, Ḥusayn ibn 'Abdullāh, *Tadābīr al-Manāzil*, pp. 32-38.
7. A'rāfī, 'Alī -Reḍā, *Arā'-e Dānishmandān Musalmān dar T'alī m va Tarbiyat va Mabānī-yi Ān,*, pp. 291-294.
8. Ghazālī, Abū-Hāmid, *Kīmiyā-yi Sa'ādat*, vol. 1, p. 301.
9. Tūsi, Nasīr al-Dīn, *Akhlāq Nāsirī*, pp. 217-219.
10. Fayḍ al-Kāshānī, Muḥsin, *al-Maḥajja al-Baiḍā' fī Tahdhīb al-'Iḥyā'*, vol. 3, pp. 67 and 96-135.
11. Tabātabā'ī, Sayyid Muḥammad Ḥusayn, *Tafsīr al-Mīzān*, vol. 4, p. 285.
12. Tabātabā'ī, *Tafsīr al-Mīzān*, vol. 4, pp. 289 and 544-547.
13. This theme was expanded by Bertalanffy, wherein the family is studied as a unit, with each individual being a part of an inclusive system (Siemon, F., *Key Concepts and Theories in Family Therapy*, p. 253).
14. Muṭahharī, Murtaḍā, *Ta'līm va Tarbiyat az Nazar Islām*, pp. 266-267.
15. Qur'an 49:10.
16. Muṭahharī, Murtaḍā, *Akhlāq Jinsī dar Islām va Jahān Gharb*, pp. 46-47.
17. Sārūkhānī, Bāqir, *Muqaddamih-yi bar Jāmi'i Shināsī-yi Khānivādih*, p. 136.
18. 2:102, 187, 228, 229, 231, 222, 223; 3:14; 4:3, 34, 35, 128, 129, 21; 24:32; 30:21; 58:1-4; 66:1, 5, 11; 64:14; 25:74.
19. 17:23, 24; 12:12, 8, 92, 100; 2: 132.
20. 4:1; 8:75; 33:50; 24:24.
21. 66:6.
22. 20:132.
23. 18:46.
24. Including the advice of the prophets to their children, and their prayers for them. For example, see Qur'ān 2:132 and 14:40.
25. Including Noah's praying for his son to be saved (Qur'ān 11:46) and Abraham's prayer for his father (9:114).
26. Forsyth, D. R., *Our Social World*, p. 362.
27. Minuchin, S., *Families and Family Therapy*, pp. 20-26.
28. Goldenberg, I. and Goldenberg, H. *Family: An Overview*, pp. 13-16.

29. Ibid.
30. Sārūkhānī, *Muqaddamih-yi bar Jāmi'i Shināsī-yi Khānivādih*, pp. 23-24.
31. Najafī, Muḥammad-Ḥasan, *Jawāhir al-Kalām*, vol. 29, pp. 5-8.
32. The Qur'ān *states*: *Every people has a marriage.* In this connection, one can mention cases in which religious leaders in Islām opposed those who said that the marriage of individuals in other cultures was unacceptable, and that they were in an adulterous relationship, since the marriage had been performed contrary to the marriage conditions recognised in Islām. See Kulaynī, Muḥammad ibn Ya'qūb, *Kāfī*, vol. 1, p. 353.
33. They have taken a strong pledge from you (Qur'ān 4:21).
34. Majlisī, *Biḥār al-Anwār*, vol. 100, pp. 267-269.
35. Divorce must be pronounced twice and then (a woman) must be retained in honour or released in kindness (Qur'ān 2:229), and Release them in kindness (Qur'ān 2:231).
36. Qur'ān 30:21.
37. Rashīd Reḍā, Muḥammad, *Tafsīr al-Minār*, vol. 4, p. 460.
38. Al-Ḥurr al-'Āmilī, *Wasā'il al-Shī'a*, vol. 14, p. 17.
39. Ibid., p. 14.
40. Ibid., p. 52.
41. Michel, Thomas, *Christian Theology*, p. 94.
42. Saif, Sūsan, *Te'ori-yi Rushd Khānivadih Muqaddamih-yi bar Jāmi'i Shināsī-yi Khānivādih*, p. 86.
43. Al-Ḥurr al-'Āmilī, *Wasā'il al-Shī'a*, vol. 14, p. 8.
44. Ibid., p. 5.
45. Majlisī, *Biḥār al-Anwār*, vol. 100, p. 221.
46. Ibid., pp. 285, 289.
47. Al-Ḥurr al-'Āmilī, *Wasā'il al-Shī'a*, vol. 14, p. 79.
48. Majlisī, *Biḥār al-Anwār*, vol. 100, p. 275; ibid., p 267.
49. Al-Ḥurr al-'Āmilī, *Wasā'il al-Shī'a*, vol. 17, p. 121.
50. Khumeinī, Sayyid Rūhullāh, *Taḥrīr al-Wasīla* , Issue 13, p. 388.
51. Amānī, Mehdī, Jam'īyyat Shināsī-yi 'Umūmī , p. 62.
52. Āzād, Paimān, *Zīndigī bidūni Iḥsās Gunāh*, pp. 170-173.
53. Najafī, *Jawāhir al-Kalām*, vol. 29, p. 146.
54. Ibid., p. 200; Banī-Hāshimī, Sayyid Muḥammad-Ḥasan, *Tawḍīḥ al-Masā'il Marāji'*, vol. 2, p. 386.
55. Al-Ḥurr al-'Āmilī, *Wasā'il al-Shī'a*, vol. 14, p. 25.
56. Ibid., p. 74.

57. Ibid., p. 7. Nūrī-Tabarsī, Ḥusayn, Mustadrak al-Wasā'il va Mustanbat al-Masā'il, vol. 14,, p. 37.
58. Qu'ran 30:21.
59. Aḥmadī, Sayyid Aḥmad, *Ravānshināsī-yi Nawjavānān va Javānān*, pp. 44-48, 1.
60. Al-Ḥurr al-'Āmilī, *Wasā'il al-Shī'a*, vol. 14, p. 39.
61. Kulaynī, *Kāfī*, vol. 2, pp. 79-80.
62. Nūrī, *Mustadrak al-Wasā'il*, ch. 1.
63. Ibid., ch. 2.
64. Al-Kulaynī, *Kāfī*, vol. 5, p. 347.
65. Al-Ḥurr al-'Āmilī, *Wasā'il al-Shī'a*, vol. 14, p. 52.
66. The age pyramid is a chart showing the distribution of population according to age. If a large number of individuals in a society are of an older age group, the population is then considered old (Amānī, *Mabānī-ye Jam'īyyat Shināsī*, p. 24, 1998).
67. Javān, Ja'far, *Jughrāfiyā-yi Jam'īyyat Iran*, p. 285.
68. Kāzimīpūr, Shahlā, *Barrisī Dimographic Taghyīr Sinn Izdivāj*, p. 71.
69. Muḥsinī, Manūchihr, et al, *Izdivāj va Khānivādih dar Iran*, pp. 146-175.
70. Al-Ḥurr al-'Āmilī, *Wasā'il al-Shī'a*, vol. 14, p. 24.
71. Qur'ān 24:32.
72. Al-Ḥurr al-'Āmilī, *Wasā'il al-Shī'a*, vol. 14, p. 24.
73. Mason, Paul Henry, *Child Development and Personalī ty*, p. 533.
74. Qur'ān 24:32.
75. Majlisī, *Biḥār al-Anwār*, vol. 101, p. 87.
76. Tabrisī, Faḍl ibn Ḥasan, *Majma' al-Bayān fī Tafsīr al-Qur'ān*, under Qur'ān 24:33, p. 220; Narāqī, Mullā Mahdī, *Jāmi' al-Sa'ādāt*, vol. 29, pp. 8-17.
77. Al-Kulaynī, *Kāfī*, vol. 2, p. 79; Ibid.
78. *Nahj al-Balāghah*, Aphorism 474.
79. Al-Ḥurr al-'Āmilī , *Wasā'il al-Shī'a*, vol. 14, p. 5.
80. Ibid., p. 8.
81. Ibid., p. 79.
82. Sārūkhānī, Muqaddamih-yi bar Jāmi'i Shināsī-yi Khānivādih, pp. 33-38.
83. Siddīq-Awra'ī, Ghulām-Reḍā, , *Jāmi'i Shināsī-yi Masā'il Ijtimā'ī Javānān*, pp. 91-99.
84. Ādharbāyjānī, Mas'ūd et al, Ravānshināsī-yi Ijtimā'ī ba Nigāhī bi Manābi' Islāmī, p. 250.
85. Sārūkhānī, *Muqaddamih-yi bar Jāmi'i Shināsī-yi Khānivādih*, pp. 51-52.
86. Ibid., pp. 63-64.

87. Ādharbāyjānī, Mas'ūd et al, *Ravānshināsī-yi Ijtimā'ī ba Nigāhī bi Manābi' Islāmī*, pp. 256-257.
88. Ministry of Culture & Islamic Guidance, *Arzish-hā va Nigarish-hā-yi Iranian*, pp. 38-39.
89. Ibid.
90. Sārūkhānī, *Muqaddamih-yi bar Jāmi'i Shināsī-yi Khānivādih*, p. 62.
91. Ibid., pp. 40-72.
92. Ādharbāyjānī, Mas'ūd et al, Ravānshināsī-yi Ijtimā'ī ba Nigāhī bi Manābi' Islāmī, pp. 256-261.
93. Sārūkhānī, *Muqaddamih-yi bar Jāmi'i Shināsī-yi Khānivādih*, p. 41.
94. Al-Ḥurr al-'Āmilī, *Wasā'il al-Shī'a*, vol. 14, p. 14.
95. ibid., pp. 20, 34.
96. Nūrī, *Mustadrak al-Wasā'il*, vol. 14, p. 169; Al-Ḥurr al-'Āmilī, *Wasā'il al-Shī'a*, vol. 14, p. 78.
97. Al-Ḥurr al-'Āmilī, *Wasā'il al-Shī'a*, vol. 14, p. 59; Majlisī, *Biḥār al-Anwār*, vol. 100, p. 231.
98. Majlisī, *Biḥār al-Anwār*, vol. 100, p. 237.
99. Qur'ān49:11; Al-Kulaynī, *Kāfī*, vol. 5, p. 344.
100. Majlisī, *Biḥār al-Anwār*, vol. 100, p. 237;Al-Ḥurr al-'Āmilī, *Wasā'il al-Shī'a*, vol. 14, p. 13.
101. Ibid., p. 14.
102. Ibid., p. 15.
103. Ibid., p. 22.
104. Al-Suyūtī, Jalālal-Dīn, *al-Durr al-Manthūr*, vol. 1, p. 152.
105. Al-Ḥurr al-'Āmilī, *Wasā'il al-Shī'a*, vol. 14, p. 20.
106. Ibid., p. 4.
107. Al-Suyūtī, Jalāl al-Dīn, *al-Durr al-Manthūr*, vol. 1, p. 152.
108. Al-Ḥurr al-'Āmilī, *Wasā'il al-Shī'a*, vol. 14, p. 13.
109. Ibid; Majlisī, *Biḥār al-Anwār*, vol. 100, p. 231.
110. Tabrisī, Ḥasan ibn Faḍl, *Makārim al-Akhlāq*, p. 199; Majlisī, *Biḥār al-Anwār*, vol. 100, p. 238.
111. Qur'ān 2:221; Nūrī, Mustadrak al-Wasā'īl, vol. 14, p.161.
112. Ibid., p. 17.
113. Majlisī, *Biḥār al-Anwār*, vol. 100, p. 235.
114. Al-Ḥurr al-'Āmilī, *Wasā'il al-Shī'a*, vol. 14, p. 43; Majlisī, *Biḥār al-Anwār*, vol. 100, p.235; p.237.
115. Majlisī, *Biḥār al-Anwār*, vol. 100, p. 236.
116. Al-Ḥurr al-'Āmilī, *Wasā'il al-Shī'a*, vol. 14, p. 54.

117. Majlisī, *Biḥār al-Anwār*, vol. 100, p. 236.
118. Al-Ḥurr al-ʻĀmilī, *Wasā'il al-Shī'a*, vol. 14, p. 32. Marriage with relatives also occurs very often in the practice of the Imams.
119. Farīd, Murtaḍā, *al-Ḥadīth*, vol. 1, p. 184; Ibid.
120. Muḥammadī-Reyshahrī, Muḥammad, *Mīzān al-Ḥikmah*, p. 2258, vol. 5; Al-Kulaynī, *Furū' al-Kāfī*, vol. 5, p. 332.
121. Al-Ḥurr al-ʻĀmilī, *Wasā'il al-Shī'a*, vol. 14, p. 19.
122. Ibid., p. 29; Muḥammadī-Reyshahrī, *Mīzān al-Ḥikmah*, Ḥadīth 7848.
123. Ibid., p. 14.
124. Ibid., p. 18; Farīd Tunikābunī, Murtaḍā, *al-Ḥadīth*, vol. 1, p. 177.
125. Ibid.
126. Good women are for good men, and good men for good women, Qur'ān 24:26.
127. Tabātabā'ī, *Tafsīr al-Mīzān*, vol. 15, p. 115.
128. Ḥaqdūst, 'Alī -Akbar, et al, 'Barrasī-yi Dīdgāh Dānishjūyān 'Ulūm Pizishkī Pīrāmūn 'Avāmil Mu'aththir dar Izdivāj', in *Andīshih va Raftār Quarterly*, vol. 2, No. 3
129. Good women are for good men, and good men for good women, Qur'ān 24:26.
130. Al-Ḥurr al-ʻĀmilī, *Wasā'il al-Shī'a*, vol. 14, p. 30, and Hadiths 23, 22, 21, 17, 15, 14.
131. Qur'ān 2:221.
132. And if you know them to be believers, then do not return them to the disbelievers; they are not lawful [wives] for them, nor are they [the disbelievers] lawful [husbands] for them. But give the disbelievers what they have spent. And there is no blame upon you if you marry them when you have given them their due compensation. And hold not to marriage bonds with disbelieving women, Qur'ān 60:10; Al-Kulaynī, *Kāfī*, vol. 5, p. 358.
133. Najafī, *Jawāhir al-Kalām*, vol. 34, vo. 30, p. 93.
134. Ādharbāyjānī, Mas'ūd et al, *Ravānshināsī-yi Ijtimā'ī ba Nigāhī bi Manābi' Islāmī*, p. 162.
135. Majlisī, *Biḥār al-Anwār*, vol. 71, p. 171.
136. Ibid., vol. 69, p. 404; Ibid., p. 408.
137. Al-Ḥurr al-ʻĀmilī, *Wasā'il al-Shī'a*, vol. 14, p. 54.
138 Majlisī, *Biḥār al-Anwār*, vol. 100, p. 224.
139. Ibid., p. 244; p. 247.
140. Ibid., vol. 75, p. 93.
141. Ibid., vol. 71, p. 373.

142. Ibid., p. 392.
143. Ibid.
144. The fornicator does not marry except a fornicator or polytheist, and none marries her except a fornicator or a polytheist idolater, and that has been made unlawful to the believers, Qur'ān 24:3.
145. Majlisī, *Biḥār al-Anwār*, vol. 100, p. 372.
146. Nūrī, *Mustadrak al-Wasā'il*, vol. 14, p. 191.
147. Some of these defects are set forth in the Civil Code, Articles 1120-1125.
148. Al-Ḥurr al-'Āmilī, *Wasā'il al-Shī'a*, vol. 14, p. 51.
149. Muttaqī Hindī, 'Alā' al-Dīn, *Kanz al-'Ummāl*, Ḥadīth 17166.
150. Majlisī, *Biḥār al-Anwār*, vol. 74, p. 187.
151. Ibid., vol. 100, p. 235.
152. Al-Ḥurr al-'Āmilī, *Wasā'il al-Shī'a*, vol. 14, p. 13.
153. And of His signs is that He created for you from yourselves mates that you may find tranquility in them; and He placed between you affection and mercy." Qur'ān 30:21.
154. Al-Ḥurr al-'Āmilī, *Wasā'il al-Shī'a*, vol. 14, p. 13; p. 21; p. 22; narrations on pp. 22-24.
155. Ibid., p. 60; narrations in ch. 36, pp. 59-61.
156. Ibid., p. 61.
157. Ibid.
158. Ibid., p. 33.
159. Ibid., p. 31.
160. Ibid., p. 33.
161. Ibid., p. 33.
162. Ibid., p. 30.
163. Maslow, Abraham, *Motivation and Personalī ty*, p. 79.
164. Majlisī, *Biḥār al-Anwār*, vol. 100, p. 372.
165. Ibid., p. 373.
166. Ibid., vol. 75, p. 367.
167. Qumī, Sheikh 'Abbās, *Muntahā al-Āmāl*, vols. 1 and 2.
168. Such as: And marry the unmarried among you and the righteous among your male slaves and female slaves, Qur'ān 24:32.
169. And whoever among you cannot [find]the means to marry free, believing women, then [he may marry] from those whom your right hands possess of believing slave girls, Qur'ān 4:25.
170. O mankind, indeed We have created you from male and female and made you peoples and tribes that you may know one another. Indeed, the most noble of you in the sight of Allāh is the most righteous of you, Qur'ān 49:13.

171. Majlisī, *Biḥār al-Anwār*, vol. 100, p. 379.
172. Such as the marriage of Imām Sajjād(as) to female slaves.. Ibid., p. 374.
173. Al-Ḥurr al-'Āmilī, *Wasā'il al-Shī'a*, vol. 14, p. 372.
174. Majlisī, *Biḥār al-Anwār*, vol. 22, pp. 265 and 437.
175. Sārūkhānī, *Muqaddamih-yi bar* Jāmi'i Shināsī-yi Khānivādih, p. 63.
176. And marry the unmarried among you and the righteous among your male slaves. If they should be poor, Allāh will enrich them from His bounty, Qur'ān 24:32.
177. Nūrī, *Mustadrak al-Wasā'il*, vol. 12, p. 214.
178. Ibid., p. 173.

CHAPTER 2

THE PSYCHOLOGICAL EFFECTS OF MARRIAGE

Throughout history, getting married and starting a family has always had a broad effect on various aspects of life and is not limited to a particular domain. By accepting this fact, in this chapter we examine the psychological effects of marriage on the lives of individuals. Then, by taking one aspect, that of widening social relationships, we will deal with family relationships and their consequences.

1. Satisfying Sexual Desire

Sexuality and the corresponding physical organs play an important part in human life. In order to sustain a healthy and peaceful mind, the first step is to acknowledge one's sexual feelings and those of others. Ignoring this can seriously upset the individual.[1] In the philosophy of psychology, desire is one of the forces within man, part of which has to do with sexuality.[2] Nevertheless, in most societies until a few decades ago – and before people like Freud – sexual matters were a cultural taboo. For example, research on students showed that most of them cannot ask their parents questions regarding sexuality, because the parents would either be angry and accuse their children of bad manners and having bad influences, or feel inferior and confused and then give the wrong answers or pretend ignorance. Although the parents' motivation is to protect the children, making sexual matters mysterious creates problems for the future.[3] The solution to this is proper sex education, and first of all, the belief that information on sexuality is dirty or embarrassing needs to be changed. In order for this to happen, the boundaries between the private space – the family – and the wider world should be clearly defined. Within the private domain of the husband and wife, it is desirable, and sometimes necessary, to share sexual talk in a healthy and legitimate way in order to help each other. If any major question or problem arises between them, they should under certain circumstances visit a psychologist or physician, otherwise the problem might become more severe. According to the teachings of Islām, reticence in this respect should be avoided,[4] and in response to certain questions put to them, the divine religious leaders would sometimes give answers that contained sexual remarks.[5] However, any discussion of these things in public should be indirect and within the necessary limits. What was said in respect of the importance of modesty in Islām refers to this.[6] Therefore, in Islamic texts, sexual issues are mentioned metaphorically and explicit descriptions are avoided. For example, in the Qur'ān, *mubāshirat*[7] means the physical skin contact between two people, being a "raiment"[8] for each other, and *rafath*[9] refers to various types of sexual pleasure.[10] The next step is to create a positive understanding of the sexual relationship and the resulting love. In this respect, the individual takes pleasure in his sexual feelings and those of his spouse, and does not feel a need to suppress them. Otherwise, there are likely to be problems with the fulfilment of sexual desires within the marriage, and even sexual disorders, a tendency to be attacked to people of the same sex, or sexual crimes. Things like this have often resulted from sexual repression. Moreover, the suppression of legitimate sexual feelings can cause problems with emotions and relationships.[11] Some like Freud have gone further, and explained personality and mental development in terms of the sexual instinct and its concentration in various parts of the body. Although some critics consider Freud's views exaggerated and extreme,[12] in general the importance of sexuality and its effective role in human behaviour cannot be denied, and ignoring or repressing it can cause mental imbalance.

The teachings of Islām are in accord with human nature[13] and take all physical and mental needs into consideration, and certain points regarding sexuality are mentioned in many verses of the Qur'ān. Loving, sexual relationships and the beauty they give to life are explicitly mentioned in the Qur'ān,[14] and there is even mention of the Prophet's love of women; the sexual relationship is accentuated[15] to the degree that the Prophet of Islām said: "In the world, I love perfume and women."[16] When there is mention of sexuality in Islamic texts, it is often addressed to men. This may be due to deference towards women:[17] "Modesty is better, but it is the best in women," and as it has been said that modesty has ten elements, nine of which concern women and one man.[18] Another reason is the apparently active part men take in these matters, and the assumption that women are more passive in this respect. We will deal with this more when discussing the family in Islām. Nonetheless, an important dimension of human life is seeking pleasure, which culminates in the sexual relationship.[19] The teachings of Islām have affirmed this, and even incorporated it with the afterlife. The divine religious leaders have said that, both here and in the next life, people do not take pleasure from anything more than they do from sexual union.[20] Hence, Islām has a positive outlook to this, and even gives it a spiritual dimension. The divine religious leaders have in numerous cases mentioned the reward in the afterlife for sexual relationships, which has sometimes surprised the people.[21] The divine religious leaders have equated the reward for sexual relationships with that of difficult religious duties such as *jihād* and the purification from sin,[22] thus investing it with a positive religious outlook and thus giving people an encouraging outlook towards these relationships and more pleasure in them. Reinforcing this attitude allays any feelings of guilt. Although the teachings of Islām resort to different methods to accommodate the pleasure of the sexual relationship, spurious customs and an incorrect religious interpretation of ethical questions can result in a sense of guilt. An advantage that Islām has over religions which have negative views about sexuality[23] is that it gives it a positive value. The fulfilment of sexual desire does not contradict chastity and piety, in the light of which one can satisfy this desire adequately, thus avoiding uncomfortable negative emotions, deprivation or strict repression. Nevertheless, attending to a need is not the same as unconditionally provoking it.[24]

According to the points mentioned, Islām accepts sexual satisfaction only within marriage, where it is considered the main support; therefore if for any reason it is not possible, the marriage can be easily dissolved.[25] Disease or disability in a man that impedes his sexuality entitles a woman to cancel a marriage, as provided in Article 1122 of the [Iranian] Civil Code and according to religious texts.[26] Moreover, it is a basic duty of each partner to satisfy the sexual needs of the other. In this connection, neither may refuse to have sexual intercourse with the excuse of performing worship.[27] The teachings of Islām not only stress the importance of establishing the sexual relationship, but also consider the pleasure of both sides. Therefore, advice is given to both partners in which the pleasure of the other person is emphasised. The woman is advised to submit to the relationship as much as possible, even if she is not in a peak condition.[28] Moreover, the woman should prepare herself with makeup, beautiful clothes and nice perfume,[29] while setting aside any modesty or inhibition during the sexual act[30] in order to fulfil the sexual needs of the man within the religious law.[31] At certain times of the day and night, she is expected to make these preparations.[32]

The teachings of Islām contain advice for making sexual intercourse pleasurable for the woman as well. The first point is the good physical condition and appearance of the man. A clean body and the wearing of perfume are things that appeal to the other person. In general, the man should be as much prepared for the woman as he expects her to be for him.[33] Another point is to take one's time. Men are advised to do this in order to fulfil the psychological needs of the woman and give her more pleasure.[34] In this respect, verbal and nonverbal communication[35] is used.[36] Foreplay is encouraged,[37] and the man is advised not to rush, so that the woman has her pleasure.[38] Attention to these points will make the sexual act more pleasurable for both sides. Otherwise, psychological problems and issues of compatibility will inevitably arise.[39] In the Qur'ān, after the decree permitting sexual intercourse during the nights of Ramaḍān, the man and the woman are described as raiment for each other.[40] This expression can be interpreted to mean that in the sexual relationship, each may protect the other's purity[41] if the relationship is satisfactory for both sides. In addition, this expression can be more appropriately interpreted as meaning that the relationship should be mutual, and that the two parties should cooperate.[42]

After the official marriage, Islamic teaching permits the couple various legitimate ways to satisfy their sexual desires. Nevertheless, men are advised to avoid any activity which might cause mental or physical harm to the woman. In this respect, it is the woman who brings happiness to the man and should not be abused.[43] The woman should make known any activity that is unpleasing to her;[44] even though it may well be technically permissible, it could be potentially damaging.[45] Sexual exchange is one of the most important elements of the relationship between the man and the woman, and involves close intimacy. In the sexual relationship, all kinds of immediate and remote problems emerge in the deepest form possible, the effects of which cause widespread changes beyond the matter of sexuality.[46] The teachings of Islām also mention such effects. The interaction of body and mind, which is the basis of relaxation with which the individual reaches peace of mind,[47] results in physical pleasure and the alleviation of certain tensions in the body, and this has been asserted by the divine religious leaders.[48] As well as causing happiness, the sexual exchange is also effective in eliminating depression and lethargy.[49] Conversely, impotence or the avoidance of sex may result in irritation and anger.[50] The divine religious leaders have shown ways to reinforce sexual desire and to maintain an interest in sexuality.[51] In this connection they have given advice for solving problems in sexual relationships[52] and for special circumstances.[53] Generally speaking, they explicitly uphold the idea of sexuality.[54]

In respect of human reproduction,[55] the Islamic teachings include recommendations regarding the method,[56] time[57] and place,[58] and some of the conditions concerning each partner. It has been emphasised that these things should be accompanied with the name of God and a request for healthy children.[59] There are also things mentioned in the teachings which concern the unborn child, such as the mental state of each partner during the sexual act, any words spoken[60] or thoughts,[61] one's behaviour,[62] feelings of peace or anxiety,[63] as well as the manner, place and time.[64] For example, it has been said that if the sexual act is on the night before a Friday, the child to be born will have the flair of a good speaker.[65]

A final point is psychological and physical hygiene. The teachings of Islām have many recommendations in this respect.[66] The general advice regarding the sexual relationship stresses moderation and control according to the age of the individual. This also affects a person's health and life experience.[67] Moreover, excessive sex can have an undesirable psychological effect, and this is also mentioned by the divine religious leaders.

2. Peace of Mind

An important goal of marriage is for the husband and wife to gain peace of mind from their close relationship. The Holy Qur'ān mentions this in several verses, for example:

> *And of His signs is this: He created for you helpmeets from yourselves that ye might find rest in them, and He ordained between you love and mercy;*[68] and *He it is Who did create you from a single soul, and therefrom did make his mate that he might take rest in her.*[69]

The relationship and attraction between the husband and wife is based on three factors:

The first involves similarities in mentality and basic physical form, which are more than simply being of the same kind.

The second includes physical and psychological differences, including hormonal differences. These differences make the man and the woman appeal to and approach each other. Moreover, having complementary personalities provides the ground for this. Similarities and complementarities are two important factors in interpersonal attraction,[70] which most exegetes have asserted when interpreting the pacifying relationship of husband and wife.[71]

Part of the mutual attraction has to do with sexuality, which becomes manifested in the sexual relationship and desire.

The third factor is the human need to seek a bond.[72] The man and the woman stimulate each other positively, and in times of trouble are companions who support each other. With such a bond between them, they can more easily face the uncertainties of the future. In their relationship with each other the need for mutual appreciation is fulfilled.

The study of the psychological conditions of young people prior to marriage shows how marriage can bring peace of mind. Before marriage, the individual is somehow restless and anxious due to sexual needs. Friendships during youth cannot provide perfect peace of mind. On the other hand, sexual acts outside lawful marriage have intensified the idea of mutual love within marriage, and the kindness and love of a companion in life is one of the most important motivations for marriage.[73] It is evident that mutual kindness, sympathy and acceptance are necessary ingredients in life.[74] The attraction of strong complementary feelings cannot be fully realised other than in marriage.[75] As already mentioned, passages in the Qur'ān assert the peace of marriage. In fact, it can be said that the closest human relationship is the affective relationship between husband and wife, through which worries and troubles can be reduced. Therefore, the family can be an important source of the relief of tension.[76]

The role of the husband and wife relationship becomes clearer if it is damaged or absent. The most stressful of times are those when family relationships are damaged or they collapse altogether. If the death of a spouse results in 100 degrees of tension, then divorce scores 73, separation from a spouse 65, sexual problems 39, as well as the tension generated by family quarrels.[77] Such things are more stressful than other events in life. Therefore, the best way to tackle stress is for the husband and wife to have a satisfactory relationship. If support is needed, the husband and wife are the best companions for each other.[78] Studies show that financial help, emotional support and cooperation are three important factors in family life, although the first two are said to be more important.[79]

Islamic texts interpret the affection between the husband and wife as fellowship and verbal interaction.[80] In describing this very close relationship, the Holy Qur'ān uses a very beautiful and subtle metaphor: *They are raiment for you and ye are raiment for them.*[81] Here, "raiment" is a source of peace, and there is an analogy with "night," in that both the night and the marital bond bring peace.[82] Also, a raiment in the literal sense has different functions; it covers the private and sensitive parts of the body, it protects against cold, heat and exposure. In addition, it is nowadays a significant personal ornament, a symbol of national or professional identity, and a reflection of the personality. The husband and wife have similar functions for each other. Each can cover the defects of the other, protect them from danger, and beautify each other.[83]

According to research, women are regarded as mothers, spouses, and intimate friends who generate happiness. The wife can be the biggest source of satisfaction, and this has a close inverse relationship with depression.[84] Fellowship and affection in the family also exist between the parents and the children. The affection of the mother and child is taken as a matter of course.[85] Most parents are happy with their children and they laugh together.[86] In general, marriage and family life form the perfect arena for affection, fellowship and peace. It is of interest that the model of intimacy and affection among adults is similar to that which they experienced with their parents.[87]

The affective bonds between adults, especially a married couple, are a continuation of the affective bonds between the child and his parents, but at a different level, since marriage is an experimental ground for forming these bonds.[88]

In this respect, childhood affection is very much related to spousal affection. Research shows that the model of mother and child affection depends on the degree of physical, visual and verbal contact and the mother's awareness of and response to the child's needs. If this relationship provides safety, the child will enjoy positive emotions, empathy, high self-esteem and peaceful interaction with peers and adults in the future. When such a person approaches their spouse, they feel comfortable about relying on them, and can generally have a satisfactory and committed long-term relationship.[89] Those with a sufficient degree of affection experience security, intimacy, are attentive to their spouse and have empathy with them. They are better equipped to withstand external pressure, since they can rely on the support of the other and are more satisfied in marital life.[90] Couples who feel protected benefit from the comfort of intimacy and a lack of anxiety, and find it easy to support one another. They are more responsible towards and sensitive to their partner and consequently have a higher degree of marital satisfaction and health.[91]

Therefore, it is evident that there should be an emphasis in the teachings of Islām on marriage and the peace of mind and tranquillity resulting from it, with affection being but one of the various psychological aspects.

3. Growth and Development of the Personality

Marriage has important effects on the growth of the personality and spiritual perfection. From the spiritual point of view, the divine religious leaders have asserted that a half of a person's faith involves marriage,[92] and the value of that person's acts of worship will be several times greater than those of someone who is unmarried.[93] From another point of view, morality and chastity are better protected by marriage.[94] The term "raiment," referring to the husband and wife, indicates their mutual protection against moral and sexual corruption.[95] This not only increases the person's spiritual rank, but also improves his personality. If someone does not marry, he may be led astray due to the pressures of sexual desire. The results are feelings of guilt and inferiority, and damaged self-esteem. This reduction of self-worth forms an obstacle to growth and perfection.

Nevertheless, we should bear in mind that even if someone can control themselves morally without getting married, they would still be deprived of the accompanying growth and development. They will have abandoned what is natural for mankind, and in particular, the example of the most perfect of people in the past, such as the prophets and the divine religious leaders. Those such as Jesus Christ, Yaḥyā and the Virgin

Mary are exceptions, since Mary's pregnancy took place without any sexual relationship, and the birth of Jesus Christ is unique. Therefore, remaining unmarried should not be a model for others. In this respect, Muṭahharī mentions those who controlled their desires without getting married and technically reached high positions, but one can see in them a kind of defect or naivety. It seems that there is a kind of spiritual perfection that cannot be attained other than in the school of the family. It is interesting that marriage, despite its association with sexuality, has a perfecting, developmental aspect, and is therefore a recommended tradition in Islām.[96]

An important factor for the developing personality is a sense of self-worth. The husband and wife usually love and praise each other,[97] and this increases their feelings of self-worth. As already mentioned, marriage clears the way for mental stability and the fulfilment of sexual desire. The proper fulfilment of these desires is another factor in strengthening one's self-esteem. The process of becoming a spouse and then a parent is considered a kind of perfection of the personality. As Muṭahharī has mentioned, the role of marriage in developing one's personality[98] makes the person feel others as a part of himself. Piaget sees the movement from egocentrism to decentration in the course of child development as the cause of ascending to a higher phase,[99] and this can also be applied to marriage. An altruistic attitude of sacrifice towards one's spouse and children is a manifestation of this development.

4. Preparing the Ground for Bringing Up a Child

An important function of marriage is to perpetuate one's own kind and bring them up for a life in society. This is greatly emphasised in Islām.[100] The Prophet encourages people to get married and places importance on reproduction, and sees this as a source of merit in himself.[101] Most people are interested in continuing their family line and have children of their own. This feeling is stronger in women, and some authors reify this by invoking certain verses[102] of the Qur'ān. One such verse points to Moses' mother, whose devotion was entirely for her son, and because of their separation, she was so upset and anxious that she could save herself only with God's blessing.[103] Nevertheless, the biological relationship between the mother and the child – both of whom at a certain stage form a single biological entity – and the full biological dependence of the child on the mother during the months when the mother suckles the child, creates the deepest of affective bonds. There is also a strong emotional relationship with the father, although not so intimately biological. Parent and child affective relationships are satisfying, enlivening and bring peace, and they are the source of the affective relationship between the child and his future spouse, as well as towards society as a whole.[104] Moreover, it has been said that the source of many other affective relationships, such as friendship, empathy and a willingness to help others is found in the family.

Islām attends to this psychological need for having children, and there are many prayers in Islamic texts in this respect. In many cases, those who were unable to have a child consulted the divine religious leader, who would give them advice that included certain prayers.[105] The Qur'ān also considers it good to pray for having children.[106] The divine religious leaders said that having children is a source of happiness in life, and that a person is happy with a child who is similar to him in morality, behaviour and appearance.[107] One who does not seek children deprives himself of a strong social support, since a child is often the best support.[108] These affective needs are all fulfilled within marriage and the family. Research shows that children born of illegitimate sexual relationships or artificial insemination without a legal marriage have many emotional problems, including a sense of shame and emotional ambivalence towards the mother.[109] Regarding fatherless children:

> "The child's personality develops under strong influence from the parents. The absence of either or both of them will have an undesirable effect on the child's development and will make him susceptible to psychological diseases or behavioural problems."[110]

During the period 1994-97, 345 articles were published on the effects of the father's absence on children. The effects can be direct, such as having no male role model, or indirect in the case of support. In addition, the father's absence has a wider emotional, economic and social effect on the family.

Generally speaking, psychological disorders in illegitimate children are directly related to those of the mother.[111] The deprivation of a satisfactory affective relationship with either or both parents will have harmful consequences for a child, and this can be observed in research relating to the children of collapsed families or divorce.[112] Research shows that the rates of psychological imbalance, attempted suicide, self-harm and substance addiction are higher in children of single-parent families, particularly if it is the mother who heads the family. Research confirms the consequences of the father's absence in the development of the male identity, success at school and social confidence. Aggressive tendencies, low self-esteem, anxiety, criminal behaviour and depression are more frequent in such cases.[113] It is in consideration of these points that Islām stresses the importance of having children within marriage, when everyone concerned may benefit from the good psychological effects of having children. This is why the divine religious leaders have counselled so much on children and the effects in the afterlife of having children.[114]

5. Expanding Social Relationships Through Blood Ties

Getting married expands one's social environment. Through marriage, two branches of new relationships are formed, and with the birth of children, blood relationships are expanded. In addition, new bonds are established with various individuals. The Qur'ān points out these two types of relationship.[115] In this connection, the more people marry outside the extended family – not their cousins, for example – the greater the increase in relationships. In the discussion of family relationships, we examine the role of marriage in expanding the social sphere. In the present era, the nuclear family has developed, urbanisation has increased, and larger distances are covered, as was mentioned in the definition of the family. The teachings of Islām consider the family inclusive of other relatives who are part of the family system, and this compensates for the limitations resulting from the nuclear family. We will now examine the various aspects of family relations.

5.1. The Importance of Family Relations

Present social conditions and the increasing industrial developments of recent centuries have reinforced the nuclear family, in such a way that, by getting married, the individual separates from the main family and the relationship usually becomes increasingly weaker. This is a situation that for various reasons threatens the family institution. From an economic point of view, the newlywed couple should try to work hard to provide for their immediate family life, bearing in mind that in most cases they are deprived of help from their original families. In addition, from an affective point of view, the nuclear family is deprived of the social and emotional support of the original families in times of trouble. All these things can cause emotional problems and increase pressure. In the past, a connection with the original family prevented many problems. Nowadays, because of the complexities of industrial society, the extended family has all but disappeared. Today, the husband and wife living independently is unavoidable, nor would it be appropriate within Islām to prevent it being so. The nuclear family thus forms the primary family unit, although the individual is still part of the second- and third-level family, that is, his parents' family and the extended family. This interdependence entails certain responsibilities as well as rights. The teachings of Islām emphasise family relationships in order to support the small family, help it grow and solve its problems. By reinforcing the hierarchy of family relationships, one can take significant steps in order to solve family problems, or at least reduce them. At the same time, the individual's responsibilities towards the second- and third-level family should also be fulfilled.

Part of Islām's focus on family relations is for this reason. Therefore, many aspects of Islamic teachings emphasise the maintenance and continuation of family relationships, while certain verses in the Qur'ān and words of the divine religious leaders stress the positive effects of these ties, and the unfavourable consequences of terminating them. God has said that one's responsibilities regarding the divine injunctions are as important as those in family relationships.[116] The Prophet said:

> "The best behaviour in religion after belief in God is establishing family relationships."[117]

The various Islamic laws concerning worship, as well as economic and social matters, show how highly Islām regards family relationships. Certain acts of worship are invalidated if they adversely affect family relationships.[118] The inheritance law demonstrates the priority of relatives, with certain conditions pertaining to financial duties such as *zakāt* (alms for the poor), and the responsibility of some relatives in legal or criminal matters, such as the blood money of paternal kinsmen.[119] In addition, according to the divine religious leaders, visiting one's relatives and *jihād* are the best paths to God, with the former sometimes considered more important.[120]

5.2. Types of Family Relations

Visiting relatives consolidates various ties. What should exist in all such relationships is a kind of commitment to the relatives. This involves suitable conversation, emphasising with any of their problems and, if necessary, providing advice and financial help. However, if one is indifferent or inattentive towards relatives, even if they are visited, one's Islamic duty not fulfilled. Bearing this in mind, we would like to mention various types of relationship. The first type is done in a way that one connects with them. In the teachings of Islām, visiting one's relatives is stressed by the divine religious leaders to the extent that they say: "If it is necessary to travel for one year to visit a relative, then do so,"[121] and this is because it is a religious duty.[122] The failure of relatives to visit one other amounts to failing in this duty. Just talking to and greeting each other means that a relationship is in place to a certain extent, but this alone is not enough. Also, occasionally upsetting relatives by one's words or actions has undesirable consequences, as will be mentioned. The minimum that one should do is to avoid any upsets.[123] The more extensive one's relationships, the more one has fulfilled God's commands.

Visiting one's relatives prepares the ground for social support. Initially, a basic form of support is the expression of affection and talking about the issues and problems in life. Consulting them on different matters, using their experience and gaining useful information about family life are among the cognitive effects of such visits. Having parties and giving food is at a higher degree. According to the divine religious leaders, attending to the welfare of one's relatives, which includes feeding them, is said to be rewarded in many different ways, and God will greatly reward the person who works with his life and property to maintain family relationships. Financial aid to relatives has also been recommended.[124] Even lending money to relatives to ease their financial problems is considered a good example.[125]

5.3. Family Relations Following the Marriage

After they marry, the husband and wife form a new family unit within a particular framework that excludes the parents of both spouses. The husband and wife now have a kind of independence, and the privacy of their life should be respected. Any strong dependence of either of them on their parents will create problems within the new unit, as some psychologists have noted.[126] Any exchange of information from within this unit should be done according to the religious values and the mutual agreement of the parties involved.

While observing these conditions, it is necessary to maintain the relationships with the original families and acknowledge the rights of the parents. After getting married, the husband and wife confront two kinds of affective dependency. There is the dependence on parents and original family members such as brothers and sisters, as well as on the spouse. Both kinds of dependency have their own strengths. Dependence on the original family is rooted in blood, and the dependence on the spouse is based on deep affection. Usually, the individual faces a conflict when faced with these two dependencies, especially when one side seeks to monopolise the relationship. Under such circumstances, the couple needs to continue an appropriate relationship with the parents and other relatives, fully considering the rights of the parents, as well as observing the spouse's rights. Many couples embarking upon a new life sacrifice the rights of one side for the other in times of trouble. However, the difficult but important task is to acknowledge the rights of both parties. For example, if the man's parents have expectations of him that infringe upon the rights of his wife, he should overlook the wishes of his parents while still respecting them. The applies also to the woman. In order to fulfil these obligations, the husband and wife should moderate their attitudes. If they both admit and respect an affective attachment to the original family, they will never underestimate or sever it. The parents of each partner should understand their needs and allow for their independence, and understand that the emotional attachment of the newly married couple for each other might conflict with their own attachment.

After continuing the relationship with the original family, it is also a duty of the husband and wife to establish good relationships with the relatives of their spouse, especially the parents. Although visiting one's own parents does not include relatives by marriage, having good relationships with the relatives of one's spouse has an important and effective role in reinforcing the relationship of the couple. Islām provides guidelines for reinforcing one's relationships by marriage, according to which one's in-laws are considered as one's own parents,[127] and it is necessary to afford them due respect. An interesting point in the English language is that the words for the in-laws, such as "father-in-law," "mother-in-law" or "brother-in-law," demonstrate their similarity with one's own father, mother and brother. Such terms are very useful for a smooth relationship with the spouse's relatives. On the other hand, one's own parents should have an appropriate relationship with their son- or daughter-in-law. If the parents consider their son- or daughter-in-law as their own child, the affective relationship will be much stronger. This understanding was also the practice of the divine religious leaders.[128] Obviously, attention to the relationships with one's spouse's relatives, or failure therein, affects both the husband and wife. Therefore, in order to maintain mutual relationships and prevent problems in the family, the husband and wife should both observe the rights of each other's parents and relatives.

5.4. The Effects of Family Relations

Family relationships have many effects on people's lives as well as life after death, as mentioned in the religious texts. According to the divine religious leaders, visiting one's parents lengthens one's life more than any other activity.[129] It has also been said that one's life will be lengthened by establishing family relationships.[130] Moreover, it has been said that visiting one's parents will prevent problems[131] and an unfavourable death.[132] Physical health has also been given as an effect of visiting one's relatives.[133] The elimination of poverty,[134] improved sustenance,[135] and the flourishing of families[136] and communities[137] are other effects of having good family relationships. Establishing such relationships will improve people's conduct[138] and behaviour[139] and give them joy and peace of mind.[140] Moreover, the family relationship will increase a person's popularity.[141] One can even observe that even those of little faith or those in error who maintain family relationships benefit in worldly effects, such as financial increase. Indeed, it can therefore be said that if a person has stronger faith, the effects will be better.[142]

One can provide a psychological explanation for the effects of family relationships. People face all kinds of pressures in life, in the light of which social support plays an important role, and a major part of this comes from family relationships. These connections provide the space for the emotional expression that promotes peace of mind.

In addition to this, these relationships will help the person cope with internal issues. Self-expression is a means of tranquilising mental problems. At the same time, one enjoys the empathy and guidance of others. During family visits, through the process of emotional expression, negative and imaginary thoughts are modified,[143] and depression can be reduced to a certain degree. In view of the importance of combating tension for physical and psychological health, and the considerable effect of family relationships in this respect, one can to a certain extent explain the way family ties can lengthen one's life and improve one's health.

Part of the communal support involved concerns help if there is financial pressure, and Islamic teachings supply the necessary advice.[144] An example is the lending of money to relatives, which is several times more meritorious than giving money away,[145] even though lent money will return to the lender, while money given away does not. In this case, the Qur'ān mentions that God will reward the lender several times more than the person who gives money away.[146]

Conversely, if someone refuses to lend money to someone in need while capable of doing so, God will deprive him of the fragrance of paradise.[147] Moreover, feeding one's relatives[148] and supporting them financially without recompense is very much encouraged.[149] For instance, it has been said in a religious narration that the giving of money to relatives who are in financial trouble is given the highest reward.[150] According to Islām, in certain cases people have to solve the financial and subsistence problems of their close relatives. Otherwise, they have failed to abide by God's command and are therefore sinful.[151] Inheritance issues, which are also decided according to the status of the relationship, constitute a law which in certain cases can help solve the financial problems of the relatives.[152]

Without a doubt, visiting one's relatives is greatly rewarded in the next life, and the divine religious leaders refer to this in order to encourage people to maintain such relationships. Examples of this are: "This will ease the evaluation of one's deeds on the Day of Resurrection,"[153] "It will cause God's anger to subside,"[154] "It will bring the person close to God on the Day of Resurrection,"[155] "It will help the person cross the Bridge of the Path, which is a difficult stage on the Day of Resurrection, and will easily take him to Heaven,"[156] "Its reward is more swift than the reward of any other action,"[157] and "It will protect the person against sins."[158] One who fulfils the rights of his relatives with his property and life will be greatly rewarded by God, and for each step that he has taken, will be given the reward of a thousand good deeds and forgiven a thousand bad ones; it is as if he had worshipped God for a hundred years in patience, in the hope of reward.[159] It has also been said that there is a level in Paradise that no one reaches other than the just Imam and the one who has patiently fulfilled his family obligations.[160]

5.5. The Effects of Cutting off Family Ties

In addition to emphasising the desirable worldly and otherworldly effects of establishing and maintaining family relationships, Islām also provides prescriptions for deterring people from cutting these ties. Interesting items of advice, found less often in other religions and cultures, concern re-establishing family ties with those who have been cut off. This is according to leading religious figures, including the Prophet and Imām 'Alī , as found in the following: "Even if your relative chose to stay away from you, you should establish ties with him,"[161] "Even if your brother violates your rights, you should maintain your relationship with him,"[162] and "One of the best moral deeds in this and next world is to establish a relationship with the relative who has cut ties."[163]

Although it may seem difficult to do this, in some cases it results in a strengthening of the family, and encourages amicable respect from the person concerned. Therefore, maintaining these connections is desirable for both parties. Examples of such things can be found in the practice of the divine religious leaders.[164] It is worth mentioning that if the other person insists on cutting ties, it has an undesirable effect only on him, while the person who has attempted reconciliation will be protected from any bad consequences.[165]

The teachings of Islām also stress the consequences in this world and the next of cutting family ties in order to reduce the number of people who feel trapped and compelled to do so. According to verses in the Qur'ān, those who cut family ties are deemed losers,[166] and can expect God's wrath in the next world.[167] By cutting family ties, one is both depriving the rest of the family of support, and depriving oneself of the attention of many people;[168] one is deprived of their emotional, social and financial support and creating conditions in which poverty,[169] a short life,[170] sudden death,[171] severe problems, disasters[172] and defenselessness are inevitable,[173] and as already stated, other undesirable consequences in worldly life.[174] Cutting family ties prepares the ground for the destruction of the family.[175] Another effect is a weakening of the family economy, because the greater the problem, the less room there is for cooperation and progress, since some of the material assets will be allocated to the problem; and in certain cases, money and property are put at the disposal of the wrong people, and it then makes it possible for them to dominate the other relatives.[176]

The cutting of family ties will adversely affect a person spiritually and have consequences in the next world. The person who inattentive towards the family is considered impious.[177] Families who cut off relationships will be deprived of spiritual success, including the blessings of being with the angels.[178] Other consequences are remoteness from God's blessings on the Day of Resurrection,[179] distance from Heaven[180] and being deprived of its fragrance.[181] As there is no acceptable excuse for failing to observe family duties,[182] he who does so has committed the ugliest of sins,[183] and therefore will not enter Heaven.

All these warnings demonstrate the importance of maintaining family relationships. The teachings of Islām intend that people should have the advantage of the psychological, social and financial support that such relationships provide. Therefore, the divine religious leaders worked hard to encourage what should be done and deter what should not be done in this respect, so that people might enjoy the advantages to be found therein.

5.6 Levels of Family Relations in Islām

According to certain verses in the Qur'ān, there are various levels within the family, with the higher levels having more rights.[184] Among other things, inheritance is divided according to these levels. If we consider the newly formed family, the Islamic scale of family relationships from the standpoint of the newlywed couple are as follows:

1. Parents, children and grandchildren;
2. Grandparents and great grandparents;
3. Siblings and their children i.e. nephews and nieces (immediate or otherwise);
4. Parents' siblings, i.e. uncles and aunts (immediate or otherwise);
5. Children of parents' siblings, i.e. cousins.

The first four groups are considered closely related, which means that intermarriage between them would amount to incest.[185] Moreover, when visiting these people, certain religious injunctions, such as wearing the *ḥijāb* (the Islamic veil), may not apply,[186] and this illustrates the closeness of these relatives. In a similar fashion, certain rules such as the *ḥijāb* are lifted for close relatives such as the spouse's parents, marriage to whom is prohibited. Apparently, one of the reasons for having rules that define whom one may marry is to protect the family relationships.[187] The importance of the connections with relatives of the first four levels has resulted in rules concerning others. For example, one does not need permission to enter the house of anyone in these four groups and cook food, whereas one needs permission to do so in the houses of others.[188]

In establishing the various types of family relationships as mentioned, it is necessary to bear these matters in mind. For example, if the parents encounter economic problems, the children should help them as much as they can. As well as the obligation to visit them, other relatives have a priority according to their status in financial matters. Admittedly people these days have to take into consideration several contemporary problems concerning communication and transport, but generally the children can visit the parents once a week, the siblings once a month, and so on throughout the other levels.

5.7. Problems in Family Relations

The teachings of Islām are meant to protect these relationships. While mentioning the difficult conditions concerning the Resurrection, some verses of the Qur'ān say how relatives are separated from each other. One therefore remains alone, disconnected from one's parents, spouse and children,[189] and on this day they cannot offer any help.[190] Such descriptions of the Day of Resurrection are expressed in order to help people gain insight, comply with the divine injunctions and observe the rights of others. It can generally be said that any family relationship that fails to abide by God's commands is wrong. In other words, individuals should act justly, even though it may appear at first to be disadvantageous to them or their relatives.[191] In judicial matters such as giving testimony, it is necessary to observe justice, even if it results in loss to oneself or one's relatives. A problem in our society is the use of family relationships for social or administrative advantage. People appoint their relatives to jobs, even if that person is unqualified for the responsibility. An emphasis on a person's abilities would deter this from happening, and be within the boundaries of justice and truth. According to the Qur'ān, everyone is responsible for his own behaviour,[192] and no one else can shoulder the burden of that responsibility.[193] Therefore, it is necessary in all these cases to observe people's rights and duties. The way Imām 'Alī treated his brother, Aqīl, when he was in severe financial difficulties and asked for a bigger share of the public treasury[194] is a great lesson.

Nonetheless, it is possible that family visits might provide an opportunity for damaging people's reputations, if they are the object of gossip, mockery or blame in conversation, which is strongly criticised in the teachings of Islām, and for which there are penalties in this world and the next.[195] During family visits, there is ample opportunity to talk with and learn from each other, but sometimes it can lead to verbal abuse. Whereas having prayers and Qur'ān readings, and learning from the experience of one's elders – who, according to the divine religious leaders are like prophets among one's relatives[196] – can add to a positive, spiritual dimension to family visits.

Another possible source of harm is the undue and sometimes harmful interference in the lives of others, which perhaps frequently occurs. Giving social or financial support someone does not allow interference in their life or imposing one's own views on them. The divine religious leaders have said that the most valuable aspect of family relationships is the avoidance of doing harm to each other,[197] which is nevertheless something that can result from undue interference.

Rivalry in worldly matters is another harmful aspect. One should attend to the advice of Islām in avoiding luxury,[198] and a way to do this is to encourage competition in good deeds and spirituality instead.[199]

The family should not be a cause of ignoring God's commands. It is harmful if bad behaviour emerges in a family gathering and the divine commands are overlooked. The Qur'ān emphasises the emotional characteristics of the family, and seriously warns against those who prefer the friendship of the family to the friendship of God and their sacred duties.[200] Moreover, the Qur'ān describes one's family and children as a means of testing an individual.[201] This raises one's awareness so that one keeps to the religion as well as family responsibilities.

We address the Prophet and the divine religious leaders in prayer with words such as:

> "May my father and mother [or 'may I and my family'] be a sacrifice for you,"[202]

and this expresses how we love them more than our own families. These words are in fact a practice which ensures that people uphold the commands of God and the divine religious leaders as much as possible, as well as observing the rights of their relatives. All this can reduce some of the harm caused in the family that might result from a failure to adhere to the divine commands.

Notes

1. Satir, Jane, *Making Humans in Psychology of the Family*, (Tehran: Rushd Publications, 1370 A.H). p. 131.
2. Khājavī, Muḥammad, *Tarjumih Asfār*, vol. 2/4, pp. 85-87.
3. Satir, Jane, *Making Humans in Psychology of the Family*, p. 131.
4. Al-Ḥurr al-ʿĀmilī, *Wasā'il al-Shīʿa*, vol. 14, p. 15.
5. Ibid., pp.38, 72,75,77, 83 and 84.
6. Al-Kulaynī, *Kāfī,* vol. 2, p. 606; Majlisī, *Biḥār al-Anwār*, vol. 68, p. 331; Majlisī, *Biḥār al-Anwār*, vol. 5, p.197, see the narrations that emphasise keeping the sexual relationship in confidence. Also see Qur'ān 24:58, regarding the need for children to ask for permission to enter the parents' room at three times of the day and night. This all indicates how important public decency is.
7. "So now, have relations with them and seek that which Allāh hath decreed for you, Qur'ān 2:187.
8. They are raiment for you and you are raiment for them, Qur'ān 2:187.
9. It is made lawful for you to go in unto your wives on the night of the fast, Qur'ān 2:187.
10. Ismāʿīlī, ʿAlī , *Javān, Angīzih va Raftār Jinsī* , p. 40.
11. Satir, Jane, *Making Humans in Psychology of the Family*,), pp. 132-134.
12. Daftar Hamkārī Ḥawzah va Dānishgāh, *Maktabhā-yi Ravānshināsī va Naqd ān*, p. 321.
13. Certain verses of the Qur'ān emphasise this, such as 30:30: So direct thy face [O Muḥammad] toward religion, inclining to truth. [Adhere to] the nature [framed] of Allāh, in which He hath created man. Also Al-Kulaynī, *Kāfī,* vol. 5, p. 494.
14. Beautified for mankind is love of the joys [that come] from women, Qur'ān 3:14.
15. Al-Ḥurr al-ʿĀmilī, *Wasā'il al-Shīʿa*, vol. 14, p. 10 and p. 4.
16. Majlisī, *Biḥār al-Anwār*, vol. 73, p. 649.
17. Farīd Tunikābunī, Murtaḍā, *Nahj al-Fasāḥa*, p. 425.

18. Majlisī, *Biḥār al-Anwār*, vol. 71, p. 336.
19. Al-Ḥurr al-'Āmilī, *Wasā'il al-Shī'a*, vol. 14, p. 10.
20. Ibid.
21. Ibid., p. 77.
22. Ibid., p. 76; Nūrī, *Mustadrak al-Wasā'il*, vol. 14, p. 150.
23. Ackner, R. A., *Selection of Russell's Thoughts, Psychology of Marital Relations*, pp. 121-136.
24. Muṭahharī, *Akhlāq Jinsī dar Islām va Jahān Gharb*, p. 55.
25. According to the laws of Islām, deficiences that impede the sexual satisfaction of either party may result in the cancellation of the marriage. Khumeinī, Sayyid Rūhullāh, *Taḥrīr al- Wasīla*, vol. 2, pp. 292-293.
26. Rāstī, Zahrā, et al, *Inḥilāl Nikāḥ bi Vāsitih-yi 'Ayb*, pp. 31 and 61.
27. Forbid not the good things which Allāh hath made lawful for you," Qur'ān 5:87; Al-Ḥurr al- al-'Āmilī, *Wasā'il al-Shī'a*, vol. 14, p. 8; and for the woman, p. 117.
28. Ibid., p. 112.
29. Ibid.
30. Ibid., p. 15.
31. Ibid., p. 14.
32. Ibid., p. 112.
33. Ibid., p. 183.
34. Ibid., p. 82; p.83; p. 83.
35. Jazā'irī, Sayyid 'Abdullāh, *Tuḥfa al-Sunniyyah*, p. 277.
36. Ibid.; Majlisī, *Biḥār al-Anwār*, vol. 52, p.327; Al-Ḥurr al-'Āmilī, *Wasā'il al-Shī'a*, vol. 14, p. 77.
37. Nūrī, *Mustadrak al-Wasā'il*, vol. 14, pp. 179, 221.
38. Mūsilī, Aḥmad ibn 'Alī , *Masnad ibn Ya'lā*, vol. 7, p. 209; al-Haythamī, 'Alī ibn Abī Bakr, *Majma' al-Zawā'id*, p. 295
39. 'Akk, Khālid 'Abd al-Raḥmān, *Ādāb al-Ḥayāt al-Zawjiyyah*, pp. 413-416.
40. It is made lawful for you to go in unto your wives on the night of the fast. They are raiment for you and ye are raiment for them, Qur'ān 2:187.
41. According to the author of the exegesis *Majma' al-Bayān*, "raiment" here refers to sexual relations between the man and the woman and the man (Tabrisī, *Majma' al-Bayān fī Tafsīr al-Qur'ān*, vol. 1, under Qur'ān 2:187).
42. 'Akk, Khālid 'Abd al-Raḥmān, *Ādāb al-Ḥayāt al-Zawjiyyah*, p. 421.
43. Al-Ḥurr al-'Āmilī, *Wasā'il al-Shī'a*, vol. 14, p. 120.
44. Majlisī, *Biḥār al-Anwār*, vol. 101, p. 29; Will ye commit abomination such as no creature ever did before you? Qur'ān 7:80; Ibid.

45. Tabātabā'ī-Yazdī, *'Urwah al-Wuthqā*, vol. 2, p. 808; Here are my daughters! They are purer for you, Qur'ān 11:78; Majlisī, *Biḥār al-Anwār*, vol. 100, p. 29.
46. Siemon, F. B., *Key Concepts and Theories*, p. 190.
47. Fatḥī, Rasūl, *Relax Therapy*, pp. 158-200.
48. Majlisī, *Biḥār al-Anwār*, vol. 100, p. 291.
49. Nūrī, *Mustadrak al-Wasā'il*, vol. 14, ch. 14, p. 169; Ibn Sīnā (Avicenna), Ḥusayn ibn 'Abdullāh, *Qānūn*, vol. 1, p. 31; Al-Ḥurr al-'Āmilī, *Wasā'il al-Shī'a*, vol. 14, p. 37.
50. Majlisī, *Biḥār al-Anwār*, vol. 101, p. 46.
51. Ibid., pp. 80-83; Al-Ḥurr al-'Āmilī, *Wasā'il al-Shī'a*, vol. 14, p. 85.
52. Al-Ḥurr al-'Āmilī, *Wasā'il al-Shī'a*, vol. 14, pp. 34-38.
53. Ibid., p. 72.
54. Ibid., pp. 75-76.
55. Seek that which Allāh hath ordained for you, Qur'ān 2:187.
56. Al-Ḥurr al-'Āmilī, *Wasā'il al-Shī'a*, vol. 14, p. 85 regarding looking, and p. 84 regarding the relations.
57. Ibid., pp. 80, 88, 90, 91, 93 and 187.
58. Ibid., pp. 84 and 98.
59. Ibid., pp. 79, 81, 82 and 96.
60. Ibid., pp. 86-87.
61. Ibid., p. 188; Majlisī, *Biḥār al-Anwār*, vol. 100, p. 282.
62. Ibid., p. 189.
63. Majlisī, *Biḥār al-Anwār*, vol. 36, p. 415, vol. 40, p. 169, vol. 60, pp. 251 and 359.
64. Al-Ḥurr al-'Āmilī, *Wasā'il al-Shī'a*, vol. 14, pp. 89, 94, 95, 99, 187, 189 and 190.
65. Ibid., p. 190.
66. Ibid., pp. 80, 98, 99, 191 and 192; Majlisī, *Biḥār al-Anwār*, vol. 59, pp. 261 and 327.
67. Majlisī, *Biḥār al-Anwār*, vol. 100, p. 295.
68. Qur'ān 30:21.
69. Qur'ān 7:189.
70. Ādharbāyjānī, Mas'ūd et al, *Ravānshināsī-yi Ijtimā'ī ba Nigāhī bi Manābi' Islāmī*, pp. 256-261.
71. Including Zamakhsharī, Maḥmūd ibn 'Umar, *Kashshāf*, vol. 3, p. 472; Rashīd Reḍā, *Tafsīr al-Minār*, vol. 9, p. 518; Tabātabā'ī, *Tafsīr al-Mīzān*, vol. 16, p. 166.
72. Ādharbāyjānī, Mas'ūd et al, Ravānshināsī-yi Ijtimā'ī ba Nigāhī bi Manābi' Islāmī, p. 248.
73. Although life together may pave the way for mutual love to a certain extent, since this is not always the norm in many cultures, and is also a shaky

relationship in which either party might have another sexual partner, this can never be a good background for mutual affective and psychological support.

74. Bornstein, F.C., Marriage Therapy, (Izdivāj Darmānī),, pp. 12-13.
75. Rashīd Reḍā, *Tafsīr al-Minār*, vol. 9, p. 518.
76. Mazāhirī, Muḥammad 'Alī et al, 'Muqāyasah-yi Bihdāsht Ravānī dar Zawjhā-yi Jashnhā-yi Izdivāj Dānishjū'ī va Zawjhā-yi 'Ādī', in *Anjuman Irani-yi Ravānshināsī Quarterly*, p. 53.
77. Di Matteo, M. *Health Psychology*, vol. 2, pp. 525-534.
78. Ibid., p. 764.
79. Argyle, Michael, *The Psychology of Happiness*, p. 141.
80. Al-Ḥurr al-'Āmilī, *Wasā'il al-Shī'a*, vol. 14, p. 2.
81. Qur'ān, 2:187.
82. And have appointed the night as a cloak, Qur'ān 78:10; Tabrisī, *Majma' al-Bayān fī Tafsīr al-Qur'ān* , vol. 1, p. 504.
83. Makārim Shīrāzī, Nāsir, *Tafsīr Nimūnih*, vol. 1, p. 473, under exegesis of the same verse.
84. Argyle, Michael, *The Psychology of Happiness*, p. 142, p. 128.
85. Mansūr, Maḥmūd and Parīrukh Dādsitān, Dīdgāh Piaget dar Gustarih-yi Taḥavvul Ravānī, vol. 2, pp. 150-154.
86. Argyle, Michael, *The Psychology of Happiness*, p. 135.
87. Ibid., p. 128.
88. Bīshārat, Muḥammad 'Alī and Manīzhih Fīrūzī, 'Muqāyasah-yi Zanān va Mardān Nābārvar bar Ḥasab Sabk Delbastigī va Sāzish Ravānshinākhtī bā Bārdārī' in *Ravānshināsī va 'Ulūm Tarbiyatī Journal*, p 29.
89. Ādharbāyjānī, Mas'ūd et al, Ravānshināsī-yi Ijtimā'ī ba Nigāhī bi Manābi' Islāmī, pp. 267-268.
90. Bīshārat, Muḥammad 'Alī and Manīzhih Fīrūzī, 'Muqāyasah-yi Zanān va Mardān Nābārvar bar Ḥasab Sabk Delbastigī va Sāzish Ravānshinākhtī bā Bārdārī' in *Ravānshināsī va 'Ulūm Tarbiyatī Journal*, p 39.
91. Ibid., p. 4.
92. Al-Ḥurr al-'Āmilī, *Wasā'il al-Shī'a*, vol. 14, p. 5.
93. Ibid., pp. 6-7.
94. Nūrī, *Mustadrak al-Wasā'il*, vol. 14, pp. 150, 154 and 159.
95. Tabātabā'ī, *Tafsīr al-Mīzān*, vol. 2, p. 44.
96. Muṭahharī, Murtaḍā, *Ta'līm va Tarbiyat az Nazar Islām*, pp. 166, 266-267.
97. Argyle, Michael, *The Psychology of Happiness*, p. 128.
98. See: Ch. 1, the view of Professor Muṭahharī.

99. Mansūr, Maḥmūd and Parīrukh Dādsitān, Dīdgāh Piaget dar Gustarih-yi Taḥavvul Ravānī, p. 359.
100. Al-Ḥurr al-'Āmilī, *Wasā'il al-Shī'a*, vol. 14, p. 33.
101. Ibid., p. 3.
102. Including Qur'ān 46:15 and 31:14.
103. And the heart of the mother of Moses became void, and she would have betrayed him if We had not fortified her heart, that she might be of the believers, Qur'ān 28:10-13; 'Uthmān Nijāti, Muḥammad, *The Qur'ān and Psychology*, p. 47.
104. Siemon, F. B., *Key Concepts and Theories in Family Therapy*, p. 202.
105. Al-Ḥurr al-'Āmilī, *Wasā'il al-Shī'a*, vol. 15, p 100.
106. Qur'ān 3:38-48, 19:3-10 and 25:74: Our Lord! Vouchsafe us comfort of our wives and of our offspring.
107. Al-Ḥurr al-'Āmilī, *Wasā'il al-Shī'a*, vol. 15, pp. 95 and 96.
108. Ibid., p. 96.
109. *Nīsī, 'Abd al-Kāẓim* et al, *'Muqāyasah-yi 'Amalkard Taḥsīlī, Salāmat Ravānī va Jismānī-yi Dānishāmūzān Pisar Fāqid Pidar va Vājid Pidar'in 'Ulūm Tarbiyatī va Ravānshināsī Journal* of *Shahīd* Chamrān University, *vol. 8, Nos.* 3-4 (*1380 A.H)*, p. 67.
110. Ibid.
111. Adams, Paul, et al, *Psychology of Fatherless Children*, pp. 54-58.
112. Teyber, Edward, *Children of Divorce, (Bachchi-ha-yi Talāq)*
113. Muḥibbī, Sayyidah Fātima , "The West and the Phenomenon of Single-Parent Families," translated by Hājar Ḥusaynī, Fātima Bakhtiārī, *Women*, issue 24.
114. But the good deeds which endure are better in thy Lord's sight for reward, and better in respect of hope, Qur'ān 18:44; Al-Ḥurr al-'Āmilī, *Wasā'il al-Shī'a*, vol. 15, p. 95.
115. And He it is Who hath created man from water, and hath appointed for him kindred by blood and kindred by marriage, Qur'ān 25:54.
116. Qur'ān 4:1; Al-Kulaynī, *Kāfī*, vol. 2, p. 150.
117. Majlisī, *Biḥār al-Anwār*, vol. 71, p. 97.
118. Such as a recommended fasting by a child without the father's permission. See Tabātabā'ī-Yazdī, *Urwat al-Wuthqā*, vol. 2, p. 243.
119. According to Islamic law, if someone kills another by mistake, it is the duty of men in the family such as the mother's and the father's brothers to pay blood money to the victim's family. See: Aḥmadī, Dhikrullāh, Nahād Āqilih dar Huqūq Kaifarī-yi Islām, pp. 17-32.

CHAPTER 2

120. Majlisī, *Biḥār al-Anwār*, vol. 75, p. 58.
121. Majlisī, *Biḥār al-Anwār*, vol. 71, p. 103.
122. Ibid., p. 114.
123. Ibid., p. 103.
124 For example, it is so in fitr religious tax. See: Tabātabā'ī-Yazdī, *'Urwah al-Wuthqā*, vol. 2, p. 365.
125. Ibid., p. 138.
126. Barker, Phillip, *Basic Family Therapy*, p. 11.
127. Amīnī, 'Abd al-Ḥusayn, *al-Ghadīr*, vol. 1, p. 369.
128. Al-Ḥurr al-'Āmilī, *Wasā'il al-Shī'a*, vol. 14, p. 42.
129. Nūrī, *Mustadrak al-Wasā'il*, vol. 15, ch. 11.
130. Al-Kulaynī, *Kāfī*, vol. 3, p.221 ; Majlisī, *Biḥār al-Anwār*, vol. 71, p. 108.
131. Al-Kulaynī, *Kāfī*, vol. 3, p. 229.
132. Majlisī, *Biḥār al-Anwār*, vol. 71, p. 88.
133. Ibid., vol. 47, p. 194.
134. Ibid., vol. 71, p. 88.
135. Al-Kulaynī, *Usūl Kāfī*, vol. 3, p. 229.
136. Majlisī, *Biḥār al-Anwār*, vol. 71, p. 138; Al-Kulaynī, *Usūl Kāfī*, vol. 3, p. 222-223.
137. Ibid., p. 211.
138. Ibid., p. 221.
139. Ibid., Ḥadīth 4.
140. Ibid., p. 222.
141. Ibid., p. 223.
142. Ibid., p. 226.
143. " Aḥmadī, Muḥammad Reḍā, 'Naqsh Silih-yi Rahim dar Bihdāsht Ravānī', Ma'rifat, Vol. 10, No. 46 (1381 A.H) , pp. 29-38.
144. Majlisī, *Biḥār al-Anwār*, vol. 47, p. 229.
145. Ibid., vol. 71, p. 101.
146. Qur'ān 57:11; Majlisī, *Biḥār al-Anwār*, vol. 100, p. 140.
147. Majlisī, *Biḥār al-Anwār*, vol. 100, p. 138.
148. Including Qur'ān 90:15.
149. Majlisī, *Biḥār al-Anwār*, vol. 71, p. 88.
150. Ibid., vol. 71, p. 103.
151. Qur'ān 2:180 and 215.
152. Verses in the Qur'ān relating to inheritance.
153. Al-Kulaynī, *Usūl Kāfī*, vol. 3, p. 229.
154. Majlisī, *Biḥār al-Anwār*, vol. 71, Ḥadīth. 32.

155. Ibid.
156. Ibid., p. 118.
157. Ibid., p. 121.
158. Ibid., p. 131.
159. Ibid., p. 89.
160. Ibid., p. 90.
161. Al-Kulaynī, *Usūl Kāfī,* vol. 4, p. 48.
162. Majlisī, Biḥār al-Anwār, vol. 71, p. 165.
163. Ibid.
164. Including the way Imām Sādiq(as) and 'Abdullāh ibn Ḥasan behaved as in *Usūl Kāfī,* vol. 3, p. 227.
165. In *Biḥār al-Anwār*, vol. 71, the consequences of cutting family ties have been mentioned, including p. 133.
166. Qur'ān 2:27.
167. Qur'ān 13:25.
168. Majlisī, *Biḥār al-Anwār*, vol. 71, p. 101.
169. Ibid., p. 91.
170. Al-Kulaynī, *Usūl Kāfī,* vol. 4, p. 48.
171. Majlisī, *Biḥār al-Anwār*, vol. 71, p. 94.
172. Ibid.
173. Ibid., p. 104.
174. Al-Kulaynī, *Usūl Kāfī,* vol. 4, p. 47.
175. Majlisī, *Biḥār al-Anwār*, vol. 71, pp. 9 and 99.
176. Al-Kulaynī, *Usūl Kāfī,* vol. 4, pp. 48, 49.
177. Qur'ān 4:1 can be thus interpreted.
178. Muḥammadī-Reyshahrī, *Mīzān al-Ḥikmah*, vol. 4, pp. 2020-2022.
179. Ibid.
180. Ibid.
181. Al-Kulaynī, *Usūl Kāfī,* vol. 4, p. 50.
182. Ibid.; Muḥammadī-Reyshahrī, *Mīzān al-Ḥikmah*, vol. 4, p. 2016.
183. Muḥammadī-Reyshahrī, *Mīzān al-Ḥikmah*, vol. 4, p. 2020.
184. Qur'ān 8:75 and 33:6.
185. Qur'ān 4:23.
186. Qur'ān 24:31.
187. Majlisī, *Biḥār al-Anwār*, vol. 71, p. 110.
188. Qur'ān 24:24.
189. Qur'ān 80:34.
190. Qur'ān 60:4.

CHAPTER 2

191. Qur'ān 5:106, 6;152.
192. Every soul is a pledge for its own deeds, Qur'ān 74:38.
193. The phrase nor doth any laden bear another's load occurs five times in the Qur'ān: 6:164, 17:15, 39:7, 35:18 and 53:38.
194. *Nahj al-Balāghah*, Sermon 224.
195. Qur'ān 49:11.
196. Fattāl al-Nīshābūrī, Muḥammad ibn Aḥmad, Raudat al-Wā'izīn , p. 476.
197. Al-Kulaynī, *Usūl Kāfī*, vol. 3, p. 222.
198. Qur'ān 57:20.
199. Qur'ān 3:133, 57:21.
200. Qur'ān 9:24.
201. Qur'ān 8:28, 64:14.
202. Such expressions are quite common in *Mafātīḥ al-Janān* by Sheikh 'Abbās Qumī prayers with the Prophet and the .

CHAPTER 3

THE PILLARS OF THE FAMILY

In order to realise the objectives of marriage as defined by Islām, all the family members have special responsibilities, and they should adjust to one another in ways that help fulfil these objectives as much as possible. In this chapter, we deal with these different relationship and their responsibilities, which form the supports of the family.

1. The Mutual Responsibilities of Husband and Wife

The first duty of the married couple is to be compatible with each other, for their similarities are the basis of their life together. Nevertheless, they are two different and unique personalities with their own temperaments, affections, motivations and values. The husband and wife should gradually set aside some of their individual opinions and preferences in order to accept the other person.[1]

1.1. Primary Compatibility

Islamic teachings contain guidance for the husband and wife, based on various aspects of their psychology. According to the divine religious leaders, two important points are mentioned regarding women, bearing in mind the psychological differences in men and women. The woman's personality is different to that of the man, and he should not evaluate the woman according to what he sees in himself, nor should he expect her to be the same as him. If the man ignores this, he will harm the woman.[2] It is therefore necessary for the man to accept the woman with all her characteristics, and coordinate himself with her in certain respects. In addition, the divine religious leaders have described the woman as *rayḥāna*,[3] which implies tenderness and sensitivity. The wife does not have the virile qualities of the "hero," which means that the husband is the chief servant of the household in terms of management and courageousness. The contrast between the two can be interpreted as meaning that the more aesthetic, peaceful and affective elements are dominant in the woman, and less determination is expected of her.

On the other hand, men usually experience more pressures than women due to particular social conditions, since, in the family system, the responsibility of financial affairs of the family devolves upon the man. Men in society undergo difficulties which can reduce their threshold of tolerance, thus provoking aggression. In addition, the hormonal composition of men means that certain kinds of aggressive behaviour emerge for gaining superiority.[4] The woman should accept this and adapt to it. Only then can she psychologically support the man. If each partner pays attention to the characteristics of the other, it would greatly help their mutual understanding. Therefore, each should activate the positive and sometimes hidden aspects of the other and correct the negative ones. However, if instead of accepting the spouse the way they are, one highlights their weak points and tries to impose certain rules, then conflict will arise.[5] In other words, the family is composed of various individuals who will draw closer together if basic common principles are followed. Failure to recognise one's relatives as individuals, and trying to impose a uniform family atmosphere, will create heavy emotional pressures and feelings of alienation, and could even result in the breakdown of the family.[6]

1.2. Continuity of Optimum Relations

Following the initial discovery of compatibility between the couple, it is important for them to maintain a satisfactory relationship. The criteria for this are to be found in the Qur'ān and in good company.[7] The Qur'ān uses the word *ma'rūf* ("common good") more than twenty times for various aspects of family relationships, the most important of which is that of the husband and wife. Some have said that the decisive factor in marriage is *ma'rūf*,[8] but in most of the related verses the word is used more extensively, in connection with all aspects of family relationships. Some sages have considered *ma'rūf* to be the pattern for proper behaviour in society,[9] or *ma'rūf* to mean desirable behaviour within the framework of religion.[10] The divine religious leaders also connect it with various concepts, such as kindness,[11] good associations with the family and others,[12] and generally any deed that is good and in accordance with the divine commands.[13] *ma'rūf* Therefore, an appropriate definition of *ma'rūf* is behaviour that is accepted by the people of a society and in accordance with the *Sharī'a*, which are accord with the nature of the husband and wife.

In Islamic texts, the man and the woman are advised to prepare the ground for an appropriate relationship. The responsibilities of the man to his wife include providing for economic needs,[14] fulfilling emotional needs,[15] respecting and revering the woman,[16] treating her well,[17] kindness, understanding[18] and forgiveness.[19] Being caring and wise consultants, the divine religious leaders employed different methods to help men fulfil their family responsibilities. A very fine description is that women are like a gift entrusted to men.[20] It has been pointed out that many women give their trust regarding several matters to other women,[21] whereas Islām usually advises differently.[22] It is evident that, if the man considers his wife a gift entrusted to him, he will treat her well. Another matter is that women are physically weaker than men,[23] which can be seen in how in the modern world men's and women's competitions are held separately. In view of this natural reality, the divine religious leaders advise that women should be treated appropriately, and with piety and restraint.

Another way that the divine religious leaders encourage men to treat their wives properly is by mentioning things that matter a great deal, such as taking honest pleasure in life in a way that brings happiness and a good[24] and a long lifetime.[25] Yet another matter to consider is the social persona of the individual. For example, the correct treatment of one's spouse is a sign of a person's honour and dignity.[26] Most importantly, the good treatment of one's spouse indicates the degree of one's faith. According to the divine religious leaders, anyone who treats their spouse well has a higher degree of faith.[27] Therefore, the Prophet said: "I, more than all people, treat my wives nicely".[28]

The example set by the divine religious leaders regarding their wives encourages good behaviour in the family. They respected their privacy[29] and valued their personalities and spirituality, and gained spiritual help from them.[30] They would cooperate with their wishes within the boundaries of *Sharī'a* and the family,[31] and any bad behaviour was met with patience and understanding.[32] Even today, this model can be very effective for men as the best way of dealing with one's spouse. In Chapter 6, the practice of the divine religious leaders will be studied separately.

On the other hand, the responsibilities of women in the family are also very important, so much so that the teachings of Islām consider the most important responsibility of the woman after her religious duties to her responsibility towards her husband.[33] The most fundamental duty of the woman is to fulfil the emotional and sexual needs of the man, which, in terms of value, is considered equal to the man's most difficult duty, i.e. *jihād*.[34] The expression of love towards the spouse[35] is considered a duty of the woman according to the Qur'ān.[36] In addition, women are also expected to provide for their husbands' happiness in life as much as they can. This can be considered a very effective factor in consolidating the family and a good relationship between the husband and wife. In this respect, the woman's patience when faced with problems,[37] not telling her husband what to do, and helping him in social and economic problems[38] can pave the way for a good relationship between them.

In brief, the responsibilities of the husband and wife are considered equal according to the following Qur'ānic verse, although more is sometimes expected of the wife:

> *And women shall have rights similar to the rights against them, according to what is equitable, but men have a degree (of advantage) over them.*[39]

Therefore, it is the woman's role to listen to the man,[40] and this is examined further in the section on the levels of the family in Islām.

2. Responsibilities of the Parents

After the responsibilities the husband and wife have towards each other are their responsibilities as parents. The birth of the first child is a major development, as the parents have to consider the presence of another person within the home. The way they behave towards each other provides the child with a model for their own future relationship with the opposite sex. The child will learn from them various ways of expressing emotions, and how to communicate with a partner in times of trouble.[41] With the birth of a child, the husband and wife should gradually balance their responsibilities to each other and towards the child. The source of many problems in families that have a child shortly after marriage is the balancing of these responsibilities, and this will be perused in the discussion on family problems and solutions.

It is the duty of the parents to bring up their children and introduce them to society step by step. In early childhood, food and protection are of prime importance. Later on, teaching and guidance become more important, and in adolescence they should be prepared for independence. As the child spends most of his time with the family up until adolescence, the family is the most important factor in his growth and development. There has been a great deal of psychological research into the educational role of the parents, the influence of siblings and the family atmosphere.[42] Here we will briefly examine the duties of the parents from the Islamic point of view.

The first thing to consider is the sanctity and spiritual value of the parents. They have been given value in the eyes of God and have an important religious function. For instance, regarding maternal duties, the Prophet says:

> "When a woman becomes pregnant, she is given a reward equal to that of fasting and prayer, and to that given to one doing *jihād* with his property and life on God's path."

When she delivers the baby, no one can understand the grandeur of her reward. When she breastfeeds the baby, every time that the baby sucks the milk an angel tells her: "All your sins are forgiven; start afresh."[43] In a similar fashion, some of the father's actions have a sacred character.[44] This understanding has two important effects on the parents: in the first place, it makes them work more to fulfil their parental responsibilities, and secondly, they will find their actions of spiritual value. Consequently, any difficulties involved will be alleviated to a certain extent. Moreover, this understanding will cause the parents to consider their family duties similar to other religious duties, and not see any interruption therein.

The second point is attending to religion in the relationship between the parents and the child prior to conception and birth. The teachings of Islām include points regarding the behaviour of the husband and wife, including types of nutrition and their chastity,[45] while providing important advice for the mental and religious health of the children.[46] As already mentioned, the conditions at the time the baby is conceived affect the child's personality.[47] Moreover, certain advice is given for the mother during pregnancy, part of which relates to food and its effect on the child, and partly to her behavioural patterns.[48]

The third point is the attention that Islām gives to all aspects of the child's development, with special recommendations for the parents regarding nutrition and physical, cognitive, affective and social development. It is recommended that the child be breastfed from the time of birth, since nothing is better than the mother's milk. The cognitive, physical and religious effects of breastfeeding are emphasised. Therefore, women who are mentally or physically defective, foul-mouthed, very ugly, eat non-halal food, drink alcohol or are enemies of the divine religious leaders should not breastfeed a child,[49] all of which in effect covers the same ground as the criteria for choosing a spouse.[50] In spite of the fact that powdered milk is often used nowadays as a substitute, these recommendations illustrate the effect of the initial feeding on all aspects of the child's personality. Indeed, research has so far proved only the physical and emotional effects on the infant of breastfeeding.[51] Concerning the fulfilment of the child's material needs, it is emphasised that properly acquired, not illegal, property should be used, because this will have an undesirable effect on the child's character and behaviour.[52] Certain advice has been given regarding the type of food for children, insofar as it should be halal,[53] with an emphasis on certain fruits and other foodstuffs.[54]

A fourth point concerns the affective relationship between the parents and their children. In this regard, Islām provides both theological and other advice which provides for the mental health of children. Psychologists very much emphasise the emotional needs of children, and their most interesting advice is to give positive and unconditional affective attention to the child, for this has a strong influence on the child's mental health in later life.[55] The divine religious leaders have given the following advice in this respect:

> "Talk kindly and sympathetically to children;[56] look at them kindly[57] and stroke their heads,[58] kiss and embrace them, since parents gain merit in Heaven for each time they kiss the child[59] (although the age and development of the child should be taken into consideration); play with children;[60] treat them kindly, in a way understandable to them,[61] and avoid expressing anger and inappropriate emotions;[62] value them and address them respectfully and kindly."

Islām emphasises justice and fairness when dealing with the emotions of children.[63] The Prophet of Islām calls upon parents to treat their children fairly.[64] Evenness in the expression of emotions towards children, whether in actions or words, prevents certain negative complexes developing, such as feelings of inferiority and jealousy.[65] Regarding the improper treatment of women and female children at the time of the Prophet Muḥammad, traces of which persist today,[66] the teachings of Islām advise that more attention be given to the female children. The Prophet said:

> "One who enters a bazaar to buy a gift for his family is like one who gives gifts to those in need. He should give gifts to girls before boys, because he who makes his daughter happy is rewarded as if he had liberated a slave from among the children of Isma'il, and if he makes his son happy, it is as if he had cried in fear of God. Such a person will be sent by God to Gardens of Paradise full of blessings."[67]

He also said that God is kinder to girls than to boys.[68]

Positive emotional attention to the girl should be considered more from two points of view. Firstly, one is enjoined by Islām to guard against inappropriate, domineering attitudes towards them and treating them less kindly. Secondly, girls are more sensitive to the emotions of others, as the Prophet said:

> "Girls are such good children. They are tender, warm and becoming, ready to serve, friendly, bring blessings and are clean in themselves and with other things."[69]

Psychological research also demonstrates the higher sensitivity of girls to the expression of affection.[70] Nonetheless, a greater expression of affection towards girls should not result in discrimination against or inattention to the male children. The parents should also react appropriately to the affective needs of boys.

It should be mentioned that in the teachings of Islām, an excessive expression of love towards children is not encouraged,[71] as it results in the family being centred on the child and the child depending heavily on the family, leaving the child with a lack of self-determination. Very mild punishment is approved of in certain circumstances, including not talking to the child, although not for a long period.[72] In Islām, beating children[73] is prohibited. It has been said that nothing angers God as much as injustice to children and women.

3. Responsibilities of Children

In the same way that the ground for the development of children is the family, they also have responsible roles that they should gradually be taught. As for the upbringing of children, two undesirable methods can be observed throughout history. Prior to the present century, the raising of children and encounters with them were often accompanied by impositions and pressure, and the rights of children were rarely taken into account. In the contemporary era, gradually more attention has been shifted towards children, so much so that this has often been done to excess, and in the West this has resulted in a child-centredness that imposes more on the parents.[74] In order to maintain coherence and efficiency within the family, Islām considers two aspects of the relationship, one from the parents' perspective and the other from that of the children. While children do not have any legal or religious responsibilities at an early age (approximately the first 8 to 10 years), the parents are in charge of the upbringing and education of the children.

3.1. Duties of Children Towards the Parents

We should begin the discussion with a special understanding of these duties. First of all, there is the spiritual aspect and sanctity of these duties; not only is a good relationship with the parents considered the best religious practice,[75] but it is also the time when other aspects of religion are introduced.[76] God's satisfaction depends on the satisfaction of the parents, and God will be dissatisfied if the parents are dissatisfied.[77] The Qur'ān puts the parents' rights on the same level as sacred responsibilities:

> *We have enjoined upon man ... Give thanks unto Me and unto thy parents.*[78]

If the parents are dissatisfied with the child, very undesirable consequences will await the child in this world and the afterlife.[79] Also, the prayers of the parents for the child are very effective.[80] All this shows that, an appropriate relationship between the child and the parents is integral for the spiritual happiness of the child.

Secondly, there is the comparison between the duties of the children and those of the parents, which extend throughout the lifetime of the parents and even after. According to Islām, both male and female children should, after starting their own families, continue fulfilling their various responsibilities, such as economic and psychological support for their parents, especially in old age,[81] when certain responsibilities increase. These duties extend after death, and if one observes one's parents' rights while they are alive, but fails to do so after they die, it will bring them dissatisfaction.[82]

Thirdly, there is the unconditional nature of these duties. This means that even if the parents are lacking in religiosity or misguided,[83] or fail to observe the children's rights,[84] the children are still responsible towards them.

A fourth point is the greater responsibility of the children towards the mother, as also emphasised in the words of the divine religious leaders, where, in addition to highlighting the mother's rights,[85] kindness to her should to be twice of that towards the father.[86] In order to encourage people to establish a good relationship with their mothers, the Qur'ān speaks of the pains that mothers undergo:

> *And We have enjoined upon man [care] for his parents. His mother carried him, [increasing her] in weakness upon weakness, and his weaning is in two years,*[87]

and also:

> *And We have enjoined upon man, to his parents good treatment. His mother carried him with hardship, and his gestation and weaning [period] is thirty months.*[88]

Regarding the mother's rights, the Prophet said:

> "If you are with and serve her for as many days as there are grains of sands and drops of rain in life, you can still not make up for the hard work and pain that she underwent during pregnancy."[89]

A fifth point is the importance of the great responsibility children have towards their parents, as already mentioned. Now, after the above points, it is time to further elaborate on the duties of children. They should talk to their parents softly, kindly, and in a low voice.[90] Since it is inappropriate to cause annoyance to or be aggressive towards the parents, children should try to avoid even the slightest[91] form of harsh talk,[92] and always address their parents respectfully.[93] Children should not call their parents by their names. Rather, they should use such titles as "Mother" or "Father."[94] The reason for this is perhaps that the basis of the relationship, and the most important factor binding parents and children, is the parent and child blood relationship, as signified by the words "father" and "mother." If a child calls his parents by name, it is as if the close parental relationship is not put in its proper place, or at least is not given its due importance. And if it should continue for a long time, the polite affective relationship will be gradually weakened, resulting in a failure of duties. In this connection, it is interesting to know that even the Prophet himself asked Fātima to call him "Father," rather than "the Prophet."[95] In verbal interaction with others, the child should avoid any cause for verbal insult to his parents.[96] Moreover, he should always pray for them, even if they are not on the right path.[97]

As for nonverbal interaction, the most important factor is humility towards one's parents. The Qur'ān uses a beautiful metaphor to encourage people to show the utmost humility towards their parents:

> *And lower to them the wing of humility out of mercy, and say: My Lord, bestow on them Your Mercy as they did bring me up when I was small.*[98]

Therefore, it is inappropriate for a child to walk ahead of his parents,[99] sit in front of them[100] or lean on them.[101] The child should not stare[102] at his parents or look at them angrily, even if they have treated him unjustly.[103] On the other hand, if he looks at his parents kindly, it is deemed as an act of worship,[104] and in this case divine blessings descend upon him.[105] Kissing the parents is also like an act of worship.[106] In addition, the child should never cut off all connection with his parents or refuse to talk to them.[107]

Parents usually come across problems as they approach old age, and therefore the religious texts emphasise attending to them in their old age.[108] In general, it has been said that children should fulfil the needs of the parents before they are asked.[109]

It would be fitting to explain here the reason why many teachings in Islām greatly emphasise the rights of the parents. In the family system, the parents, especially the mother, make the most investment in their children. This has been so for all people throughout history. Both parents help emotionally, economically and socially to prepare for the growth and development of their children, but the mother makes the most sacrifice. However, she also gains the most from her investment in the form of the child. The needs of children are fulfilled only through the parents, because the institutions that take care of children, even when they are of a good standard, cannot provide the necessary material and psychological support at all hours of the day and night. In addition, a lack of this emotional investment causes certain disorders in children, which sometimes take a long time to remedy, if it can be done at all.[110] As previously mentioned, a child needs positive and unconditional attention, which the parents are able to provide, in order for them to enjoy a high degree of self-esteem.[111] In many cases, disfunction in the family is due to the parents failing in their duties. Considering all the above points, parents have a vital role to play. Obviously, in order to fulfil their duties properly, they need to be encouraged and rewarded. Since they cannot expect material support from the children for many years, giving them respect and paying more attention to them can motivate them, and to a certain extent give them more pleasure in fulfilling their duties.

3.2. Duties of Children Towards Each Other

The family is the place where children grow and their personalities develop; negotiation, cooperation, competition, support, friendship and conflict are learned through one's siblings.[112] The relationships that siblings have with each other seriously affect their future social responsibilities and relationships. It seems that when children are still small and have not attained full emotional independence, the main responsibility for fashioning satisfactory relationships between them lies with the parents. Nonetheless, any intrusion by the parents in these matters should be balanced, in such a way that the children are not left on their own to face undue pressure, nor should too much control be exercised, for too much interference in their privacy is to be avoided. It seems that the teachings of Islām adopt a moderate stance for nurturing a strong family.[113]

One can see in the teachings of Islām points about sibling relationships that are more applicable to adulthood, although one should be familiarised with them from childhood in order to internalise relationships. There are many references to brotherhood, most of which are founded on religion, and include sibling relationships by marriage, because they should be likened to brotherhood in order to illustrate the importance of the relationship between two believers.[114] These relationships are described under the title of family ties and also depend on hierarchy. Those involved should always provide each other with affective, psychological and material support. Emotionally, visits between them brings them peace of mind, because they then have a sense of belonging and similarity, which prepares the ground for peace between them,[115] emotional release[116] and happiness.[117] Meanwhile, older children, such as the elder brother, have the special role of standing in for the parents in their absence.[118] Therefore, they should give more psychological and material support to the younger siblings, who in return offer them special respect. The material support of siblings for each other is also of special importance, so much so that two brothers are likened to two hands washing each other.[119] As is common, even in contemporary societies, men generally have a higher income than women, and therefore more emphasis is put on the brother's psychological and material support than that of a sister.[120] Sibling relationships should also continue after the death of the parents, so that the affective and psychological shortfall left by the parents absence can be compensated. These relationships should not be cut off, and even if one side cuts themselves off, the other should continue. As mentioned, an interesting point also considered in the teachings of Islām[121] and the practice of the divine religious leaders[122] is the establishing of relationships with relatives who have abandoned someone. Obviously, in such conditions the other side will also be encouraged to do their part for there to be a stable affective relationship.[123]

4. Hierarchy in the Family

Like other social systems, the family is an organisation, and in an organisation each individual has a special position that indicates his power and influence on the others, for there is no organisation within a society where all the individuals are at the same level.[124] Many family experts, such as Minuchin and J. Hay-Lee, assume that the apparent hierarchy within the family supposes its efficiency. This governs the relative health of the family, and a family therapist like Minuchin describes the purpose of therapy as "putting the parents behind the steering wheel." Order and coherence within the family depend on a suitable hierarchy.[125]

Hierarchy invests more authority in certain family members, and an adequate, harmonious authority is necessary for this. If authority is assigned to someone who lacks the power and means, things will become difficult or impossible, and roles should be delegated accordingly in the family system. The previous discussions revealed that the parents have the highest and most important function, and therefore more authority. In this connection, along with most family therapists,[126] the teachings of Islām stress that the parents should manage the family, and that it is necessary to cooperate with them.[127] Disobedience to them is only permitted if they persist in sin and polytheism, and even then it is necessary to treat them appropriately and politely.[128] In order to protect the authority, facilitate the role and lessen the burdens of the parents, Islām considers certain acts of worship become invalid if discontent is caused to the parents.[129] God's pleasure is subject to the pleasure of the parents, whose anger will result in the anger of God.[130]

If this hierarchy is not observed, and the parents do not have sufficient authority and others make decisions independently, the family will lose its cohesion, because the axis of the family, i.e. the parents, will be unable to manage the family, which may be seriously damaged due to conflicting ideas. Perhaps this is why the Prophet said: "Oh, God, I seek refuge in You from the child who acts like my god,"[131] that is, the child who gives orders to his parents to which the parents submit.

In addition to the authority of the parents, the teachings of Islām give greater authority to the husband. This is explicitly stated in the Qur'ān:

> *Men are the protectors and maintainers of women, because Allāh has given the one more (strength) than the other, and because they support them from their means. Therefore the righteous women are devoutly obedient."*[132]

There is another verse in the Qur'ān that says:

> *And women shall have rights similar to the rights against them, according to what is equitable; but men have a degree (of advantage) over them.*[133]

In many of the words of the divine religious leaders, the most important responsibility of the woman is to cooperate with the husband. The Prophet said:

> *"The husband's right over the wife is for her to obey him and not go against him, not to give alms from the properties of the house without his permission, not to fast without his permission, not to leave home without his permission."*

The Prophet was asked: "Who has the greatest right over the wife?" and he said: "Her husband."[134] In addition to the need for the man's authority in the family, it is also necessary for the woman to acknowledge it. Imām 'Alī said:

> *"If a woman observes your authority, it is better than if she sees you broken and weak."*[135]

According to verses in the Qur'ān, the words of the Prophet and his household, Islamic jurisprudence and the Iranian Civil Code (Article

1105), the husband is the head of the family.[136] This entails making decisions regarding family matters and considering the interests of the family, some of which, according to legislation, include deciding where to live, taking control of finances, and having legal guardianship of the children. In explanation of this law, it has been said that every group should have a leader to coordinate various tasks, so that his opinion is deferred to in order to protect the unity of the group if there is any disagreement.[137] If the family does not have someone at its head, if there are even minor differences, some other higher authority is needed, and this jeopardises coherence within the family. Therefore, the man is placed in charge of the family in order to maintain stability, and to take into account the interests of the others without this necessarily being an advantage for the husband. It is more of a social duty which brings happiness to the family and should not be abused. The man should not go against accepted social norms or the interests of the family by using undue force or exploiting his authority.

The word "authority" in the Qur'ān has a wide scope:

A. The man should properly fulfil the wife's physical and psychological needs, so that she may have peace of mind.

B. In running the affairs of the home, the man should understand the woman,, support her, and run the family accordingly.[138]

These are principles that provide for the freedom of the wife and children within the norms of *Sharī'a* and common practice.[139] The man's authority does not prevent the wife and children from participating in family matters, and this will be mentioned in the discussion on consultation within the family. However, the man's authority means that he has the final say in matters on which the others disagree, because it is at last necessary to have one person decide and the others accept the decision.[140]

It is apposite to now examine and explain the reasons why the man is placed in charge of the family. Particular powers and understanding are needed to manage the financial and social concerns of the family, and having the final say in things that cannot be resolved, and to cope with the tension and anxiety involved. This responsibility should obviously be undertaken by one of the parents, and for various reasons the man is considered more suitable. The woman, because of certain natural characteristics, is stronger than the man in affective matters.[141] The woman's affective attraction and ways of interacting with the man are also superior. For example, women are twice as capable of empathy than men.[142] There is also a deep affective bond between the mother and the child that begins during pregnancy and infancy, the result of which means that the mother has a greater role in fulfilling the child's needs.

Therefore, giving the woman guardianship of the family would generate problems for her in two respects. Firstly, due to her psychological characteristics, she has a more emotional approach to life, which in itself is good, yet sometimes detached reasoning is more effective when facing various problems. There could be disagreement in times of decision-making, as has been mentioned in a discussion of management in various organisations.[143]

Secondly, making the woman the guardian of the family would put excessive responsibility on her, bearing in mind her roles as mother and wife. Women would then inevitably have greater difficulty fulfilling all their responsibilities.[144]

Another point made in the Qur'ānic verses mentioned above[145] is the question of finance. According to the laws of Islām, the man is responsible for providing for the living costs of the family. As many family decisions are governed by financial interests, it is fitting that the person in charge of finances to make the decisions, since this could affect the efficiency of money management. Generally speaking, considering the different constitutions of men and of women, one can conclude that, if provident, intelligent and perceptive enough, men are better prepared to act as guardian of the family and maintain order within the family to prevent its collapse.

5. Boundaries within the Family

The psychological paradigm of each family member is important, and concerns the limitations on the range of activities within subsystems of the family, which we may define as boundaries. In theories of family therapy, certain structuralists led by Minuchin explained the concept of the boundary and its role in the family. After presenting this view, we will elaborate on the boundaries within the family. According to rules set by every family, individuals discover what is permissible for them, what can be done with caution, and what is forbidden. If someone does what they are not supposed to do, other members of the family will react in order to correct him, and he will either accept this or challenge it. The family members are generally aware of the topography involved.[146]

5.1. Boundaries within the Family According to Structuralism

A. The Concept of Boundaries within the Family

A boundary is a hypothetical border that serves to protect, distinguish and integrate the family as a whole, so that there is a system within which every family member functions. A boundary is a metaphor for the special associations that regularly occur between systems. The boundaries of a subsystem consist of rules that determine who is part of the subsystem and what part they play in it. In the family system, these boundaries are psychological, and concern such things as the verbal and nonverbal relationships between individuals and their emotions. Those who are in a particular interactive relationship and those who are outside it are indicators of these boundaries.[147] For example, the adjustment of a married couple to new conditions requires freedom from the interference of others in the family or those outside the family. In the case of children, the development of skills for negotiating and reaching agreement with their peers requires the noninterference of the parents in the subsystem of the children.[148]

In order for the family to function properly, the boundaries of the subsystems should be clear, so that the members of each subsystem can fulfil their roles without disturbance, while maintaining contact with those in other subsystems. The combination of the subsystems is not as important as the clarity of the boundaries of the subsystems. For example, the subsystem of the parents, if consisting of a grandmother or a "parent-like child," as long as the lines of responsibility and authority are clear, can function well. The clarity of the boundaries is a useful indicator for evaluating the functioning of the family. Some families concentrate on their own members in order to construct a small world for themselves. In such a case, intercommunication increases and results in a tightly-knit family system.[149]

In terms of degrees of flexibility, the boundaries in some families are too vague or too rigid, and communication between the subsystems becomes difficult and weakens the supporting role of the family. This is known as "intertwining" and "rupture." All families will be somewhere on this scale, and in most of them, both unclear (intertwined) and rigid boundaries can be found.

B. Boundary Problems

Many family problems can be traced to defects in these boundaries. We just referred to the two extremes of intertwined (unclear) and ruptured (too rigid) boundaries, both of which can cause damage. For example, the intertwined subsystem of the mother and children may push the father aside and ultimately cut him off (rupture). Disallowing independence to children is one of the undesirable effects of intertwined boundaries. The family of intertwined subsystems may become paralysed, because increased attachment means a loss of independence. Failing to distinguish the subsystems weakens the independent exploration and control of difficulties. Consequently, cognitive and affective skills will be hampered, especially in children. The members of the subsystems in the ruptured family may act independently, but will suffer a loss of loyalty, connection, interdependence and mutual support.[150]

C. Making Boundaries in Treatment

There are boundary-making techniques for rectifying these problems. In order to maintain the independence of family members, and at the same time keep them connected to the family, one should examine individual boundaries and boundaries between the systems. Individual independence can be maintained and reinforced by simple rules. For example, no one should talk on behalf of another, or claim to have the only true picture of things that have happened within the family in the past. Children should be considered individually, and have privileges according to their status. The boundaries between the subsystems should be sufficiently strong, and the husband and wife subsystem should be protected against interference from the children or older members of the family. Indistinct boundaries of the husband-wife sub-system is a common cause of disorder, and the private matters of the husband and wife should remain within their sub-system, separate from other members of the family.[151]

5.2. Boundaries in the Family According to Islām

A comparison of this viewpoint with Islamic thought shows that both have a relatively similar concept of the boundaries of the relationships and their protocols. Both views share the concept of each person's individual psychology.[152] The idea of the boundary is used for establishing distance from or closeness to other family members, such as the husband being closer to his wife than he is to his son. Moreover, Islām agrees upon there being both flexible and firm boundaries. The teachings of Islām define certain limits governing the relationships one has with other family members as well as outsiders. Observing these rules creates better relationships within the family, and improves the way the family functions in the wider world

A. Boundaries within the Family

Islamic teachings consider it necessary for there to be boundaries between individuals and between the subsystems within the family. The husband and wife as a subsystem should have a separate room in the house, and other members of the family should not enter this private space at certain times of the day. The Qur'ān says in this connection:

> *O ye who believe! Let those whom your right hands possess, and the (children) among you who have not come of age ask your permission (before they come to your presence), on three occasions: before morning prayer; the while ye doff your clothes for the noonday heat; and after the late-night prayer: these are your three times of undress: outside these times it is not wrong for you or for them to move about attending to each other: thus does Allāh make clear the signs to you: for Allāh is full of knowledge and wisdom. But when the children among you come of age, let them (also) ask for permission.*[153]

These verses, the words of the Prophet and his household and the other teachings all acknowledge special times of privacy for the husband and wife subsystem.[154]

Everyone, both young and old, should allow this privacy. This psychological space allows for personal problems between the husband and wife to be resolved, and for their emotional support of each other. In addition, the other subsystems also need space and time that the parents should not encroach upon. As the children approach adolescence, their need for privacy is greater. Although this concerns both boys and girls, it seems that a girl needs more privacy due to fewer opportunities for privacy outside the family, and consequently others should not intrude upon her.[155]

According to Islām, there should be boundaries between the male and female children, for each need a psychological space of their own. The sleeping areas of the parents, sons and daughters should all be separate, and each child should have a bed of their own.[156] In addition, the contact between siblings in adolescence should be subject to certain controls,[157] in order to prevent causes for inappropriate behaviour.

Privacy is a foundation for mutual trust, and this concerns the boundaries within the family. In the teachings of Islām, privacy is a very important condition of faith, which people are encouraged to nurture in order to reach perfection.[158] It is a basis for health and balance in the family, whereas excessive openness is ill-advised, for privacy within the family is a vital issue. Matters relating to the private relationship between the husband and wife should be kept within the husband and wife subsystem.[159] The Qur'ān praises women who keep the secrets of their husbands, saying:

> *Righteous women ... guard in (the husband's) absence what Allāh would have them guard.*[160]

The Qur'ān tells of an incident in which two of the Prophet's wives disclose a private secret. God announces this behaviour to be a deviation and tells them to repent of their improper act.[161] Needless to say, this also applies to men. Family privacy also concerns one's faults, which should be kept secret, especially those of the husband and wife who, as previously mentioned, are "raiments" for each other and should cover each other's defects. Therefore, righteous women are obedient and guard secrets and faults, and they generally reprimand others that do not do so. However, disclosure may be the only way of correcting a fault. Nonetheless, gossiping is described in the Qur'ān as like eating the flesh of a dead brother.[162] Since it is private and there is less control over it, the family environment offers an opportunity for doings personal things, but discussing them outside the family is considered gossip and is prohibited. In addition to the fact that the secrets and faults of the family should not be conveyed to others, the family environment itself should not be a place for such talk. One should not even discuss the positive characteristics of one's close relatives outside the family, or even in certain cases to others with the family. The teachings of Islām put a special emphasis on keeping secrets, and warn against their disclosure.[163] If speaking of the positive characteristics of a family member is going to result in jealousy, then one should remain silent, as demonstrated in the story of Yūsuf (Joseph) and his brothers in the Qur'ān.[164]

B. Boundaries of the Family and Society

Other limits are set for family members, including what applies to the wife leaving the house with her husband. Also, the father has guardianship over the children until they reach puberty, and should monitor their coming and going. Moreover, the man in the family should monitor the entry of individuals who are not morally reliable.[165] It seems that if the wife leaves the house only as often as necessary and gives priority to home affairs, she will invest more in the affective and spiritual development of the entire family. Indeed all these limits should be balanced and logical, and any excessive control by the man in the family can provoke mental imbalances in other family members.[166] The teachings of Islām also define the boundary of the home, which is not unconditionally open, and those wishing to enter it should do so with permission. This rule is stated explicitly in the Qur'ān:

> *O ye who believe! Enter not houses other than your own, until ye have announced your presence and saluted those in them: that is best for you … if you are asked to go back, go back: that makes for greater purity for yourselves.*[167]

The Arabic word for "announcing one's presence" conveys the meaning of becoming familiar to something, and is interpreted as meaning that one should not enter a house without prior permission. It is noteworthy that permission should be granted even before entering the house of one's parents or offspring.[168] Another inference of this word is "more pure," which means that this rule is for maintaining the mental and moral health of those who dwell therein. The above verse also has a psychological aspect, inasmuch as it is to ensure that the inhabitants of the house are prepared for non-family members to enter. If they are not ready, they would naturally be stressed. Unreadiness may also result in the disclosure of private family matters to others. Therefore, this boundary preserves both the mental health of the family as well as private matters.

C. Boundaries in Sexual Relationships

An important key to personal development is when one coordinates steps into the world of sexual unity.[169] While recognising sexual pleasure, Islām also defines certain limits. The Qur'ān says:

> "*Who guard their modesty, except with those joined to them in the*

> *marriage bond, or (the captives) whom their right hands possess – for (in their case) they are free from blame. But those whose desires exceed those limits are transgressors.*[170]

Illegitimate sexual activity, such as adultery, sodomy and so forth, is forbidden. As we can read in the Qur'ān:

> *Nor come nigh to adultery; for it is a shameful (deed) and an evil.*[171]

These things are seriously censured, and they have severe punishments.[172]

Prohibited sexual relationships have undesirable consequences for the family, society and the individual. Adultery threatens the foundations of one's faith[173] and generates feeling of guilt that damage self-worth, and making up for it takes a long time.[174] In the family system, straying from the boundaries of the legitimate sexual relationship seriously harms the love and friendship between the husband and wife.[175] Adultery has deep psychological effects on children, the least of which is that they are more likely to imitate their parents' behaviour.[176] According to *hadith*s of the Prophet and his household(Ahl al-Bayt), among the consequences of adultery are losing the light of the face, a shortened life, poverty in this world, incurring the anger of God, and bad consequences in the next world, such as burning eternally in the fires of hell.[177] It causes other disturbances for children,[178] such as not knowing who the father is, if a child born of adultery. Such a child grows in an environment where it lacks fatherly affection, and later on is more inclined to commit adultery and other such sins.[179] The Prophet is quoted as having said: "When adultery enters a house, it ruins it."[180] Here, the ruin of the house refers to the collapse of the family. In order to protect family privacy, even minor sexual deviations are prohibited, including any provocative verbal or nonverbal expressions of a sexual nature. An illicit glance is considered adultery of the eye, and any sexual abuse of any part of the body is the adultery of that body part.[181] Moreover, along with any sexual activity outside the boundaries of marriage, sexual liaisons between two men or two women are banned in Islām.

All such behaviour is harmful in two respects. First of all, it can further encourage illegitimate sexual acts, and secondly, the behavior itself is outside the religiously legitimate boundaries. It harms the emotional relationship between the husband and wife, and causes other difficulties in addition. Therefore, it is no way to maintain a deep and intimate affective relationship between the husband and wife and achieve unity in the family.[182] In order to protect the husband and wife boundary, the teachings of Islām go a step further and consider even the thought of adultery inappropriate,[183] and say that one should think only of one's wife during sexual intercourse, otherwise there are undesirable consequences.[184]

D. The Religious Dress Code and the Limits of Relationships Between Men and Women

In order to protect the chastity and health of the family, marriage to certain blood relatives who are close or intimate (*mahram*) is considered incest. The relationships between men and women who are not close, i.e. those who may marry each other, are subject to certain rules. Women should in this case be careful of the way they dress. Proper clothing for women (*ḥijāb*) is an important issue for the health and efficiency of the family, as mentioned in the Qur'ān:

> *And say to the believing women that they should lower their gaze and guard their modesty; that they should not display their beauty and ornaments except what (must ordinarily) appear thereof; that they should draw their veils over their bosoms and not display their beauty except to their husbands [and others who are close blood relatives];*[185]

and:

> *O Prophet! Tell thy wives and daughters and the believing women, that they should cast their outer garments over their persons (when abroad): that is most convenient, that they should be known (as such) and not molested.*[186]

Women should cover the whole body except for the face and the hands from the wrists to the fingers. This precept has numerous individual and social consequences. The consolidation of the close husband and wife relationship is one of the reasons for the ruling on *ḥijāb*. It keeps sexuality within the family environment and strengthens the bond between the husband and wife. Because of the *ḥijāb*, the man's legal wife will be the only person satisfying his sexual needs.

It seems that the need for women to cover their beauty also helps to protect the family and strengthen its foundations. The woman's body has a special beauty and attraction, and is nowadays used in the West as a very effective means for advertising. Sexual harassment at work not only impedes efficiency, but has an undesirable psychological effect on the workers.[187]

Improper dress inevitably results in a man's attraction to women being over-stimulated, and men unavoidably become more interested in other women than their own wives, and likewise, women become emotionally attached to other men. For example, tests have proven that if a man sees photographs of very attractive women, he then finds his own wife less attractive,[188] which can lead to separation or divorce. Observing the religious dress code both prevents the harassment of women and helps to maintain the husband and wife relationship.

Similarly, Islām has certain rules for the way men and women look at each other and talk about things. Gazing at someone of the opposite sex[189] is considered inappropriate and a cause of transgression.[190] According to Muslim poets, the eye is the gateway of the heart, and one naturally inclines towards the thing which one finds beautiful and pleasing. Therefore, Islām warns against gazing at strangers.

Furthermore, verbal communication is a means for establishing deep affective relationships. Therefore, Islām advises women not to talk in a loud voice or provocatively,[191] and to talk to men only as much as is necessary.[192] Men should also refrain from talking provocatively and making jokes with women outside the family. The boundaries of the home are there for the family, and outsiders should not enter therein without permission, and any relationships with outsiders should be established with certain limitations.[193] A man and a woman who are unrelated to each other and alone together can provoke strong sexual feelings that few can resist, and is therefore both inappropriate and risky.[194] In order to have a satisfactory life together, a couple should protect the boundaries of their home and observe religious guidelines. Failure to protect these boundaries and allowing men and women to freely mix together can lead to illicit relationships. The Qur'ān mentions this in the story of the Prophet Yūsuf (Joseph):

> *But she in whose house he was sought to seduce him ... And (with passion) did she desire him, and he would have desired her, but that he saw the evidence of his Lord.*[195]

According to these verses, the reason this happened was that Yūsuf and Zulaikha were under the same roof. This kind of temptation would occur for most young people in the same circumstances, but only a very small percentage would refrain like Prophet Yusuf.

In addition to glances, other kinds of nonverbal communication between unrelated men and women are stated as dangerous and prohibited. Such things as shaking hands and other small matters of physical contact[196] are inappropriate, and may lead the way to sexual deviation.[197] All these rules are for protecting chastity and public morality, and deepening family relationships.

These discussions show the crucial importance of boundaries in the family in Islām. At first, these boundaries may appear as a kind of limitation, but by understanding their function of preventing harm and abnormal behaviour, one can see how important they are for protecting the well-being of the family. Moreover, any contact one has with families that keep to these boundaries will demonstrate how much pleasure and satisfaction they have in life.

An important objective in marriage is the protection of chastity and morality, and some of the boundaries help fulfil that purpose. In addition, the teachings of Islām pay attention to higher goals, relating to one's relationship with God and happiness in the afterlife, and some of these boundaries have this spiritual effect. In Islām, great emphasis is put on family relationships, which includes those related by blood to the husband and wife. Therefore, the boundary of the family is flexible, and includes the grandparents, who, if necessary, can make binding decisions on family issues within certain contexts.

Notes

1. Minuchin, Salvador, Families and Family Therapy, p. 87.
2. Al-Ḥurr al-ʿĀmilī, *Wasā'il al-Shī'a*, vol. 14, p. 123.
3. Ibid., p. 120.
4. Khudāpanāhī, Muḥammad Karīm, *Ravānshināsī-yi Physiologic*, p. 302; Carlson, N. R., *Physiology of Behavior*, pp. 479-500.
5. Minuchin, Salvador, *Families and Family Therapy*, p. 87
6. Siemon, F. B., *Key Concepts and Theories in Family Therapy*, pp. 37 and 289.
7. But consort with them in kindness, Qur'ān 4:19.
8. Including Qur'ān 2:180, 228, 229, 231-234; 4:19, 25; 60:12; 65:2, 6.
9. Bānkīpūr Fard, Amīr Ḥusayn, 'Tahlīlī bar Ravābit Dukhtarān va Pisarān Dānishjū', in Majmūʿi-yi Maqālāt Hamandīshī -yi Barrasī-yi Masā'il va Mushkilāt Zanān, vol. 2, p. 690.
10. Tabātabā'ī, *Tafsīr al-Mīzān*, vol. 2, p. 232.
11. Rashīd Reḍā, *Tafsīr al-Minār*, vol. 2, p. 374.
12. Majlisī, *Biḥār al-Anwār*, vol. 45, p. 255.

13. Ibid., vol. 74, p. 328.
14. Ibid., vol. 78, p. 303.
15. Al-Ḥurr al-ʿĀmilī, *Wasā'il al-Shīʿa*, vol. 7, pp. 251, 131.
16. Al-Ḥurr al-ʿĀmilī, *Wasā'il al-Shīʿa*, vol. 14, p. 116; Nūrī, *Mustadrak al-Wasā'il*, vol. 14, p. 251.
17. Ibid., p. 120.
18. Ibid.
19. Ibid., p. 121.
20. Beihaqī, Aḥmad ibn al-Ḥusayn, *al-Sunan al-Kubrā*, vol. 7, p. 304.
21. Al-Ḥurr al-ʿĀmilī, *Wasā'il al-Shīʿa*, vol. 14, p. 122.
22. Ibid., vol. 15, p. 206.
23. Ibid., vol.14, p. 121; ibid., p. 119.
24. Ibid., vol. 14, p. 120.
25. Majlisī, *Biḥār al-Anwār*, vol. 100, p. 225.
26. Farīd Tunikābunī, Murtaḍā, *Nahj al-Fasāḥa*, p. 318.
27. Al-Ḥurr al-ʿĀmilī, *Wasā'il al-Shīʿa*, vol. 14, pp. 9, 11.
28. Ibid., p. 122.
29. Al-Kulaynī, *Usūl Kāfī*, vol. 6, p. 476.
30. Ibid., vol. 2, p. 487.
31. Ibid., vol. 4, p. 446.
32. Qumī, *Muntahā al-Āmāl.*
33. Al-Ḥurr al-ʿĀmilī, *Wasā'il al-Shīʿa*, vol. 14, p. 115.
34. Ibid., p. 116.
35. Ibid., pp. 14 and 19.
36. Qur'ān 30:21.
37. Al-Ḥurr al-ʿĀmilī, *Wasā'il al-Shīʿa*,ch. 4.
38. Ibid., vol. 14, pp. 24 and 123.
39. Qur'ān 2:228.
40. Al-Ḥurr al-ʿĀmilī, *Wasā'il al-Shīʿa*, vol. 14, pp.112-115, 125.
41. Minuchin, Salvador, *Families and Family Therapy*, pp. 88-90.
42. Bīriyā, Nāsir, et al, *Rushd bā Nigarish bi Manābiʿ Islāmī*, pp. 854-880.
43. Al-Ḥurr al-ʿĀmilī, *Wasā'il al-Shīʿa*, vol. 15, p. 175.
44. Ibid., pp. 195 and 227.
45. Farīd Tunikābunī, *al-Ḥadīth*, vol. 2, p. 117.
46. Al-Ḥurr al-ʿĀmilī, *Wasā'il al-Shīʿa*, vol. 14, pp. 86, 87, 188 and 190.
47. The sexual relations between the husband and wife are discussed in Chapter 2.
48. Majlisī, *Biḥār al-Anwār*, vol. 66, p. 177.
49. Al-Ḥurr al-ʿĀmilī, *Wasā'il al-Shīʿa*, vol. 15, p. 188.

50. A Ḥadīth by Imām 'Alī (as)in ibid., Ḥadīth 6.
51. Isfahānī, Muḥammad Mehdī, *Taghziyi bā Shir Mādar va Mas'ale-yi Khīshāvandī* p. 55.
52. Al-Ḥurr al-'Āmilī, *Wasā'il al-Shī'a*, vol. 6, pp. 380-385; Majlisī, *Biḥār al-Anwār*, vol. 103, p. 1.
53. Qur'ān 2:168-169; Majlisī, *Biḥār al-Anwār*, vol. 5, p. 147, vol. 103, p. 7; Muḥammadī-Reyshahrī, *Mīzān al-Ḥikmah*, vol. 5, p. 147, vol. 10, p. 720.
54. Including the eating of quince, pear and melon.
55. Shokrkon, Ḥusayn, et al, *Schools of Psychology*, vol. 2.
56. Al-Ḥurr al-'Āmilī, *Wasā'il al-Shī'a*, vol. 15, p. 195.
57. Farīd Tunikābunī, *al-Ḥadīth*, vol. 3, p. 296.
58. Ibid., p. 59.
59. Al-Ḥurr al-'Āmilī, *Wasā'il al-Shī'a*, vol. 15, p. 194.
60. Ibid., pp. 203 and 295.
61. Ibid.
62. Ibid., p. 199.
63. Ibid.
64. Al-Ḥurr al-'Āmilī, *Wasā'il al-Shī'a*, vol. 15, p. 204.
65. Farīd Tunikābunī, *al-Ḥadīth*, vol. 3, p. 67.
66. For example, these articles mention discrimination against girls in the present times, Johnny Jiggs, "Superiority of the Male Child," translated by Zohre Zāhedi, the journal *Women*, issue 50; Shianti Gush, "Ominous Girls in Southeastern Asi," translated by Elhām Sādeqi, the journal *Women*, issue 7.
67. Al-Ḥurr al-'Āmilī, *Wasā'il al-Shī'a*, vol. 15, p. 100.
68. Ibid.
69. Ibid., p. 100.
70. Khudāraḥīmī, Siyāmak, et al, *Psychology of Women*, pp. 114, 129 and 130.
71. Farīd Tunikābunī, *Al-Ḥadīth*, vol. 1, p. 301.
72. Ibid., vol. 2, p. 348; Al-Kulaynī, *Furū' Kāfī*, vol. 6, p. 50.
73. Majlisī, *Biḥār al-Anwār*, vol. 23, p. 114.
74. Minuchin, Salvador, *Families and Family Therapy*, p. 89.
75. Al-Ḥurr al-'Āmilī, *Wasā'il al-Shī'a*, vol. 15, p. 205.
76. Ibid., p. 217.
77. Majlisī, *Biḥār al-Anwār*, vol. 74, p. 80; Nūrī, *Mustadrak al-Wasā'il*, vol. 15, p. 175.
78. Qur'ān 31:14.
79. Al-Ḥurr al-'Āmilī, *Wasā'il al-Shī'a*, vol. 15, pp. 216, 217.
80. Muḥammadī-Reyshahrī, *Mīzān al-Ḥikmah*, vol. 4, p. 1676.
81. Al-Ḥurr al-'Āmilī, *Wasā'il al-Shī'a*, vol. 15, pp. 216, 217; Qur'ān 17:23.

82. Ibid., p. 221.
83. Ibid., p. 207.
84. Ibid., p. 217.
85. Ibid.
86. Ibid., p. 209.
87. Qur'ān 31:14.
88. Qur'ān 46:15.
89. Nūrī, *Mustadrak al-Wasā'il*, vol. 15, p. 182.
90. Al-Ḥurr al-'Āmilī, *Wasā'il al-Shī'a*, vol. 15, p. 205.
91. Qurayshī, 'Alī -Akbar, *Qāmūs Qur'ān*, vol. 1, p. 88.
92. Qur'ān 17:23.
93. Al-Ḥurr al-'Āmilī, *Wasā'il al-Shī'a*, vol. 15, pp. 271, 220.
94. Ibid., p. 220.
95. Baḥrānī, Sayyid Hāshim, *al-Burhān fī Tafsīr al-Qur'ān*, vol. 5, p. 429, under Qur'ān 24:63.
96. Al-Ḥurr al-'Āmilī, *Wasā'il al-Shī'a*, vol. 15, p. 220.
97. Nūrī, *Mustadrak al-Wasā'il*, vol. 14, p. 179; Qur'ān 17:24.
98. Qur'ān 17:24.
99. Al-Ḥurr al-'Āmilī, *Wasā'il al-Shī'a*, vol. 15, p. 205.
100. Ibid., p. 220.
101. Ibid., p. 217.
102. Ibid.
103. Ibid.
104. Farīd Tunikābunī, *al-Ḥadīth*, vol. 3, p. 339.
105. Majlisī, *Biḥār al-Anwār*, vol. 100, p. 221.
106. Ibid., vol. 23, p. 113.
107. Al-Ḥurr al-'Āmilī, *Wasā'il al-Shī'a*, vol. 15, p. 205.
108. Qur'ān 17:24.
109. Al-Ḥurr al-'Āmilī, *Wasā'il al-Shī'a*, vol. 15, p. 205.
110. Mansūr, Maḥmūd, *Ravānshināsī-yi Genetic*, vol. 2, pp. 150-156.
111. Perin, Lawrence. A, *Personalī ty Psychology, Theory and Research* (Ravānshināsī-yi Shakhsiyyat, Nazariyah va Taḥqīq), translated by Muḥammad Ja'far Javādi and Parvīn Kadīvar (Tehran: Mu'assisah Khadamātī Farhangī Rasā, 1372 A.H).vol.2, pp. 221-223.
112. Minuchin, Salvador, *Families and Family Therapy*, p. 90.
113. Bīriyā, Nāsir, et al, *Rushd bā Nigarish bi Manābi' Islāmī*,vol. 2, p. 875.
114. The believers are but brothers, Qur'ān 49:10; Al-Kulaynī, *Usūl Kāfī*, vol. 3, pp. 241-244.

115. Quotation from Abū 'Abdullāh(as) in Majlisī, *Biḥār al-Anwār*, vol. 74, pp. 274, 280, 97.
116. Quotation from Abū 'Abdullāh in ibid., p. 287.
117. Ibid., pp. 288, 290.
118. Ibid., p. 97.
119. Fayḍ al-Kāshānī, Muḥsin, *al-Maḥajja al-Bayḍā' fī Tahdhīb al-'Iḥyā'*, vol. 3, p. 285.
120. Tirmidhī, Muḥammad ibn Isā, *al-Jāmi' al-Saḥīḥ wa huwa Sunan al-Tirmidhī*, vol. 6, p. 39; Majlisī, *Biḥār al-Anwār*, vol. 74, p. 103.
121. Majlisī, *Biḥār al-Anwār*, vol. 74, p. 102.
122. Such as the way Imām Ḥusayn treated his brother Muḥammad Hanafiyyah (Ibid., pp. 44 and 191) or the other Imams treated their relatives ('Abdūs, Muḥammad Taqī, Sīrih-yi Imāmān Shī'a, vol. 2, pp. 181, 190-194).
123. Repel [evil] by that [deed] which is better; and thereupon the one whom between you and him is enmity [will become] as though he was a devoted friend, Qur'ān 41:34.
124. Hay-Lee, J., *Family Psychotherapy*, pp. 171-179.
125. Siemon, F. B., *Key Concepts and Theories in Family Therapy*, p. 235.
126. Unless like Bu Germany, who accepts any kind of family organisation in which mutual appreciation and respect are considered.
127. Some Islamic jurisprudents consider sexual disinclination of the parents that would result in their discontentment or annoyance to be a sin (Children's House, *Our Precepts and the Children*, pp. 125, 219).
128. But if they endeavour to make you associate with Me that of which you have no knowledge, do not obey them but accompany them in [this] world with appropriate kindness, Qur'ān 31:15; 'Arūsī-Ḥuwaizī , 'Abd 'Alī ibn Jum'ah, *Nūr al-Thaqalain*, vol. 4, p. 202.
129. Such as recommended fasting by the children without the parents' consent (Children's House, *Our Precepts and the Children*, p. 221).
130. Nūrī, *Mustadrak al-Wasā'il*, vol. 15, p. 175.
131. Majlisī, *Biḥār al-Anwār*, vol. 86, p. 186.
132. Qur'ān 4:34.
133. Qur'ān 2:228.
134. Al-Ḥurr al-'Āmilī, *Wasā'il al-Shī'a*, vol. 14, p. 112.
135. Ibid., p. 120.
136. Safā'ī, Sayyid Ḥusayn and Asadullāh Imāmī, Mukhtasar Huqūq Khānivādih, p. 125.
137. Rashīd Reḍā, *Tafsīr al-Minār*, vol. 2, p. 380.

138. Such verses in the Qur'ān as Be ye staunch in justice, 4:135; and Be steadfast witnesses for Allāh, 5:8; And if ye fear that ye cannot do justice (to so many) then one (only), 4:3. This verse c
an be considered as witness to the man's just behaviour (Sajjādī, Sayyid Ibrāhīm, 'Qur'ān va Mushārikat Ijtimā'ī Zanān', in Pazhūhishhāyi Qur'ānī, Daftar Tablīghāt Islāmī, Vol. 7, Nos. 27-28).
139. But consort with them in kindness, Qur'ān 4:19.
140. Ra'ūf, Hiba, *Mushārikat Siyāsī-yi Zan*, p. 179.
141. Many Islamic experts hold such a view, such as Tabātabā'ī, *Tafsīr al-Mīzān*, vol. 5, p. 343; Muṭahharī, Murtaḍā, *Niẓām Huqūq Zan dar Islām*, p. 163; Majlisī, *Biḥār al-Anwār*, vol. 45, p. 2; Faḍlullāh, Muḥammad-Ḥusayn, *Min Waḥy al-Qur'ān*, vol. 7, p. 161. Some other experts also hold such a view. Durant, Will, *The Pleasures of Philosophy*, p. 139; Pires, Roger, *Psychology of Differences between Women and Men*; Hāshimī, *An Introduction to Psychology of Women* as quoted by Sajjādī, 'Qur'ān va Mushārikat Ijtimā'ī Zanān', in *Pazhūhishhāyi Qur'ānī, Daftar Tablīghāt Islāmī*, Vol. 7, Nos. 27-28, p. 54.
142. Ādharbāyjānī, Mas'ūd et al, Ravānshināsī-yi Ijtimā'ī ba Nigāhī bi Manābi' Islāmī, p. 350.
143. Ayman, R, *Leadership*, p. 158.
144. Ādharbāyjānī, Mas'ūd et al, Ravānshināsī-yi Ijtimā'ī ba Nigāhī bi Manābi' Islāmī, pp. 187-197, 447-450.
145. ... and because they support them from their means, Qur'ān 4:34.
146. Minuchin, Salvador, *Families and Family Therapy*, pp. 14-20.
147. Barker, *Basic Family Therapy*, p. 88.
148. Minuchin, Salvador, *Families and Family Therapy*, p. 91.
149. Ibid., p. 85.
150. Ibid., pp. 83-87.
151. Minuchin, Salvador, *Families and Family Therapy*, pp. 146-161.
152. Ibid., p. 146.
153. Qur'ān 24:58-59.
154. Al-Ḥurr al-'Āmilī, *Wasā'il al-Shī'a*, vol. 14, pp. 157, 159, 160.
155. Ibid., p. 158.
156. Ibid., p. 171.
157. Ibid., p. 152.
158. Majlisī, *Biḥār al-Anwār*, vol. 75, p. 68.
159. Al-Ḥurr al-'Āmilī, *Wasā'il al-Shī'a*, vol. 14, p. 154.
160. Qur'ān 4:34.
161. Qur'ān 66:4.

CHAPTER 3

162. Qur'ān 49:12.
163. Majlisī, *Biḥār al-Anwār*, vol. 75.
164. Qur'ān 12:5.
165. *Nahj al-Balāghah*, Letter 39.
166. Al-Ḥurr al-'Āmilī, *Wasā'il al-Shī'a*, vol. 14, p. 175.
167. Qur'ān 24:27 and 28.
168. As it was also practised by the Prophet. See Al-Kulaynī, *Kāfī*, vol. 5, p. 528; Muṭahharī, Murtaḍā, *Mas'alī h-yi Ḥijāb*, p. 131.
169. Qā'imī, 'Alī , *Niẓām Ḥayāt Khānivādih dar Islām* , pp. 52, 208-211.
170. Qur'ān 23:5-7.
171. Qur'ān 17:32.
172. Qur'ān 24:2; 4:15-16; Majlisī, *Biḥār al-Anwār*, vol. 71, pp. 17-40.
173. Majlisī, *Biḥār al-Anwār*, vol. 76, p. 26.
174. Ibid., p. 27.
175. Ibid.
176. Ibid.
177. Ibid., p. 22.
178. Ibid., pp. 24, 28.
179. Ibid., p. 11.
180. Ibid., p. 19.
181. Al-Ḥurr al-'Āmilī, *Wasā'il al-Shī'a*, vol. 14, p. 138.
182. Muṭahharī, Murtaḍā, *Mas'alī h-yi Ḥijāb*, pp. 83-89.
183. Al-Ḥurr al-'Āmilī, *Wasā'il al-Shī'a*, vol. 14, p. 240.
184. Ibid., p. 188.
185. Qur'ān 24:31.
186. Qur'ān 33:59.
187. Baron, R. A., *Social Psychology*, p. 226.
188. Ādharbāyjānī, Mas'ūd et al, Ravānshināsī-yi Ijtimā'ī ba Nigāhī bi Manābi' Islāmī, p. 253.
189. Qur'ān 24:30-31.
190. Al-Ḥurr al-'Āmilī, *Wasā'il al-Shī'a*, vol. 14, pp. 139-140.
191. Qur'ān 33:32.
192. Al-Ḥurr al-'Āmilī, *Wasā'il al-Shī'a*, vol. 14, p. 143.
193. Qur'ān 33:53.
194. Al-Ḥurr al-'Āmilī, *Wasā'il al-Shī'a*, vol. 14, p. 134.
195. Qur'ān 12:23-24.
196. Al-Ḥurr al-'Āmilī, *Wasā'il al-Shī'a*, vol. 14, p. 142.
197. Ibid., p. 185.

CHAPTER 4

GUIDELINES FOR THE EFFICIENCY AND PROPER DEVELOPMENT OF THE FAMILY

Having discussed the Islamic injunctions regarding the family under the title "The Pillars of the Family," in this chapter we will deal with the necessary guidance for efficiency and development within the family. We first of all consider the role of an appropriate religious understanding among members of the family. Then we follow up with a discussion of ethics in the family, which can be applied in many areas. Finally, we examine advice on behaviour.

1. The Role of Religious Insight in the Family

In the discussion on selecting a spouse, the need for similar religious attitudes for reaching a balance was considered. In addition, if the husband and wife have strong religious beliefs, this will consolidate the relationships between members of the family to a considerable degree, while shortcomings in this respect give rise to numerous problems, which are referred to in the Qur'ān as leading to a "narrow life."[1] This can be due to greed, fear and anxiety.[2] Therefore, religious belief plays an important role in normal life, while its absence takes away peace of mind and pleasure in life, causing anxiety, shock and longing, even if the individual has many material advantages.[3] Numerous psychological investigations have shown that religious belief engenders peace of mind and relief from tension.[4]

1.1. Belief in God

The most important religious belief is faith in the one God. The monotheistic worship of God makes one's attitude towards life meaningful and one's behaviour logical,[5] and creates a unified system of peace.[6] Belief in God will cause all behaviour and family life to be satisfying to God.[7] The person who thinks of God as watching and accompanying[8] him, even closer than his jugular vein,[9] will try to please

God by fulfilling family duties. The awareness of God's justice, and an understanding that He is not unjust[10] and does not violate anyone's rights,[11] is another cognitive reason for controlling the behaviour of the family members. The stronger this is, the fewer problems there will be, and no outside monitor or arbitrator will be needed. Paying attention to God's attributes and the sufficiency of His infinite love, kindness,[12] power[13] and support[14] for all His creatures, will have positive effects on life and the family. The kindness of family members towards each other reflects the love of God,[15] and is the basis for preventing and solving problems. Relying on God, i.e. trusting in His power in all the affairs of life, is one of the effects of belief in God.[16] A believer considers God to be controlling the world, and all changes and developments to be according to His will. When faced with problems in life, one has need of material means and a suitable psychological constitution. Putting one's trust in God provides the conditions for both of these. Sometimes a weak will, fear, sadness, anxiety or the lack of a full command over a situation makes a person unable to find ways to solve problems. Putting one's trust in God strengthens one's will, reduces the effect of disturbing psychological factors, and further enables the person to solve the problems in his life and reach balance and compatibility.[17] Families face numerous problems in life, some of which are economic, such as a low income, bankruptcy, stolen property and unemployment; others relate to the health of the family members, such as illness, disability and death; and some are to do with relationships and issues of compatibility. In such conditions, trust in God strengthens the family and its efforts. In addition, when there are material problems that seem insoluble, trust in God opens a door, and sometimes solves the problems in unexpected ways.[18] Giving guidance for gaining trust is important, and has been evaluated as being more positive in the case of women,[19] because the main responsibility for solving problems, especially economic ones, lies with the man, and it is very important that his morale be boosted by the others.

An effect of belief in God is submitting to and being satisfied with the divine will. Such a state of mind will prepare the appropriate cognitive and affective grounds. The individual should believe that all events in the world are subject to God's permission and the power that He exercises through various means.[20] Moreover, not only is God more aware of what is good for people, but He also wishes for their happiness more than they do themselves.[21] Therefore, all events happen for the good and expediency of the people. Submission to and satisfaction with the events of the world, which are at God's disposal, is desirable for every person who believes in metaphysics and in God. If the person does not follow the path of satisfaction, the situation will be more difficult.[22] This condition is more specifically useful in conditions over which people have no control, such as earthquakes, floods, terminal diseases and the death of loved ones. Such incidents create serious problems. For example, sometimes a disaster such as a death or sickness create a great deal of tension. In such circumstances, either the father or mother may blame another person, or often him- or herself, for the disaster. In some families, challenges arising from a disease or handicap of a child can be severe, and the stress can last a very long time.[23] In such a situation, if the parents submit to and are satisfied with the divine will, it is easier to face these problems. Because of this state of satisfaction, the family will see the problems as positive and perfecting, and help them adapt to an irreversible situation, thus making things easier. Much research has confirmed the effect of religious beliefs on satisfaction within marriage. Other research has found that religion is the most important factor for the stability in a lasting marriage.[24]

1.2. The Belief in the Divine Mission and Imamate

A second pillar of religious belief is that of the mission of people appointed by God[25] as prophets throughout history. Divine leadership and the substitution of prophets are known in Shi'ism as the "Imamate,"[26] and this corresponds to the completion of the mission of the prophets.[27]

In man's life, the role of belief in the principle of prophethood and the imamate has two dimensions. The first is religious education, and living life according to religious precepts. The unique way of knowing about the teachings of religion and the words of God is through the words of the Prophet and his successors, in such a way that a proper understanding of God is based on knowing and understanding the words of the religious leaders. This aspect of the role of belief in prophethood and the imamate is clarified throughout the discussions of this book. From now on, we will consider the way the divine religious leaders are modelled. The principle of assimilation, which exists in people from childhood by taking others as models, is the basic factor in learning, so that imitation has a very positive effect on children for solving problems or facing the surrounding environment.[28] In addition to this, from amongst the various methods of learning, observing a model is the most effective and lasting. As for relationships and behaviour within the family, it is also necessary to follow and assimilate to those in whom religious teachings are fully manifested. Since people need objective behavioural examples for all aspects of life in order to learn how to behave, they will inevitably be drawn towards such models. Therefore, it is useful to give suitable examples. The Qur'ān enjoins those who seek spiritual perfection to consider the Prophet as a good model in their lives.[29] The lives of the divine religious leaders also provide good examples of how to behave in all respects.

1.3. Belief in the Afterlife

A crucial aspect of religious belief is belief in the afterlife and the weighing of one's deeds on the Day of Judgment, when one is either rewarded or punished. Although belief in the Resurrection affects all aspects of one's life, here more emphasis is put on the familial aspects. Nowadays, despite scientific progress and less problems in life, stress and anxiety are on the increase. Part of the problem is due to a feeling of purposelessness in life,[30] and disbelief in the afterlife makes things worse and has an adverse effect on the family. Due to a lack of higher goals, a limited functioning of family life is considered enough, and families often fall apart. Belief in the afterlife stabilises the family and strengthens its bonds.[31] Such families then support each other emotionally and feel happy with life, even if faced with severe problems.

Another effect of belief in the Resurrection is that it motivates and encourages people. The divine religious leaders refer to the rewards and blessings in the afterlife that are given in return for fulfilling family duties. Remembering these blessings and the comfort of the afterlife then motivates the individual to consider his actions so that he acquires such blessings. For example, certain verses[32] such as the following, further increase a person's eagerness to fulfil his duties:

> *Enter the Garden, ye and your wives, to be made glad. Therein are brought round for them trays of gold and goblets, and therein is all that should desire and eyes find sweet, and ye are immortal*

therein. This is the Garden which ye are made to inherit because of what ye used to do.

A third effect is not unconnected to the previous, and is to do with dealing with problems. Despite losing a loved one, a serious disability or severe economic problems, the family would still have mental peace because of belief in the Resurrection. Sometimes problems seem insoluble, and relief can only be found by bearing in mind the rewards of the afterlife. For example, as regards economic problems, the following sayings are worth considering: "Problems are gifts from God, and destitution is kept in God's treasury";[33] "Destitution is ugly to people, but is a decoration from God on Judgment Day";[34] "Do not look down on poor Muslim and their families, because every one of them intercedes as much as those of a [large] tribe";[35] "On Judgment Day, God looks at poor people apologetically, saying, 'I swear by My grandeur that I did not make you poor in the world because of humiliation or inattention.[36] Now see what I am giving in place of what happened in the world.'"[37]

As for bereavement for the death of a child, consequences in the next world have been mentioned such as putting a strong fence by the person to protect him from Hell,[38] or Paradise being guaranteed for him.[39] It has also been said that whoever takes refuge in God in times of trouble, and remembers that he will return to Him, is guaranteed Paradise.[40] Psychologically speaking, anyone who complains about small afflictions will be stricken with greater ones.[41]

Regarding disease, it has been said that: "Not sleeping for one night due to illness or pain is better than a year of worship, and will be rewarded more";[42] and "Anyone who is sick for three days without complaining to those who visit him will be renewed. He will then be healed, and taken without sin to the region of blessings."[43]

As for nursing and helping those who are sick, it has been said: "He who stays with a sick person for one night will be resurrected with Abraham and cross the Bridge of the Path instantly. He who fulfils a need of a sick person will have his sins erased, and be as if just born from his mother.[44] Moreover, he who feeds a sick person what is pleasing to him, God will give him the fruits of Paradise."[45] All such reassurances, relating above all to the afterlife, encourage members of the family to recognise that, under difficult circumstance that cannot be remedied simply by hard work in this world, they should still persevere.

Belief in the Resurrection is also a deterrent. Many problems in the family are due to a failure to control actions that lead to the violation of the rights of the other family members, by imposing upon them or being aggressive. Belief in the Resurrection, remembering the bad consequences of violating the rights of others and failing to fulfil one's responsibilities, deters bad behaviour to a certain extent. In this connection, the Qur'ān warns believers to save themselves and their family from the fire whose fuel is men and stones.[46] For example, one of the consequences of having a bad temperament within the family is hardship for the soul in the next life, and even if the person fulfils his other duties in life, but behaves badly at home, he will suffer adversity in the next life.[47] In addition, the divine religious leaders refer to the consequences of treating one's spouse badly.[48] Consideration of the unfavourable consequences in the afterlife can to a certain extent be a deterrent against bad behaviour.

2. Moral Advice for Further Efficiency within the Family

In the discussion on the responsibilities of the husband and wife in the family, we mentioned the necessity of good manners. Here, we will examine some moral attributes that affect the family and how they can be developed.

2.1. Honesty

Honesty in the family is the emotional basis for trust. Psychologically speaking, honesty is expressed verbally and behaviourally when the person's actions correspond with what they say. In other words, the person speaks explicitly, frankly and clearly. When a person speaks dishonestly there is a conflict, since his intentions differ from what he says.

In such a case, the hearer who responds to these words or actions will be confused by what the person actually does. Sometimes, he pays attention to his words and behaviour and overlooks his motives, and sometimes, because of too much attention to the possible motives, shows an inappropriate reaction. This is a characteristic of distressed families.[49] Dishonesty in the husband or wife will drive the family atmosphere to distrust and cynicism and promote differences. The divine religious leaders emphasise honesty, because of the destructive effect that telling lies has on interpersonal relationships,[50] and they say that faith is judged by telling the truth.[51] Telling the truth prepares the ground for mutual trust and friendly, intimate relations.[52] Therefore, to develop healthy relationships in the family, verbal and physical communication (tone of voice, posture, eye contact, glances and movements) should be direct, clear and explicit, so that the words accord with facial expressions, posture and the tone of voice, while also being in harmony with subconscious moods. In fact, all one's psychological aspects should display the same thing. This will bring truth, integrity, commitment, honesty, merit and creativity when tackling problems.[53]

2.2. Optimism

Optimism is an effective moral attribute based on mutual trust. Optimism and good intentions towards God, each other and life in general, including its problems, have an important role in the health of the family. In family life, optimism has a considerable effect in preventing and solving many emotional problems. In order to create a state of optimism, the husband and wife should try their hardest to get to know each other at the beginning of their life together in order to benefit from it. In addition, they should observe the moral precepts. Family members can work towards eliminating suspicion and creating optimism by acquiring these conditions in light of mutual trust. Religious texts emphasise optimism towards one's brothers and sisters in religion and interpreting their behaviour in the best way possible,[54] and that it is a sin to be unduly suspicious,[55] because it is not religiously permissible and causes improper speech and behaviour towards others.[56] In the family also, the husband, wife and children should avoid being suspicious of each other. Any judgment or suspicion of others should be based on sound knowledge, without which the family members should be optimistic about each other. A particular interpersonal problem is the failure to understand the motives of the other person. Sometimes people misinterpret each other's actions, but Islamic precepts recommend that these should be interpreted in the best possible way. Obviously, any attempt within the family to reduce negative interpretations of each other's behaviour clears the way for good understanding and proper relationships. The psychological atmosphere within the family should be of an acute attentiveness to the positive aspects of others, and not to unduly exaggerate negativity. This will promote feelings of optimism towards each other.

Optimism towards issues in life and optimistic explanations of unfavourable events also affect one's ability to tackle problems. On the other hand, pessimistic explanations may entangle individuals in affective states and make them insecure. In such cases, physical illness becomes more likely. Optimism guides the individual towards the solution of problems. By adhering to such plans, things will often go according to the individual's desire. This will double his efforts.[57] Therefore, it can be said that a positive view of life, while affecting emotions, will improve family relationships.

Another aspect of optimism mentioned in Islamic texts, the optimism about God, also affects family life positively. A believer will consider God to be influencing all the affairs of life in the world. Now, if a person is not optimistic about God and becomes frustrated, he will be frustrated in all matters of life and cannot do anything positive or useful. Therefore, pessimism about God has been known as one of the worst sins,[58] and the divine religious leaders have encouraged optimism about God in different ways.[59] For example, it has been said that if someone has good thoughts about God, God will prepare conditions as he expects them.[60]

2.3. Contentment

Contentment and the avoidance of a life of luxury is an important moral attribute, which, according to Islamic texts, affects worldly life and the afterlife.[61] In the contemporary era, means of material welfare have increased along with the use of modern equipment and luxury goods. This has created many differences in familial living facilities. It is impossible for everyone to have a better material life, and many are left behind in this competition. Differences in income and standards of material life can cause dissatisfaction and conflict within families. In the teachings of Islām, in order to prevent or reduce such disputes, individuals are advised to be content with what they have, and to avoid luxury. One who is content will be satisfied with as much as he needs,[62] and will not pressure himself for a higher income. If the family members, especially the husband and wife, are content with the income they earn by hard work, and do not trouble themselves or others in this respect, they will be less upset and suffer less.[63] Women especially are advised to be content and to try to expect less,[64] perhaps because the man is usually the breadwinner of the family and undergoes more psychological pressure. As a result, pressure from the woman will intensify his problems.

In order to be content,[65] people should pay attention to other families who are worse off, and should communicate with them more often, rather than admiring those who are well-off, thus giving themselves pain and sorrow. Such a spirit will convert greed into the energy for spiritual and scientific development. Family members, if they manage to be content and stop yearning for a luxurious material life,[66] will be liberated from sorrow[67] and have a degree of self-esteem[68] that gives them a feeling of needlessness, even if one has many shortages.[69] This state will make life more pleasing.[70] According to the divine religious leaders, a person who is content with his income and his share in life enjoys the most pleasant life, whereas discontent[71] leads to grief and sorrow.[72]

2.4. Patience

A characteristic moral attribute of a good spouse is patience.[73] A particular level of Paradise has been described for the one who is patient.[74] Patience has to do with contentedness. However, due to its importance in the family, it is examined separately. Patience and forbearance in the face of family problems are prerequisites for solving them properly. If family members become tense due to normal problems, they are inevitably vulnerable to disputes. Patience is a most important personal attribute for preventing such problems, and is considered a principle of faith,[75] because the person who is unable to control himself may involve the others when he is in trouble, and may even expose his religious beliefs to doubt.[76] Regarding family issues, sometimes individuals face problems that take time to be resolved. In such conditions, intolerance and a lack of control will create tension for the person, and his needs will not be fulfilled. Rather, mental pressure will increase and the situation will seem more difficult than it is,[77] while patience will bring success in the long run.[78]

Sometimes the inappropriate behaviour of others makes the person react, in which case patience and forbearance is very effective for solving the problem or preventing differences. In addition, not reacting badly enables the person to behave properly at any appropriate time.[79] This is possible only with patience and self-control. Otherwise, one may react too quickly and regret it afterwards.[80]

Apart from problems in relationships, there can be physical, psychological or financial issues that cause problems within the family. Sometimes the problems can be so severe that, if the person does not get energy from spiritual and metaphysical sources, he will totally fail. The Qur'ān makes promises to those in such circumstances, and calls them to be patient, stating that they will receive God's blessing.[81] Elsewhere it tells of the infinite remuneration for patient people[82] and, above all, says that God loves,[83] accompanies[84] and is a companion[85] to patient people. All these verses further motivate the individual to control himself and be more patient. The divine religious leaders have made very clear statements that one should be patient in the face of problems: "If you are patient, God will give you a reward for every blight,"[86] "Patience is given in proportion to troubles,"[87] and "Everyone who is patient when blighted, and comprehends it in peace, will be given three hundred spiritual grades by God."[88] This last point illustrates the need to advise members of the family to be patient towards each other,[89] and concerns one's own patience as well as that of the others.

2.5. Generosity

Generosity is a valuable characteristic in the family, especially as regards men.[90] The worst of men are those who are mean.[91] As men are usually financially in charge of the family, their meanness will badly affect the comfort of the family, so much so that sometimes other family members may in their hearts wish the death of the father.[92] According to the divine religious leaders, meanness contains all the ugly attributes,[93] so much so that even a generous person who makes mistakes is loved more by God than a worshipful, but mean man.[94] In the teachings of Islām, the development and welfare of the family are greatly emphasised, and the blessings and material comfort given to man by God are considered appropriate.[95] However, the teachings of Islām make a distinction between the husband and wife in respect of generosity and meanness, and do not expect the woman to be generous.[96] This is in order for the woman to take more care of the costs, so that the family will not get into economic difficulties due to excessive spending or extravagant gifts. This is also why meanness in a woman is undesirable as it is in a man.

3. Behavioural Teachings of Islām for Desirable Family Efficiency

The teachings of Islām have various recommendations for improving family relationships. Some of these relate to both verbal and nonverbal communication between the family members. Others relate to the home environment, running the family and worshipping at home, all of which either directly or indirectly play a part in family relationships. Let us now examine these suggestions.

3.1. Verbal Communication

Certain differences are noticed between children and adult men and women in the way they establish verbal relationships. As for children, preparing the ground for talking to them critically affects the way they grow and develop. On the contrary, a lack of appropriate conditions for talking and the expression of feelings and thoughts will result in the repression of affections and cognitive abilities. The family environment is the best place for verbal development and self-expression. Conversation in the house matters more to the wife than to the husband, and he cares more about being present.[97] The teachings of Islām contain thorough guidance about the way one speaks and what is said. Firstly, family members should talk to teach other respectfully, and in a mild tone. In order to encourage individuals to talk to each other tenderly, the Qur'ān makes an analogy in order to encourage people to speak mildly, especially in the home environment.[98] A sign of respect when talking is that the husband and wife address each other by the title that they love best.[99] Secondly, expressions of love and friendship towards family members have a special importance, because they help deepen affective relationships.[100] And thirdly, the family members should verbally express their thanks to each other.[101] The expression of thanks to the parents is deemed equal to thanking God.[102] Also, the husband and wife should appreciate what they do for each other. A good attribute of women is to be thankful for and appreciative of the family.[103] On the other hand, a woman's being ungrateful has undesirable consequences in the family, especially for her.[104] The man should thank his wife well, for this will further increase their intimacy and give encouragement to the woman.[105]

In the family environment, talking of God's blessings[106] and being grateful for them are very important, for the Qur'ān mentions that being grateful for God's blessings is beneficial.[107] Part of gratitude to God is respecting the work of those who have given help, for otherwise, one has not been grateful to God.[108] This can also affect the family, because no one can fulfil the material and affective needs of an individual like the parents,[109] the spouse,[110] and sometimes the children.[111]

Some behaviour impedes verbal communication and should be avoided as much as possible, such as nagging, interrupting each other, arguments over unimportant issues, deviating from the main subject, making threats or insults, mockery, sharp criticism and talking too much.[112] The teachings of Islām mention some of this and add certain points, such as the fact that, in the presence of the family members, it is not appropriate to whisper, because this will upset the others.[113] The Qur'ān explicitly prohibits talking secretly in front of others.[114] In addition, telling lies is prohibited, as discussed earlier. Whether said seriously or jokingly, lies are considered wrong by the teachings of Islām,[115] because they damage frankness between individuals.[116] In order to discourage people from interrupting each other, the divine religious leaders give the analogy of scratching someone's face.[117] Making fun of others is prohibited in the Qur'ān, especially in the case of women.[118] In the discussion on family disputes, words that result in conflict in the family will be examined.

3.2. Nonverbal Communication

People communicate nonverbally through eye contact, facial expressions, touching and body language such as posture. The tone of the voice is also a part of this, as already mentioned.[119]

The teachings of Islām contain interesting points regarding nonverbal relationships in the family. It is important to have good manners, and part this involves nonverbal communication. In this connection, individuals are advised to greet people, especially their family, with a welcoming face,[120] because a welcoming face and nice facial expressions attract the heart,[121] increase love,[122] happiness and joy, and eliminate all vengeance.[123] As for the believer, it has been said that his inside is sad, but his outside happy and welcoming.[124] In addition, a smile on the face[125] also improves relationships. Turning one's face away damages relationships and is also prohibited by the Qur'ān.[126] The loving glances of the husband and wife to each other bring them joy.[127] Moreover, looking upon one's parents with kindness and love is a kind of worship,[128] and the parents are also encouraged to look at each other in ways that make them happy.[129] On the other hand, angry looks between members of the family, especially by the children at the parents,[130] will disturb the affective relationship between them.

As for physical postures, the teachings of Islām recommend humility in interpersonal relationships, so that positive feelings can be reinforced.[131] Humility means that the person does not consider himself better than others,[132] and this affects the physical posture very much.[133] Therefore, in the Qur'ān, while advising children to have the utmost humility towards their parents, the metaphor of "lowering the wing of submission" is used.[134] Humility creates a kind of physical posture that is the opposite of that which is manifested through vanity and a feeling of superiority, whereby the person tries to elevate himself.[135] Therefore, in order to establish ideal relationships within the family, it is necessary for individuals to show humbleness in their physical postures. In this connection, the husband should give advice about behaviour[136] that develops a physical expression of humility. A very good characteristic of women is humbleness towards their husbands,[137] whereas the worst kind is to display haughtiness before their husbands.[138]

3.3. The Home Environment

Another aspect of Islamic guidance concerning proper behaviour in the home environment is to do with the good appearance of the family members,[139] as well as that of the home itself.[140] It is advised in this respect that all members of the family, especially the husband and wife, maintain a nice appearance. This is said to increase the love between individuals.

Being at home and in the presence of the family, especially at night, is very important.[141] The Prophet said that sitting with one's family is more favourable to God than religious seclusion in a mosque in the holy city of Medina.[142] He also said:

> "Any man who spreads a dinner cloth to which he calls his wife and child, and begins the food with the name of God, and finishes it off with God's name, God's blessings will shower down on him before he takes the dinner cloth away."[143]

Nowadays, because of the industrialisation of a society in which men and women work long hours into the evening away from home, sometimes not coming home until their children go to bed, these recommendations become more important. Nevertheless, despite such problems in everyday life, it is very important for the family to spend time together and that the parents realise this important.

There are also recommendations for when the man enters and leaves the home, such as, if she has nothing important to do, how the woman should see him off by following him for a few steps and going out to welcome him.[144] This behaviour will increase the love and intimacy between the husband and wife. On the other hand, the man should also try to respond to this in some way. Shows of affection, kind words and ignoring mistakes are some of the things the man can do.[145] The man should greet the family when entering the house.[146] The husband should not enter the house suddenly or secretly. Rather, before entering the house, he should somehow notify the wife and children in advance, then the family can prepare for his arrival and avoid any inconvenient situation. On entering the house he should greet everyone, which indicates respect for them and brings peace and love[147] to the family. These are circumstances for which verses in the Qur'ān and words of the divine religious leaders very much emphasise polite verbal communication.[148]

Another important polite thing to do is giving presents on happy occasions, such as a festival day, or when returning from a trip, for this expresses love for the wife and children.[149] The Prophet said: "Give each other presents in order to increase love and remove the dust of revenge from the hearts."[150] When coming back from a trip, bring gifts for your family as you can afford."[151] This will improve the emotional relationships between family members. The important point about giving presents is the consideration paid to the receiver, which is of more value than the gift itself. Therefore, gifts are true signs of friendship and affection.[152]

3.4. Running Household Affairs

It is important to cooperate in helping around the house. The principle of cooperation is very much emphasied in Islām,[153] and is the basis for living life together. The teachings of Islām divide family duties so that each family member has a part to play in the functioning of the family.Certain things should not be done by the man, while certain others should not be done by the woman, but it is important point that they both help each other. The divine religious leaders have made some very interesting points in order to encourage the man and woman to help each other and cooperate at home. It has been said regarding women:

> "If a woman gives her husband a sip of water, it is spiritually more valuable than one year of fasting and praying at night. For each sip of water that she gives to her husband, God will give her a city in Paradise and forgive sixty of her sins";[154]

and

> "A woman who, in line with home duties, moves something from one place to somewhere else, will be remembered by God, and whosoever is remembered by God will not incur His wrath."[155]

A significant piece of active advice from the divine religious leaders concerns the man's contribution to the housework. The Prophet advised 'Alī:

> "A man who helps his wife at home will be given the reward of one year of fasting and prayer at night for as many hairs there are on his body, and God will give the reward due to patient prophets such as David, Jacob and Jesus. Oh, 'Alī , one who does not refrain from helping his family will be put by God on the list of martyrs, and also, every day and night of service, every step and physical pain, will be rewarded. Oh, 'Alī , one hour of service at home is better than a thousand years of worship, a thousand minor or major hajj pilgrimages, ..., feeding a thousand hungry people, ..., donating a thousand dinars, ... And one would not leave this world without first seeing his place in paradise. Oh, 'Alī , only those who serve their family are seekers of truth and martyrs, and men whom God wishes to give the good of this and next life."[156]

The Prophet's awareness of the desirable consequences of service at home motivates believers to consider it spiritually rewarding, and not something to be avoided with the excuse of performing other religious duties. The man is the manager of the house and indicates his role as guardian of the family. If the man follows this advice, all the family members will be encouraged to do their part, and a spirit of cooperation and affection will permeate throughout the family. From a sociological point of view, a basic principle of marriage and starting a family is joint effort, and this is not just a matter of helping individuals. Rather, the family group is the main purpose. Joint effort is an important factor in the family, according to which each member helps everyone else rather than thinking of his own wishes, and his purpose is the comfort of the entire family. In other words, the man and woman relationship in marriage is not merely based on personal needs and desires, but family goals matter as well.[157]

Further advice for men is to pay attention to the tastes, interests and wishes of the family regarding the condition of the house, food and other things inside the house. It would be appropriate if the man prefers the interests of his wife and children to his own and coordinates himself with them inside the home. Imposing his wishes on the family is a moral disease and a lack of faith.[158] Therefore, if there is a difference in taste regarding the home, it would be a sign of faith if the man accepts the opinion of the family and does not impose his own view on them. With such advice, the wife and the other members of the family will feel a positive independent identity, and this will help their talents to flourish. If one of the spouses takes control of all decision-making, the wife and children will be deprived of freedom to think independently and their dignity will be marred.[159]

An important teaching of Islām is to keep one's promise, and no one is allowed to violate this.[160] The man's fulfilment of his promises will positively affect the spirit of his wife and children by making them committed to this good characteristic, and parents will then be more respectful to them. Imām Kāẓim said:

> "When you promise something to children, make sure you fulfil it, because they think that their daily bread is given by you.[161] God will be enraged, more than anything else, by failure and injustice towards women and children."[162]

Failing to fulfil promises will have undesirable consequences on the family, because in many cases the excuse for failure will not be accepted.

3.5. Worshipping in the Family

Worship is important in Islām,[163] and one should guide one's family in spiritual matters, and protect them from error and its undesirable consequences in this and next life.[164] One can protect one's family in several ways: by encouraging them to worship and obey God, by teaching them their religious duties, and stopping them from doing unacceptable and bad things, while encouraging them to do good things.[165] In the first place, one should oneself worship properly in order to set a good example for the others. According to the religious texts, children should be advised to pray at the age of seven years.[166]

This advice can be given in various ways, some of which, such as setting a good example, will be more effective.[167] An important teaching of God to the Prophet is in advising his family to pray.[168] God advised the Prophet to order his family to pray and to be steadfast in pray.[169] Imām Bāqir said that when this verse was revealed, the Prophet would come every day to 'Alī and Fātima's house, saying: "Prayers, prayers! May God shower you with his blessings!" The Prophet would do this until the end of his life.[170] The Prophet Abraham asked God in his daily prayers to make him and his children say their prayers.[171] Prayers greatly influence the behaviour and manners of the family members, while being a cognitive and affective communication with God.[172] The divine religious leaders make an interesting analogy regarding the effect of prayers:

> "Prayers are like a clear spring full of water in which one washes oneself five times a day, to clean all dirt and contamination and to remove all filth."[173]

Praying at the various times of the day is like an intention to control that works at certain times. Prayers and other acts of worship, such as fasting, also help the proper relations among family members. The family atmosphere and environment should indicate the spiritual relationship of the individuals with God.[174] In this case, the motives, affections and knowledge of the individuals, including their understanding and interpretation of life, will be affected. In addition, worship affects the behaviour of the family members by strengthening their religious beliefs.

Notes

1. But he who turneth away from remembrance of Me, his will be a narrow life, Qur'ān 20:124.
2. Makārim Shīrāzī, Nāsir, Tafsīr Nimūnih, vol. 1, pp. 327-330.

3. Qara'ati, Muḥsin, *Tafsīr Nūr*,, vol. 7, pp. 406, 407.
4. Aḥmadī-Abharī, 'Alī , "Role of Faith and Religious Belief," *Thought & Behavior*, Appendices 9 & 10, pp. 27-33.
5. Allāh coineth a similitude: A man in relation to whom are several part-owners, quarrelling, and a man belonging wholly to one man. Are the two equal in similitude? Qur'ān 39:29; Lo! we are Allāh's and lo! unto Him we are returning, Qur'ān 2:156.
6. Verily in the remembrance of Allāh do hearts find rest! Qu'ran 13:28; He it is Who sent down peace of reassurance into the hearts of the believers, Qur'ān 48:4.
7. Lo! my worship and my sacrifice and my living and my dying are for Allāh, Lord of the Worlds, Qur'ān 6:162.
8. He is with you wheresoever ye may be. And Allāh is Seer of what ye do, Qur'ān 57:4.
9. We are nearer to him than his jugular vein, Qur'ān 50:16.
10. Qur'ān 4:40, 10:44, 9:70, and many other verses.
11. Qur'ān 18:30.
12. Your Lord hath prescribed for Himself mercy, Qur'ān 6:54; Your Lord is a Lord of All-Embracing Mercy, 6:147; Lo! my Lord is Merciful, Loving, 11:90; Lo! your Lord is Full of Pity, Merciful, 16:7.
13. Lo! Allāh! He it is that giveth livelihood, the Lord of unbreakable might, Qur'ān 51:58; Lo! Allāh is Strong, Almighty, 57:25; Power belongeth wholly to Allāh, 2:165; There is no strength save in Allāh! 18:39.
14. Will not Allāh defend His slave? Qur'ān 39:36; Allāh sufficeth as a Reckoner, 4:6; Allāh is sufficient as a Supporter, 4:45; But Allāh sufficeth for a Guide and Helper, 25:31.
15. Muttaqī-Hindī, 'Alā' al-Dīn, *Kanz al-'Ummāl*, Ḥadīth 5667.
16. And when His revelations are recited unto them they increase their faith, and who trust in their Lord, Qur'ān 8:2; Say: He is my Lord; there is no God save Him. In Him do I put my trust and unto Him is my recourse, 13:30.
17. Di Matteo, M., *Health Psychology*, vol. 2, p. 757.
18. And for those who fear Allāh, He (ever) prepares a way out, And He prepares for him from (sources) he never could imagine, Qur'ān 65:2-3.
19. Al-Ḥurr al-'Āmilī, *Wasā'il al-Shī'a*, vol. 14, p. 17.
20. There is no strength save in Allāh, Qur'ān 18:39; Of the bounties of thy Lord We bestow freely on all – these as well as those: the bounties of Thy Lord are not closed (to anyone), 17:20.
21. Al-Kulaynī, *Usūl Kāfī*, vol. 3, pp. 100, 101.
22. Ibid., p. 102.

23. Di Matteo, M., *Health Psychology*, vol. 2, p. 730.
24. Ghubārī Bunāb, Bāqir, 'Bāvarhā-yi Madhhabī va Atharāt Ānhā dar Bihdāsht Ravān', in *Andīshih va Raftār, Quarterly*, vol. 1, issue 4, 1995.
25. Each one (of them) believeth in Allāh, His angels, His books, and His messengers. "We make no distinction between one and another of His messengers," Qur'ān 2:285.
26. Such as religious narrations in respect of the verse: And warn thy tribe of near kindred, (Qur'ān 26:214), as well as the *Thaqalain* Ḥadīth and the Ḥadīth that says: "There will be twelve substitutes after me."
27. Tabātabā'ī, Sayyid Muḥammad-Ḥusayn, *Shī'a dar Islām*, pp. 180-189.
28. Bīriyā, Nāsir, et al, *Rushd bā Nigarish bi Manābi' Islāmī*, vol. 2, p. 555.
29. Ye have indeed in the Messenger of Allāh a beautiful pattern (of conduct) for any one whose hope is in Allāh and the Final Day, Qur'ān 33:21.
30. Jung, Carl Gustav, *Psychology and Religion*, pp. 12, 13, 85 and 174.
31. Hope Walker, L., "Religion gives Meaning to Life," translated by A'zam Puyā, in *Naqd va Nazar Journal*, 8th vol., issues 1 & 2, p. 141.
32. Qur'ān 43:70-72.
33. Al-Kulaynī, *Kāfī,* vol. 2, p. 260.
34. Muḥammadī-Reyshahrī, *Mīzān al-Ḥikmah*, vol. 10, p. 4662.
35. Majlisī, *Biḥār al-Anwār*, vol. 72, p. 35.
36. Ibid., p. 11.
37. Al-Kulaynī, *Usūl Kāfī,* vol. 3, pp. 361, 364.
38. Majlisī, *Biḥār al-Anwār*, vol. 82, p. 131.
39. Sadūq, Muḥammad ibn 'Alī , *al-Khisāl*, p. 180, Ḥadīth 245.
40. To Allāh we belong, and to Him is our return, Qur'ān 2:156; Baḥrānī, Sayyid Hāshim, *al-Burhān fī Tafsīr al-Qur'ān*, vol. 1, p. 364.
41. Ibn Abī al-Ḥadīd, *Sharḥ Nahj al-Balāghah*, vol. 20, p. 98.
42. Al-Kulaynī, *Kāfī,* vol. 3, p. 114.
43. Ibid., p. 115.
44. Majlisī, *Biḥār al-Anwār*, vol. 76, p. 366.
45. Ibid., vol. 81, p. 224.
46. Qur'ān 66:6.
47. Majlisī, *Biḥār al-Anwār*, vol. 6, p. 220.
48. Ibid., vol. 103, p. 473.
49. Satir, Jane, *Making Humans in Psychology of the Family*, p. 78.
50. Majlisī, *Biḥār al-Anwār*, vol. 69, p. 254.
51. It is those who believe not in the Signs of Allāh that forge falsehood, Qur'ān 16:105; Majlisī, *Biḥār al-Anwār*, vol. 75, p. 172.

CHAPTER 4

52. Āmidī, 'Abd al-Vāhid *Ghurar al-Ḥikam wa Durar al-Kalim*, Ḥadīth 11038.
53. Satir, Jane, *Making Humans in Psychology of the Family*, pp. 92 and 97.
54. Al-Kulaynī, *Kāfī,* vol. 2, p. 269.
55. Avoid suspicion as much (as possible); for suspicion in some cases is a sin, Qur'ān49:12.
56. Al-Kulaynī, *Kāfī,* vol. 2, pp. 265-266.
57. Di Matteo, M. *Health Psychology*, vol. 2, pp. 582-584.
58. Muttaqī-Hindī, *Kanz al-'Ummāl*, Ḥadīth. 5849.
59. Majlisī, *Biḥār al-Anwār*, vol. 70, pp. 336 and 385.
60. Ibid.; Al-Kulaynī, *Kāfī,* vol. 2, p. 72.
61. For example, in the interpretation of the Qur'ānic verse "him verily we shall quicken with good life," (16:97), Imām 'Alī (as) said: "A good life is the same as a life of contentment," (*Nahj al-Balāghah*, Aphorism 229).
62. Al-Kulaynī, *Kāfī,* vol. 2, p. 139.
63. Nūrī, *Mustadrak al-Wasā'il*, vol. 15, p. 224.
64. Al-Ḥurr al-'Āmilī, *Wasā'il al-Shī'a*, vol. 14, p. 18.
65. Al-Kulaynī, *Kāfī,* vol. 8, p. 244.
66. Nor strain thine eyes in longing for the things We have given for enjoyment to parties of them, the splendour of the life of this world, Qur'ān 20:131.
67. Āmidī, *Ghurar al-Ḥikam wa Durar al-Kalim*, p. 941.
68. *Nahj al-Balāghah*, Letter 30; Āmidī,, *Ghurar al-Ḥikam wa Durar al-Kalim*, p. 391.
69. *Nahj al-Balāghah*, Sermon 192.
70. Āmidī, *Ghurar al-Ḥikam wa Durar al-Kalim*, p. 391.
71. Ibid., p. 393.
72. Majlisī, *Biḥār al-Anwār*, vol. 66, p. 390.
73. Al-Ḥurr al-'Āmilī, *Wasā'il al-Shī'a*, vol. 14, p. 124; Shafī'ī Māzandarānī, Sayyid Muḥammad, *Razi Khushbakhtī*, p. 101. A similar Ḥadīth is available in Muttaqī-Hindī, *Kanz al-'Ummāl*, Ḥadīth 43347.
74. Majlisī, *Biḥār al-Anwār*, vol. 101, p. 70.
75. *Nahj al-Balāghah*, Aphorism 82.
76. Majlisī, *Biḥār al-Anwār*, vol. 48, p. 92.
77. Dirāyatī, Mustafā, Mu'jam Ghurar al-Ḥikam wa Durar al-*Kalim*, p. 577; *Nahj al-Balāghah*, Sermon 217; Majlisī, *Biḥār al-Anwār*, vol. 71, p. 95.
78. *Nahj al-Balāghah*, Aphorism 153; Ibid., Sermon 26.
79. Majlisī, *Biḥār al-Anwār*, vol. 78, p. 79.
80. *Nahj al-Balāghah*, Aphorism 413.
81. Qur'ān 2:155.
82. Qur'ān 39:10.

83. Qur'ān 3:146.
84. Qur'ān 2:153, 249; 8:46, 66.
85. Qur'ān 3:125.
86. *Nahj al-Balāghah*, Aphorism 292.
87. Ibid., Aphorism 144.
88. Al-Kulaynī, *Kāfī,* vol. 2, p. 91.
89. And (join together) in the mutual teaching of Truth, and of patience and constancy, Qur'ān 103:3.
90. Al-Ḥurr al-'Āmilī, *Wasā'il al-Shī'a*, vol. 14, p. 18.
91. Ibid.
92. Ibid., vol. 15, p. 249.
93. *Nahj al-Balāghah*, Aphorism 378.
94. Al-Ḥurr al-'Āmilī, *Wasā'il al-Shī'a*, vol. 15, p. 253.
95. Al-Kulaynī, *Furū' Kāfī,* vol. 6, p. 447.
96. *Nahj al-Balāghah*, Aphorism 234.
97. Tannen, Deborah, *Speech Differences in* Women and Men, (Tafavuthā-yi Kalāmi Dar Zan va Mard), pp. 95-100.
98. And lower thy voice, for the harshest of sounds without doubt is the braying of the ass, Qur'ān 31:19.
99. Al-Kulaynī, *Usūl Kāfī,* vol. 2, p. 643. This relates to the relationship between two friends, but also covers the husband and wife relationship, because their friendship is usually the most intimate of all friendships. See also, Mustafavī, Sayyid Javād, Bihisht Khānivādih, vol. 1, p. 17.
100. Al-Ḥurr al-'Āmilī, *Wasā'il al-Shī'a*, vol. 14, p. 10.
101. Bernstein, F. Ch., *Marriage Therapy*, *(Izdivāj Darmānī),* p. 161.
102. Show gratitude to Me and to thy parents: to Me is (the final) goal, Qur'ān 31:14.
103. Al-Suyūtī, Jalāl al-Dīn, al-Durr al-Manthūr,vol. 1, p. 152.
104. Al-Ḥurr al-'Āmilī, *Wasā'il al-Shī'a*, vol. 14, p. 115.
105. Ibid.
106. But the bounty of thy Lord – rehearse and proclaim, Qur'ān 93:11.
107. Any who is (so) grateful does so for the profit of his own soul, Qur'ān 31:12.
108. Al-Ḥurr al-'Āmilī, *Wasā'il al-Shī'a*, vol. 74, p. 68.
109. Majlisī, *Biḥār al-Anwār*, vol. 74, p. 68.
110. Nūrī, *Mustadrak al-Wasā'il*, vol. 14, p. 169.
111. Narrations relating to the role and importance of the child in life, which are mentioned in Chapter 2.
112. Bernstein, F. Ch., *Marriage Therapy*, *(Izdivāj Darmānī),* p. 161.
113. Al-Kulaynī, *Usūl Kāfī,* vol. 2, p. 660.

114. Qur'ān58:7-10.
115. Al-Kulaynī, *Usūl Kāfī*, vol. 4, p. 37.
116. Āmidī, *Ghurar al-Ḥikam*, Ḥadīth 747-1181.
117. Al-Kulaynī, *Kāfī*, vol. 2, p. 660.
118. Let not some men among you laugh at others: it may be that the (latter) are better than the (former): not let some women laugh at others: it may be that the (latter) are better than the (former): nor defame nor be sarcastic to each, nor call each other by (offensive) nicknames, Qur'ān 49:11.
119. Satir, Jane, *Making Humans in Psychology of the Family*, pp. 45-63.
120. Al-Kulaynī, *Kāfī*, vol. 2, p.107.
121. Āmidī, *Ghurar al-Ḥikam*, p. 91.
122. Al-Kulaynī, *Kāfī*, vol. 2, p.107.
123. Āmidī, *Ghurar al-Ḥikam*, p. 92.
124. Ibid., p. 91.
125. Al-Kulaynī, *Kāfī*, vol. 2, p.188.
126. And swell not thy cheek (for pride) at men, Qur'ān 31:18.
127. Al-Ḥurr al-'Āmilī, *Wasā'il al-Shī'a*, vol. 14, p. 37; Nūrī, *Mustadrak al-Wasā'il*, vol. 14, p. 169.
128. Ibid., vol. 15, p. 205.
129. Farīd Tunikābunī, Murtaḍā, *al-Ḥadīth*, vol. 1, p. 299.
130. Al-Ḥurr al-'Āmilī, *Wasā'il al-Shī'a*, vol. 15, p. 217.
131. Āmidī, *Ghurar al-Ḥikam*, Ḥadīth. 4613.
132. Deilamī, Aḥmad, et al, Akhlāqī Islāmī, p. 140.
133. According to Imām Sādiq(as), a sign of humility is sitting in a place that is lower than where one belongs. Al-Kulaynī, *Kāfī*, vol. 2, p. 122.
134. And, out of kindness, lower to them the wing of humility, Qur'ān 17:24.
135. Narāqī, Mullā Aḥmad, *Mi'rāj al-Sa'ādah*, the discussion on "Vanity."
136. Such as the importance of offering greetings upon entering the house, which indicates humility.
137. Al-Ḥurr al-'Āmilī, *Wasā'il al-Shī'a*, vol. 14, pp. 14, 15.
138. Ibid., p. 18.
139. Ibid., p. 183.
140. Muḥammadī-Reyshahrī, *Mīzān al-Ḥikmah*, vol. 10, p. 193.
141. Al-Ḥurr al-'Āmilī, *Wasā'il al-Shī'a*, vol. 14, p. 122.
142. Iḥsānbakhsh, Sādiq, Āthār al- Sādiqain, vol. 15, p. 293.
143. Al-Ḥurr al-'Āmilī, *Wasā'il al-Shī'a*, vol. 16, p. 422.
144. Majlisī, *Biḥār al-Anwār*, vol. 76, pp. 3, 4 and 11.
145. Mustafavī, Sayyid Javād, Bihisht Khānivādih, vol. 1, p. 30.

146. Majlisī, *Biḥār al-Anwār*, vol. 76, pp. 3-11.
147. Tabātabā'ī, *Tafsīr al-Mīzān*, vol. 10, p. 20.
148. But if ye enter houses, salute each another – a greeting or blessing and purity as from Allāh, Qur'ān 24:61; Their greeting therein will be: "Peace!" 14:23; Al-Ḥurr al-'Āmilī, *Wasā'il al-Shī'a*, vol. 14, pp. 158, 161.
149. Majlisī, *Biḥār al-Anwār*, vol. 77, p. 140; Āmidī, *Ghurar al-Ḥikam*, Ḥadīth 1909.
150. Majlisī, *Biḥār al-Anwār*, vol. 75, p. 44.
151. Majlisī, Muḥammad-Bāqir, *Ḥilyat al-Muttaqeen*, 418.
152. Dihkhudā, ' Alī Akbar, Amthāl va Ḥikam , vol. 1, p. 167.
153. Help ye one another in righteousness and piety, Qur'ān 5:2.
154. Al-Ḥurr al-'Āmilī, *Wasā'il al-Shī'a*, vol. 14, p. 124.
155. Majlisī, *Biḥār al-Anwār*, vol. 101, p. 106.
156. Ibid., p. 132.
157. Rosenbaum, Heidi, *The Family as a Structure against the Society*, p. 94.
158. Al-Ḥurr al-'Āmilī, *Wasā'il al-Shī'a*, vol. 15, p. 250.
159. Ḥusaynī, 'Alī Akbar, *Akhlāq dar Khānivādih*, p. 136.
160. Al-Ḥurr al-'Āmilī, *Wasā'il al-Shī'a*, vol. 15, p. 207.
161. Ibid., p. 201.
162. Ibid., p. 202.
163. Guard strictly your (habit) of prayers, Qur'ān 2:238; Celebrate Allāh's praises, standing, sitting down, Qur'ān 4:103.
164. Save yourselves and your families from a Fire whose is men and stones, 66:6.
165. Majlisī, *Biḥār al-Anwār*, vol. 71, p. 86.
166. Al-Kulaynī, *Kāfī*, vol. 3, p. 409.
167. *Nahj al-Balāghah*, Aphorism 73.
168. Sadūq, Muḥammad ibn 'Alī , *Man lā yahḍaruh al-Faqīh*, vol. 1, pp. 210, 638.
169. Enjoin prayer on thy people worship, and be constant therein, Qur'ān 20:132.
170. Baḥrānī, Sayyid Hāshim, *al-Burhān fī Tafsīr al-Qur'ān*, vol. 5, p. 202.
171. O my Lord! make me one who establishes regular prayer, and also (raise such) among my offspring, Qur'ān 14:40.
172. For prayer restrains from shameful and unjust deeds; and remembrance of Allāh is the greatest (thing in life) without doubt, Qur'ān 29:45.
173. Ibn Abī al-Ḥadīd, *Nahj al-Balāghah*, Sermon 199.
174. It has been emphasised by the divine religious leaders that a place should be set aside in the house for prayer. Also, certain animals should not be kept at home, nor should certain pictures that take spiritualī ty and blessings away from the home (Majlisī, *Biḥār al-Anwār*, vol. 73, pp. 159-162).

CHAPTER 5

THE TEACHINGS OF ISLĀM AND FAMILY PROBLEMS

A family consists of individuals with mutual responsibilities. These individuals will have material, affective and social needs that should be fulfilled in the family environment. Apart from this, the family members usually spend most of their time together, and do not have this much interaction with anyone else. Nowadays, contact between some family members, such as the children and their parents, has become less, but their interaction in time has become longer, because life expectancy has increased, and sometimes three generations live with each other for years.[1] The family members, as with many other social groups, usually consist of individuals from different age groups and different sexes. All these factors create a basis for more difference between the family members than in any other social group. Indeed affective relationships and attachments are much deeper in the family than in any other social group. "The family as a group joins its members with a feeling of intimacy, cooperation and collaboration, i.e. the relation of the family members is based on intimacy and social life within the group. Intimacy is the basic indistinguishable feature of the family. It is the same attribute that distinguishes it from other social groups."[2] If the attachments in the family are not weakened, many differences can be resolved. In this part, we will examine factors regarding family differences, and then provide solutions to prevent or eliminate some of them.

1. Factors Affecting Family Conflicts

In a study of the factors involved in family problems, which sometimes result in the total collapse of the family, there are numerous cases resulting from mental, social, cultural, religious, economic and physical issues. We will now briefly examine them, while admitting the different roles they play.

1.1. Psychological Factors

An important factor in family differences concerns issues of the cognition and intelligence of the spouses. Defects in social or rational development result in behaviour that is not well thought out and inappropriate in various circumstances. Moreover, reacting appropriately to others also requires proper development, and failure in this can cause differences between the husband and wife. In many cases, individuals are not sufficiently aware of each other's duties and rights, and therefore sometimes fail in fulfilling their duties and observing the rights of the others. A young age is another factor. After a while, with the relative subsiding of sexual emotions, insufficiencies or incompatibilities appear.[3] Research has shown that the age of marriage in women upon divorce is significantly lower in women compared to others.[4] A large difference in the IQs of the man and the woman is another cause of differences between the two. Since it is shown that intelligence affects compatibility, a difference in the level of intelligence will create a difference in behaviour. In addition, mutual understanding will be difficult in the case of different levels of intelligence, and certain behaviour will be misinterpreted.[5]

Some differences between the husband and wife are to do with their verbal and nonverbal relationship. Certain factors disturb their interaction, as in other social interactions. Many individuals think that others are aware of their intentions. As a result, they fail to properly communicate with them verbally, and they tend to speak to them in a figurative or indirect way. The use of such vague words as "this," "that" or "the thing" impedes mutual understanding. When explaining or expressing something, people use words that connote judgment, and therefore inevitably come to form a judgment. Another point is that some individuals use few words to express their gratitude, while being more explicit when criticising or finding fault, and are less shy in doing so.[6] The two-level relationship mentioned earlier is an important factor in family dispute. Islamic texts refer to the destructive effect of disputes in human relations, including the fact that they make the passage of life difficult,[7] weaken the affective relations between individuals,[8] create hypocrisy,[9] entail a kind of feeling of superiority[10] and vengefulness,[11] downgrade people,[12] and generally result in the breaking off of relations between people.[13] As with the disputes between the husband and wife, everyone seeks superiority and often unknowingly refuses to behave properly, and even when they feel that they are right, it is recommended that disputes be avoided.[14]

In nonverbal communication, haughtiness is a cause of disputes. Haughtiness is usually manifested physically in the person's body. Apparently, self-centredness and an inability to accept others' characteristics is a major obstacle to mutual understanding and cooperation in family life. Failure to recognise the individuality of the others and futile attempts to authoritatively impose assimilation will ruin the family atmosphere, resulting at least in alienation, and ultimately the collapse of the family. Therefore, Islamic texts deprecate haughtiness and self-centredness,[15] saying that if a person has the slightest degree of haughtiness, he will not enter Paradise.[16]

In affective relationships, inattention to the needs of others will result in differences and dissatisfaction in life. Sometimes the affective relationships of someone in the family are stronger with people outside the family. This poses a serious problem, for if someone cannot find satisfaction of their emotional needs within the family, inattentiveness, hatred and selfishness can develop.[17]

The failure to satisfy sexual needs is another factor that causes marital disputes. Inattention to the sexual needs of one's partner results in disinclination or frigidity, harms the spousal relationship and causes anger and frustration towards one's spouse and life in general, aggressive behaviour and finally depression. One of the most difficult situations is when the spouse is frigid, disinclined or sexually disordered. The other partner inevitably bears the situation under pressure, because of social, economic and family conditions, the responsibility for children and concerns about the future. Sometimes the failure to fulfil each other's sexual needs causes complications such as finding fault with each other, dissatisfaction with life, not talking to each other for long periods, blaming each other, making threats of separation, expressing boredom and pretending sickness.[18] The satisfaction of sexual needs outside marriage another cause of dispute between the husband and wife that can be seen in society. Research in Iran showed that from among couples applying for divorce, 11% mentioned disobedience and 2% frigidity or impotence as the reason for their application.[19] Islamic texts emphasise the importance of the sexual relationship in the family system, and the effect of its evasion by either spouse or sexual indulgence outside marriage in causing disputes.[20] The man's unpreparedness or inappropriate behaviour in this regard,[21] preoccupation with others[22] or inattention to the needs of the woman,[23] in addition to the woman's bad behaviour in either words or actions that have sexual connotations, damage the proper sexual relationship of the husband and wife, and prepares the ground for problems in the family and its collapse.[24]

1.2. Social and Cultural Factors

Every family has a specific customs of its own concerning attitudes, behaviours, traditions and relationships with others.[25] The husband and wife have been brought up in two separate families with different preferences, interests and tastes. As a result, some characteristics should be accommodated and others set aside. Failure to take this into consideration will cause problems. The style of upbringing differs in every family, so that making jokes or annoying behaviour may differ, and this in turn can be problematic.[26]

Another important factor concerning the habits of the original families of the husband and wife is interference by others in the affairs of the new family. 27% of divorce applicants in Iran consider the undue interference of relatives and acquaintances as the cause.[27] It is the second most frequent cause of divorce, and as mentioned in the discussion of family relationships, it is damaging to family relationships. Indeed, relatives should especially provide proper social and emotional support for the newly founded family.

Urban life and industrial development is a cause of differences within the family. The contrast of this way of life with previous lifestyles can easily be seen in the development of marriages.[28] Widening social relationships, moving away from the support of the original families, problems within the nuclear family, and cultural differences between men and women provides for the education of women and other effects of industrial development in modern societies. Any of these can cause differences within the family. Different standards of education can result in different expectations, and this will make mutual understanding more difficult.

Modern life in industrially advanced societies deeply affects the social environment. Nowadays, people interact extensively with others with different characteristics, which is sometimes unhealthy and harmful. In social interaction, people inevitably assimilate the characteristics of others, either consciously or unconsciously.[29] Family members, especially the husband and wife, may be affected by the people they associate with and adopt ways that can result in differences within the family. The teachings of Islām pay attention to the profound effects of associating with others.[30] For example, associating with ignorant people,[31] criminals, or simply those who are badly behaved[32] has been prohibited.

An aspect of the environment that affects the family even more than social relationships are the mass media, especially radio and television. When the family comes together in the evening for dinner and conversation the television is usually switched on, and this interrupts family communication. Low-income and less educated families use the TV more often, while others may spend their leisure time doing sports, traveling, reading and other activities.[33] These days, much opportunity for family interaction is spent watching TV. Regardless of any positive effect of watching TV, such as being educational, raising public awareness, giving guidance, or even simply bringing the family together at home,[34] the negative effects should not be overlooked. Family life as shown on Iranian TV differs from the traditional family. This can easily be seen in the relationships between the husband and wife, the parents and children, the recognition of the nuclear family, and the relations between siblings.[35] All this can lead to conflict within the family. Therefore, the role of TV in this respect should be taken seriously.

1.3. Economic Factors

Financial issues are a significant cause of family differences. According to research in Iran, 12% of those applying for divorce said that livelihood was the reason, 4% said unemployment, and 11% living costs. In addition, 49.6% said that their salary at the time of divorce was not enough to cover their living expenses.[36] Poverty and unemployment weigh heavily on men, and is a source of conflict. Islamic texts also mention this problem as a cause of pressure on the family,[37] and its consequences in this and next life.[38] In addition, high material expectations within the family can also cause conflict. If the man is unable to fulfil the increasing demands of the family, he will either react strongly, thus preparing the ground for inappropriate behaviour, or else in desperation he will give in and lose control of the finances. In either case, the family will face serious problems. On the other hand, a surfeit of luxury can result in haughtiness.[39] Sometimes, if a family suddenly gains wealth, they forget their past, become rebellious and engage in disputes. Too much attention to luxury and the appearances of life leads to inappropriate human relationships[40] and alienates people. In such a case, moral and religious values are replaced by materialism. As some people are insatiable in this respect,[41] they are never satisfied with life and other people.[42] They become ungrateful and relationships cool off and turn towards hatred.[43] Issues relating to the man or the woman's employment may also be a cause for some differences. Having certain jobs may seem inappropriate within a particular culture and result in conflicts. Women's work outside home, because of its heavy responsibilities, especially in our culture, may prevent the woman from carrying out her family responsibilities and cause differences, and in some cases may make her independent and cause her to separate from the family. The issue of single mothers in some countries is due to this desire for independence, which has threatened family integrity. Conversely, too much work results in less presence at home and thus harms emotional relationships and leads to difference

1.4. Physical Factors

The bad health of one of the partners requires a great degree of attunement between a couple, which other family members may not be like-minded. Severe mental disorders require a higher degree of attunement. Infertility in either partner may result in a cold emotional atmosphere in the family. Having a child expresses perfection in the man and a flourishing of the woman.[44] Not having children is a serious problem for some families and sometimes cannot be resolved. The aesthetic characteristics of personal appearance are also an important issue in the family, and may emerge as a result of complications after marriage, such as disability and disease. This problem appears more in those who marry without paying attention to personal appearance, but for whom it later becomes an issue. Addiction is a psychological and physical matter, and is the third most frequent cause of disputes and applications for divorce in Iran, accounting for 18% of divorce applications.[45] It results in abnormal behaviour and eventual incompatibility. If the father becomes an addictia, he will lead his wife into addiction in order to preserve their relationship and prevent the collapse of the family. Studies show that many women patiently struggle till the last moment in order to save the family. After a time, out of the fear of embarrassment they get used to the conditions and bear severe economic problems. Ultimately, the woman sometimes either seeks divorce due to incompatibility, or is helplessly led towards other abnormal behaviour. Under these circumstances, the foundations of the family are shaken and the home becomes unsafe. In such families, a dangerous fate awaits the children and they end up as criminals through copying their parents. Under extreme circumstances, if the family is not rescued, it becomes necessary to remove the children from the family environment in order to prevent their moral and social decay.[46]

1.5. Religious Factors

Negligence of religious matters within the family has a negative effect and can cause disputes. Part of this has to do with failing to observe the religious precepts in the husband and wife relationship, as was examined earlier. All kinds of dispositions and actions which are considered bad in Islām damage relationships in the family, and here we mention the most common ones.

Causing irritation to one's parents and upsetting them[47] sometimes results in the collapse of the family structure and a strong and unbalanced reaction by the parents towards the children. Regarding the duties of children, the effects of this in this world and the next have been mentioned. Attributing unchaste acts, especially to pure women, can easily disturb the spouses by creating hostility. Therefore, the Islamic teachings, whilst strongly reprimanding such things,[48] attempt to prevent such behaviour. The consumption of alcohol, which results in abnormal behaviour,[49] and has undesirable physical and mental consequences, also causes problems. This behaviour, which has been strongly prohibited in Islām, can hurt the family in two ways. It can disturb the relationship of the spouses by disrupting their sexual relationship and causing violent behaviour towards the wife, and frustrate the wife's role as wife and mother and threaten her social position. It may also result in undesirable behaviour in the children, such as incest, and create a defective and diseased generation, while damaging their care and social adaptation, lowering their social position, and ultimately threatening the economic security of the family.[50] Giving up one's religious duties, especially the daily prayers will inevitably adversely affect the lives of individuals. Gossiping is revealing someone's defects in their absence, as a result of which the person will lose respect and their interpersonal relationships will be harmed. The Qur'ān compares this behaviour to eating one's dead brother's flesh,[51] so that people will be disgusted by it. Gossiping is also a source of quarreling in the family, because proper criticism should be done openly and without sarcasm in the person's presence, and without any intention of humiliating or insulting them. Passing a person's words to a third person[52] can worsen the differences already existing between two people.[53] Sometimes individuals say things about someone in their absence that would never be said in their presence. Passing the tale on will further inflame arguments.[54] This is therefore highly disapproved of in Islamic texts.[55]

Improper singing and illegitimate entertainment also disturbs family relationships.[56] Such singing includes material that refers to illegitimate behaviour and has a tone and song to match.[57] Sometimes by hearing such songs a person can develop moods whereby such improper behaviour emerges, including illegitimate sexual acts.[58] Obviously, it is these songs that prepare the person to behave in such ways. Important responsibilities may also be ignored upon hearing such songs, and the way set for family quarrels.[59] One such forbidden entertainment is gambling,[60] which, in addition to economically damaging the family, will hurt the individual's self-esteem, because sometimes the gambler sacrifices his own honour and that of his family for gambling.[61]

Some kinds of entertainment, although not prohibited, may result in disputes under certain circumstances. Sometimes people go to extremes and fail to properly fulfil their family responsibilities, thus clearing the ground for improper relations. In addition, entertainment may disturb important decision-making,[62] and sometimes create hostility[63] and shake religious beliefs.[64] Excessive entertainment can prevent individuals from acting properly and reasonably,[65] and make it difficult to achieve one's goals.[66] Indeed, entertainment in itself is desirable, especially in the company of the family, and is emphasised by the teachings of Islām,[67] but it is important to avoid too much entertainment so as not to deter people from their responsibilities[68]

An important cause of family disputes is using unusual and unjustified ways of establishing relationships, especially between the husband and wife. Islamic texts refer to cases in which methods such as sorcery have been used in order to bring about emotional attraction, solve problems or to cause quarrels. Fortune telling is another practice of this kind.[69] As a result, a person can develop a frame of mind that makes them prone to abnormal behaviour and the situation becomes worse.[70] A difference in the degree of faith and the comprehension of religion can also result in conflicts. Sometimes, the husband and wife do not know each other sufficiently at first, and after a while they discover differences of opinion and fail to agree, and then tension grows between them. Research in the city of Kerman has in fact shown that difference in religious beliefs is a cause of marital breakdown.[71]

2. Ways to Prevent Family Disputes in the Teachings of Islām

All the factors mentioned above can result in a sense of incompatibility and negativity which later gets worse, and in the particular case of the husband and wife, result in legal separation. However, this is not always the case, for such things merely open a door for the possibility. There are means of prevention in the preliminary stages, and these will be examined in this section. Some of these methods have already been examined in more detail in other sections, and so here more focus is put on their effects.

2.1. Attention to the Selection of an Appropriate Marriage Partner

It is an important duty of the son or daughter before marriage to know of the necessary characteristics of a spouse and to ensure that the intended person has them. This can prevent many differences later on. An emphasis on similar types and a comparable knowledge of Islām is a way to prevent IQ-related and cultural differences, such as a difference in religious belief or even levels of faith. The cause of the incompatibility of a couple has to do with their differences in feelings, knowledge and behaviour. The more similar they are in these respects, the fewer their differences will be. Some differences have to do with abnormal behaviour caused by a bad temper or other inappropriate characteristics, as well as such behaviors as alcohol drinking and gambling. Such things usually emerge in individuals at the time of marriage, or at least there are signs of them. In view of the severe damage that can be done to the individual and the family, the teachings of Islām have serious warnings regarding the selection of a marriage partner. Sexual activity outside the permissible limits also comes into this category. If any of these things emerge, one should think further about selecting such an individual. The phrase in the Qur'ān that says: *Good women are for good men, and good men for good women,*[72] is actually meant to give some insight into the selection of a spouse. In addition, certain problems of an economic nature, such as the kind of employment or level of income, can be predicted to a certain extent at the time of selecting a partner. Evidently, marrying such an individual, if done with awareness and insight, will provide a basis for solving the problems and differences.

2.2. Training the Spouses

Some family problems result from unawareness about duties and ways to establish relations and solve problems. One important strategy in solving family problems is the psycho-educational approach, which consists of the following stages:[73]

A. Clarifying goals and values. This part illustrates the aim of each partner, their expectations from each other and the way to balance them. Attention to the cultural and religious values of each other matters greatly.

B. Teaching how to communicate and exchange ideas while clarifying any inefficiency in communication skills. Teaching skills such as listening, clarifying the concept of ego or individual identity, feedback, asking for something, expressing oneself, and the positive aspects of verbal communication.

C. Teaching the skills of negotiating and entering into a contract. In this section, the principles of fairness and equality is considered.

D. Using techniques to adjust one's time. This is essential, especially for families where both the husband and wife work. These techniques help to determine priorities, plan for the family and work, and make realistic decisions.

E. Using techniques to control stress. Everyone inevitably experiences stress, and these techniques help individuals to live a less stressful life. For example, for economic problems and busy urban lifestyles, people should learn methods of muscular relaxation and breath control, and have a good diet and proper entertainment.

2.3. Religious Education

Instruction on the role of religion in life and for solving the problems is an important way of preventing certain disagreements. It is important to know the teachings of Islām regarding the family in order to play one's part in the family accordingly. The solutions examined in Chapter 4 can prevent many of the problems that arise out of failing to adhere to moral values. Sometimes disputes begin through talking and behaving aggressively. Beating a family member, especially the wife, still happens quite a lot in developed countries. In France, 95% of women are victims of reported violence, out of which 51% is committed by the husbands. In the United States, it is estimated that annually two million women are beaten by their partners, half of whom require medical attention.[74] Controlling one's behaviour and speech can prevent many such anomalies. If family members, especially the spouses, help each control their speech and behaviour, the problem would be resolved much sooner. For example, if there is an argument, one of them should remain silent and advise the other to keep calm and control themselves. In this respect, the advice of the divine religious leaders can help monitor behaviour to a certain extent. For example, it has been said that if an angry person can control his behaviour, God will fill his heart with peace and faith on the Day of Resurrection.[75] Moreover, it has been said that in order to control one's anger, one should change one's physical position. For instance, if the person is standing, they should sit down, or if they are sitting, they should lie down. Gentle physical contact with the person who is angry is a very effective way of controlling aggression in the family environment.[76]

Religious education can help prevent addiction. Research has shown that religious education, adherence to religious principles, and willingness to attend religious ceremonies are inversely proportional to the consumption of narcotic drugs. Jean Buré says, "We have to accept the clear reality that the consumption of drugs rose since religious attitudes were lost in the minds of people. Therefore, religious education can help prevent and eliminate addiction."[77]

2.4. Observing Boundaries in the Family

One of the causes of family problems derives from inattention to the necessary boundaries for having healthy relationships within the family and for the corresponding behaviour. These limits were examined in chapter three. The most important factor for the husband and wife is the observance of limits in relationships with other men and women. Research has confirmed that the control of eye contact, meaningful glances and conversation is important in this respect. For example, tests have shown that when men see pictures of beautiful women, they look upon their wives less favourably,[78] and this obviously weakens the emotional relationship. The least that this would do would be to cause a colder atmosphere within the family. Another rule concerning women is to dress in a religiously acceptable way, since this affects women as well as the men who see them. Research on female beauty has proven experimentally that this prevents an increase in the perceptive threshold of women and results in a reduction in marital differences, because, with an increased perceptive threshold, men later respond to stimuli within the family and are less prone to establish other relationships.[79]

2.5. Consultation and Agreement with Others in the Family

In many cases it is relatively easy to adapt to balanced, religious principles. It is the parents' duty to ensure that actions and decisions conform with such principles, and to explain them in a suitable way. Nevertheless, in many cases, families face decisions which are difficult to reconcile with rational and religious criteria. Like any other group, in such cases the family can decide in other ways. It seems that using the opinion of the others and selecting the most appropriate solution in each case is the best method. The Qur'ān says that consultation in all the affairs of life is an attribute of devout people.[80] Even the Prophet, who was connected to the source of revelation, is advised to consult others.[81] Doubtless to say, gathering various ideas, putting them together and selecting the best one, usually results in making a better decision, approved and supported by several others.[82] On the other hand, autocracy and inattention to the views of others usually makes the individual prone to mistakes.[83] Therefore, the divine religious leaders have explicitly mentioned the undesirable consequences of autocracy, so that people are encouraged to seek the opinion of others.[84] It states in the Qur'ān:

Therefore give good tidings (O Muḥammad) to My bondsmen who hear advice and follow the best thereof.[85]

Certainly, when administrating and solving problems within the family, this principle has to be taken into consideration. It is worth mentioning that, according to the Qur'ān, even a minor affair such as breastfeeding an infant should be done in consultation with and with the consent of the parents.[86] The mother definitely has a right in determining what is good for the infant. It seems that, in other family issues also, it is appropriate to consult others in the family. It is advised in another verse that the affairs of the family, including the issues of children, should be done with proper consultation.[87] It can be said that, even in important matters and religious affairs, one should try to use proper methods with the agreement of the family. An example of this can be seen in the way the Prophet Abraham treated his son. When Abraham found out that he had been ordered by God to sacrifice his son, he obtained his son's agreement by an appropriate method, saying to him: "Oh, my son, I dreamed that I was slaughtering you. What do you think?" The son said: "Oh, father, do what you are ordered to do."[88] In this story, having the agreement of the Prophet Ismail resulted in his being given the title "God's sacrifice." In other words, the collaboration of the father and son developed them both spiritually. Cooperation in home affairs not only stabilises relationships and emotions in the family, but also affects the making of decisions and the solving of problems. If there is room for consultation in the family, it will be easier to make decisions and keep to them. As the children grow and mature, they should also be included in the process. When the divine religious leaders refer to the third 7-year period of the child's life as the ministerial stage of his life,[89] this refers to the need to share thoughts and cooperate with adolescents. Using the adolescent's views helps his thinking to develop properly, and shows respect for him that will help his growth and optimism.[90] On the other hand, failure to consult with the adolescent in the family results in less cognitive and affective development, a scattered identity and low self-confidence.

Consulting one's wife also contributes to her development and providence in contemporary times, while her influence in the family environment can play a pivotal role in solving family problems.[91] Although it is necessary to consult her regarding her own issues and those of the daughters,[92] it is also necessary to have the agreement and collaboration in other family matters.[93] According to the divine religious leaders, a principle of family life is having the wife's cooperation and employing methods to attract her love and consent, and to avoid making her unhappy by coercion or imposing one's views on her.[94]

3. Ways to Settle Family Disputes According to the Teachings of Islām

In this part, we will mention methods to use in the case of disputes, as a means of resolution rather than prevention.

3.1. Accepting the Obligations of Family Hierarchy

We have already mentioned the need for a family hierarchy. One of the effective applications of hierarchy in the family is in the solving of problems when family members fail to reach a decision and the dispute remains unresolved. In such a case, one should sometimes consider the decision of the man of the house, which is usually the husband. For example, the woman may leave the home environment with the husband's consent. Obviously, if the husband and wife disagree on this, in order to solve the difference according to the teachings of Islām, the wife should follow the husband as the most appropriate way. The same applies to the children and to the selection of the place of residence, i.e. if no agreement is reached, the husband's view is to be adhered to, because such issues involve economic costs that are undertaken by the husband. If the man cannot impose his ideas on his wife and children and insists that he should do so, higher authorities should intervene to solve the problem.

As the children grow and reach adolescence, sometimes disputes emerge connected to the failure to abide by parental authority. Psycho-historical studies refer to a model of the relationship between the parents and the child, according to which children regard their parents as servants rather than authorities, where at every stage of their development, they know better than the parents what is good and desirable for themselves.[95] This results in children expecting too much from their parents and not respecting their views, which results in a worsening of problems. As mentioned in Chapter 3, according to the teachings of Islām, children in any age group or social class[96] should respect and follow the views of their parents as far as possible, unless this requires violating religious[97] or social laws. As long as the children live within the family, they should give priority to the views of the parents in disputes and in deciding what is best for them, because the responsibility for their management lies with the parents.[98] Indeed, as already mentioned, the parents should involve family members, especially adolescents, in decision-making, so that the parents rationally consider their views, although if negotiations do not result in a single decision, it is necessary to accept the views of the parents in order to protect the coherence of the family. The parents should also avoid imposing anything on children that is against the law or common practice. In such a situation, higher authorities should deal with the problem in order to protect the interests of the children.

3.2. Solving Emotional and Sexual Problems

Sometimes the emotional relationship between the husband and wife loses its warmth due to inappropriate behaviour, such as verbal and nonverbal aggressiveness, or inattention to each other. In such a case, if they pay attention to the advice of Islām, they can solve the problems to a certain extent. Basic advice to the man is to be tolerant towards his wife under all circumstances. This general principle forces the man not to react harshly and disturb the good relationship merely because of one single inappropriate deed by the wife. Attention to some other points will also prevent the man from behaving inappropriately, such as considering the wife as someone who has been entrusted to him, the maltreatment of whom will anger God. These points are in addition to the guidance that emphasises establishing a positive affective relationship with the wife. Women are also advised to try to solve misunderstandings in the shortest time possible.[99] In this connection, it has been said that the wife should try not to extend disputes, and to finish them on the same day.[100] Moreover, the husband should try to control his reaction to the wife's inappropriate behaviour, and not question all the positive aspects of their relationship.[101] Accepting the wife's apology and forgiving her mistakes[102] will help solve the problem. In sexual relations, the wife is asked to collaborate with the husband as far as possible.[103] The man is also advised to take into consideration the wife's wishes, and not think only of his own needs. With these suggestions, many disputes can be resolved. But sometimes disputes can worsen and lead to disobedience, which we will discuss below.

The Qur'ān and the Settlement of Family Disputes

It was mentioned in the previous discussions that the husband and wife have rights and responsibilities towards each other. Disputes usually arise when one of the two refuses to carry out their spousal duties. This is known in the Qur'ān as disobedience or discord.[104] The Qur'ān uses the word disobedience for women[105] and discord for men,[106] and provides in each case an appropriate method to solve the problem. The disobedience of a woman is when she relinquishes the compulsory duties that she has towards her spouse, such as failing to fulfil his emotional and sexual desires and other emotional responsibilities, such as giving up using make-up, leaving the house without his permission, changing her modes of speech and behaviour, reacting immediately and violently, frowning and using bad language. In other words, incompatibility leads to the woman's disobedience,[107] but merely failing to run the affairs of the house does not constitute disobedience.[108] Under these conditions, the Qur'ān provides a three-stage method for solving problems, guiding the wife towards a normal family life and fulfilling her spousal duties: first of all, giving her advice, then avoiding her in bed, and finally, chastising her.[109]

Clearly, in most cases, if the man behaves kindly and honestly and intends to agree with his wife, such a problem will not arise.[110] If, despite conditions where the man is trying on the most part to make her happy, yet the woman keeps going against him, these methods of settling disputes might solve the problem in most cases.

There is another interpretation for chastising. This group believes that it is a type of mental rather than physical chastising. In such a case, the man announces that he is upset with the wife's behaviour,[111] and makes her understand that his love of her is in jeopardy, which thus indicates a strong negative affective reaction to the woman's behaviour. This interpretation seems more in keeping with the understanding of narrations of the verse on sexual disinclination, because it is usually stipulated that the physical chastising should not be painful. Such treatment can definitely not be thought of as physical chastising, because it does not cause any physical pain. Nevertheless, according to the interpretation of the divine religious leaders, what the Qur'ān means by "scourge" is not physical chastising as commonly understood, but is a special punishment that has a particular mental and emotional effect, rather than causing physical pain.[112] In general, it seems that the nature of the chastising should have an emotional impact on the woman, and is a degree beyond avoiding her in bed.

It is unnecessary to point out to the consequences of needless violence towards women. The Prophet of Islām spoke strongly against it, and said that men who do this are unethical and irreligious.[113] Throughout his life, he never punished any of his wives, servants or anyone else in this way.[114] In one instance, the Prophet advised that the marriage proposal of a man who has a tendency to beat women should be rejected, and some of the things he said in this regard are the following:

> "How do you men beat your wives and then embrace them. Are you not ashamed?"[115]
>
> "If a man hurts his wife, God will order the Guardian of the Fire to inflict seventy punishments upon him in the fires of Hell."[116]
>
> "I am surprised by the man who beats his wife, when it is he who is more deserving of being beaten."[117]

As for one of the rights that the wife has over her husband, he said: "You should not hurt the woman in the face and should not call her ugly."[118]

In general, the practice of the Prophet and the divine religious leaders is not to use violence against woman.

The most significant is that it has a strong emotional effect that alerts the woman to the problem. Otherwise, the woman may quite unintentionally continue doing something wrong and thus cause a family breakdown. One should also take into consideration that the other solutions, such as talking to her and avoiding her in bed, would have already failed, and that it is only then necessary to take the next step. Another aspect is the preventive effect of this method, for sometimes it can prevent a problem from being taken to a court of law and being publicised, which would simply turn it into a legal issue and make it worse.

It should be said that this method is not generally compulsory. Rather, it is a solution that has been provided by God as guidance.[119] Thus, one can use it by considering whether it would be effective, and having in mind the time, the situation and the personality of the woman. Moreover, it is difficult for many modern men to keep to the necessary conditions of these methods, especially that of having a corrective intention in chastising. Therefore, in the case of the woman's sexual disinclination, it is better for the man to consult family counselors and specialists. Otherwise, instead of solving the problem, he may have to violate his wife's rights.[120]

If a man fails to fulfil the material and psychological rights of the woman or, according to the Qur'ān, comes into discord, his wife should advise him and ask for her rights by reminding him of his responsibilities. If the problem is not solved, the next stage would be for her to refer to family specialists. Finally, if the problem is still not solved, she can refer to the legal authorities in order to force the man to fulfil his family responsibilities. Under the same circumstances, the Qur'ān advises the couple to reach a compromise.[121] This has to do with the modification of their expectations of each other. Indeed, they naturally seek more privileges and make fewer concessions. Under these circumstances, in order to have peace and friendship in the family, they should modify their expectations. The man would do better by adopting the practice of doing good and being pious, and avoiding any injustice to his wife. If he is negligent, he should be reminded. If he fails to fulfil his duty and resorts to using violence, higher authorities should force him to fulfil his duties, and by pressurising him, restore the woman's rights. In this respect, during Imām 'Alī 's rule, he advised a man who had violated his wife's rights, then pressured him into fulfilling his family duties.[122] Sometimes problems in the sexual relationship have to do with sexual weakness or some kinds of disease or disorder that needs to be treated. The divine religious leaders have given certain advice for improving the sexual powers, such as eating certain fruits or foods.[123] Obviously, nowadays, with the discoveries of science proper treatment is also available. If the treatment of sexual impotence fails, according to the teachings of Islām, both the man and the woman can go as far as separation in order to fulfil their emotional needs and restore their rights. The important point according to Islamic teachings is the fulfilment of the emotional needs of both parties, and this has priority over the survival of the family.

3.3. Consultation and Arbitration

Industrialisation contributes to the problems that the family faces in modern society, to which our society is no exception. The biggest structural development in the Iranian family in recent decades is change from the extended to the nuclear family, which has resulted in basic changes in the nature of the relationships between family members, the affective significance they have for each other, the concept of family itself, the family economy and the role of genders. Consequently, some collective methods of overcoming family problems by using the emotional and experiential resources of those near to us have lost their effectiveness. In such conditions, it is usually the spouses that are left to solve their own problems. On the other hand, people often do not have sufficient communicative skills and means to set about this and find answers, as a result of which, instead of solving problems, they deny them, which in the long run has bad consequences, such as alienation and disillusionment.[124]

In view of these points, it is sometimes to consult others, especially family therapists. The teachings of Islām emphasise the consideration of the views of others in all matters. Indeed, the counsellor should have the necessary qualifications for resolving family issues. Some general criteria of the counsellor are a sufficient awareness of the subject of counselling and related matters, the ability to affectively relate to others, having pure and honest intentions, patience, trustworthiness, the ability to continue the counselling, having the qualities of a good role mode, piety,[125] and respecting the beliefs and values of the married couple.

In addition to these conditions it is necessary to be familiar with the finer points of Islamic teachings, the important role of which for Iranian families cannot be denied. It is important to consider the fact that in our society certain Islamic rulings regarding the family and marriage, including those relating to some types of marriage, are not easily accepted. This will be examined in Chapter 6. Therefore, a lack of awareness regarding these laws, and using them out of context, sometimes makes matters worse. For example, we will mention later the method of using two arbitrators, selected by the families of the husband and wife, for resolving issues in line with family counselling.

If the family dispute becomes worse, and the husband and wife decide to fight each other and ignore their obligations, a difficult situation arises, referred to in the Qur'ān as "discord,"[126] and this involves hostility and not speaking to each other. If this hostility seems likely, then others should intervene in order to rectify matters. In this case, it is recommended that two arbitrators be selected representing each partner in order to resolve the situation. The selection of arbitrators by the relatives of each party has several advantages. Firstly, the relatives have a more objective view of the couple's psychological and living conditions. Secondly, having relatives as arbitrators assures that the interests of each partner are fully represented. Thirdly, the conclusions of family relations will be more readily accepted by the couple. Fourthly, relatives would support the interests of both sides more than anyone else. Fifthly, relatives are in a better position to know ways to solve the problems and restore love and trust between the couple, as well as knowing the initial causes.[127]

It would help if the two arbitrators are astute and also married, so as to be able to understand family issues well and make proper judgments. As a first step, the arbitrators should discover the root causes by asking each of the partners in private to be truthful. The husband and wife should talk frankly and explicitly about their problems.[128] If the two arbitrators cannot reach a solution, they might decide that the husband and wife should separate, or that the couple should decide for themselves. It seems that, if the arbitrators who have been selected for resolving the dispute cannot reach a solution, then the couple themselves should decide whether or not to separate, for the arbitrators cannot force them to stay together. The spouses are entirely free to enter into the marriage agreement, and they should be equally free to reconcile their differences or part from each other. The role of the arbitrators is no more than that of consultation and guidance.[129]

3.4. Separation of the Husband and Wife

The last resort when dealing with family problems is official separation or divorce. To continue with the marriage is sometimes impractical, and can cause psychological damage and abnormal behaviour. In conditions reach a deadlock, an official separation is a solution. According to Islām, separation is undesirable. It has been said that for God the most loathe some house is the one destroyed by divorce or separation. The words of the divine religious leaders confirm how ugly and disastrous divorce is, so much so that the Prophet said:

> "I have been so much advised about women that I thought perhaps divorcing a woman is not proper unless she commits adultery."[130]

However, if it is impossible to continue in a balanced and peaceful way, it is better to divorce,[131] since to continue would be harmful.[132] Islām as a religion has accepted official separation its laws because sometimes, for whatever reason, it becomes difficult for the couple to continue their life together, even though there may be incidental causes and the situation may be temporary. On the other hand, Islām has set a limit of three times for divorce, so that if a man wishes to remarry his ex-wife after the third divorce, the woman should have first married another man before remarrying her first husband.[133] This is meant to prevent repeated or unreasonable occasions of divorce. Since divorce can result in the collapse of the family and has undesirable consequences for all concerned, the teachings of Islām prescribe different ways of avoiding divorce, such as certain time limits[134] and providing sufficient evidence. In addition, after the divorce the husband and wife can resume their life together under certain circumstances during the *'iddah* period (to ensure that the woman is not pregnant) without officially remarrying, with merely a smile.[135] Also, since the wife is required by Islamic law to live in the man's house during the *'iddah* period, this might rekindle the emotional bond between them and prevent the collapse of the family. Nevertheless, if divorce is inevitable, Islām recommends that it should be carried out in a good way, showing kindness to the woman,[136] and that the woman should not be pressured into divorce and giving up her rights.[137] If the divorce is carried out agreeably and with due consideration to the wife, including the settlement of all amounts due to her according to the accepted practice, it may lead towards further marriage and the beginning of a more balanced life for both the husband and wife.

In any case, divorce has bad psychological effects. Disease and distress (68.94%), tiredness (70%), distrust, a lower performance at work, feelings of failure (75%), worries about children, irritability, suicide, social deviation, pessimism about the future, anxiety, sadness, anger and guilt are among the psychological complexities of divorce. These are just some of the statistics among divorcees.[138] However, the first means of preventing these mental states is to avoid divorce by solving the problems and optimising the relationship. Emotional, social and economic support, especially for women, can be useful in this respect. Sometimes the reactions of others are the hardest blow.[139] The couple should be taught ways to tackle stress, and with continuous counselling they can improve their prospects of compatibility.

The children of divorcees also face several emotional, social and economic problems. Most of them are unaware of the changes in the family, since the parents feel that they cannot confide in their children. Helping the children to tackle divorce in a healthy way is an important issue, since failure to do so can have harmful consequences for them. Marital quarrels are painful for all children, although boys find it harder to cope with them. They become nervous, defiant and disorderly and get involved with the police authorities twice as often as their male peers. Girls also become anxious, worried, isolated and antisocial.

According to various studies, children in the first year of separation experience anger, fear, depression and feelings of guilt. The lack of an appropriate adult role model for them later manifests in lower grades in progress and intelligence tests, and can eventually cause emotional and sexual problems that cause difficulties in their own marital life.[140] These problems require additional attention. Here we will provide solutions for children to adapt to divorce.

In the first place, the children should be familiarised with the problems of separation and divorce in advance, for then it is much easier for them to understand and accept its various stages. Therefore, the parents should warn their child a few days in advance about their separation, so that the child can prepare. Secondly, after separation, they should have a plan to regularly visit the child, and in the first week of separation they should visit the child every day, if possible. In the case of divorce, the child should be given an explanation. Research has shown that 80% of children are told nothing about the divorce. However, it is important to assure the child of a continuing relationship with the father and mother, in order to allay feelings of insecurity and doubt in the child.[141]

If the parents continue to pay attention to their emotional and financial responsibilities towards their children even after divorce, the children's problems will be fewer. The Qur'ānic principle of "abandoning in good will" is something that can maintain the relationship of care and nurture between the divorced couple and the child.

Notes

1. Carlson, J., *Family Therapy*, p. 22.
2. Rusenbaum, Heidi, *The Family as a Structure against Society*, p. 95.
3. Farjād, Muḥammad Ḥusayn, Āsībshināsī -yi Ijtimāʿī-yi Sitīzihhā-yi Khānivādih va Talāq , p. 154.
4. Mīr-Aḥmadīzādih, 'Alī Reḍā, 'Reḍāmandī-yi Zanāshuyī' in Andīshih va Raftār journal, issue 32, p. 60.
5. Askarī, Ḥusayn, Bihdāsht Ravān dar Izdivāj, p. 260.
6. Satir, Jane, *Making Humans in Psychology of the Family*, pp. 69-70.
7. *Nahj al-Fasāḥa*, Aphorism 31.

8. Āmidī,*Ghurar al-Ḥikam*, Ḥadīth 10523; Al-Kulaynī, *Kāfī,* vol. 2, p. 300, Ḥadīth 1.
9. Al-Kulaynī, *Kāfī,* vol. 2, p. 300.
10. Muḥammadī-Reyshahrī, *Mīzān al-Ḥikmah*, vol. 11, p. 5538.
11. Āmidī, *Ghurar al-Ḥikam*, p. 5524.
12. *Nahj al-Balāghah*, Aphorism 362.
13. Muḥammadī-Reyshahrī, *Mīzān al-Ḥikmah*, vol. 11, p. 5538.
14. Ibid., p. 5540.
15. *Nahj al-Balāghah*, Sermon 192; Muḥammadī-Reyshahrī, *Mīzān al-Ḥikmah*, vol. 11, p. 5076.
16. Al-Kulaynī, *Kāfī,* vol. 2, p. 309.
17. Qā'imī, 'Alī , Nizām Ḥayāt Khānivādih dar Islām , p. 294.
18. Askarī, Ḥusayn, Naqsh Bihdāsht Ravān dar Izdivāj, p. 244.
19. Farjād, Āsībshināsī -yi Ijtimā'ī-yi Sitīzihhā-yi Khānivādih va Talāq , p. 208.
20. Al-Ḥurr al-'Āmilī, *Wasā'il al-Shī'a*, vol. 18,pp.,183, 129.
21. Ibid., vol. 14, p. 183.
22. Ibid.
23. Ibid., pp. 83, 100.
24. This was discussed under "Boundaries in the Family."
25. Askarī, Ḥusayn, Naqsh Bihdāsht Ravān dar Izdivāj, pp. 196 and 261.
26. Ibid., pp. 262-263.
27. Farjād, Āsībshināsī -yi Ijtimā'ī-yi Sitīzihhā-yi Khānivādih va Talāq , p. 208.
28. Keiniyā, Mehdī, 'Avāmil Ijtimā'ī Talāq, pp. 7-17.
29. Āmidī, *Ghurar al-Ḥikam*, Ḥadīth 2059.
30. Muḥammadī-Reyshahrī, *Mīzān al-Ḥikmah*, pp. 101, 290, 348.
31. Majlisī, *Biḥār al-Anwār*, vol. 74, p. 198.
32. Āmidī, *Ghurar al-Ḥikam*, Ḥadīth 2601.
33. I'zāzī, Shahlā, *Khānivādih va Tilivīziyun* , p. 54.
34. Wahhābī, Zahrā, Naqsh Tilivīziyun dar Bizihkārī Atfāl va Nawjavānān, master's thesis, Islamic Azād University, Narāq Branch, p. 93.
35. I'zāzī, *Khānivādih va Tilivīziyun* , pp. 14-96.
36. Farjād, Āsībshināsī -yi Ijtimā'ī-yi Sitīzihhā-yi Khānivādih va Talāq , p. 208.
37. Muḥammadī-Reyshahrī, *Mīzān al-Ḥikmah*, vol. 10, pp. 4660-4662.
38. Ibid., *Selections from Mīzān al-Ḥikmah*, p. 408.
39. Nay, but man doth transgress all bounds, In that he looketh upon himself as self-sufficient, Qur'ān 96:6, 7.
40. *Nahj al-Balāghah*, Aphorism. 58.
41. Al-Kulaynī, *Kāfī,* vol. 1, p. 46; Majlisī, *Biḥār al-Anwār*, vol. 1, p. 168.
42. Ibid., *Kāfī,* vol. 2, pp. 316, 138.

43. Sadūq, *al-Khisāl*, p. 282, Ḥadīth 29.
44. Quotations from the divine religious leaders were mentioned in the discussion on "Children."
45. Farjād, Āsībshināsī -yi Ijtimā'ī-yi Sitīzihhā-yi Khānivādih va Talāq , p. 208.
46. Kār, Mihrangīz, Bachchi-ha-yi I'tiyād , pp. 24-25, 41-45.
47. (He) hath made me kind to my mother, and not overbearing or miserable, Qur'ān 19:32.
48. Those who slander chaste women, indiscreet but believing, are cursed in this life and in the Hereafter: for them is a grievous penalty, Qur'ān 24:23.
49. Qur'ān 5:90.
50. Zamīrī, Muḥammad-Reḍā, "Mashrūb Khārī Jurmī 'Alayhi Zanān va Khānivādih," in *Kitab Zanān*, issue 20, p. 203.
51. Qur'ān 49:12.
52. Muḥammadī-Reyshahrī, *Mīzān al-Ḥikmah*, vol. 13, p. 6476.
53. Muttaqī-Hindī, *Kanz al-'Ummāl*, Ḥadīth 8348.
54. Āmidī, *Ghurar al-Ḥikam*, Ḥadīth 2663; Majlisī, *Biḥār al-Anwār*, vol. 71, p. 293.
55. A slanderer, going about with calumnies, Qur'ān 68:11; Al-Kulaynī, *Usūl Kāfī*, vol. 4, p. 75.
56. Certain reasons are given in the Qur'ān and in the words of the Prophet and his household (Ahl al-Bayt), such as Qur'ān 22:30 and 31:6; Majlisī, *Biḥār al-Anwār*, vol. 79, pp. 241-252; Sadūq, *Man lā yahḍaruh al-Faqīh*, vol. 2, p. 80, Ḥadīth 177.
57. Ansārī, Murtaḍā, *Kitab al- Makāsib*, pp. 103-113.
58. Muḥammadī-Reyshahrī, *Mīzān al-Ḥikmah*, p. 4420.
59. Majlisī, *Biḥār al-Anwār*, vol. 79, p. 252; Āmidī, *Ghurar al-Ḥikam*, p. 477; ibid., p. 64.
60. Qur'ān 2:219.
61. Al-Kulaynī, *Kāfī*, vol. 5, p. 122, Ḥadīth 1, p. 123, Ḥadīth 6.
62. Āmidī, *Ghurar al-Ḥikam*, Ḥadīth 2165.
63. Ibid., Ḥadīth 3132.
64. Ibid., Ḥadīth 9815; Muḥammadī-Reyshahrī, *Mīzān al-Ḥikmah*, p. 5358.
65. Āmidī,*Ghurar al-Ḥikam*, Ḥadīth 7969; ibid., p. 460.
66. Ibid., p. 333.
67. Majlisī, *Biḥār al-Anwār*, vol. 76, p. 59; Al-Kulaynī, *Kāfī*, vol. 5, p. 50; Muḥammadī-Reyshahrī, *Mīzān al-Ḥikmah*, p. 5360.
68. Qur'ān 2:102. There is also a Ḥadīth of the Prophet in which he strongly scolds a woman for resorting to sorcery to attract her husband's love (Al-Kulaynī, *Kāfī*, vol. 2, p. 60)

69. Ḥusaynī, K, *"Padīdi Fāl va Fālgīrī dar Iran", in Irandukht*, issue 11.
70. Sālārī, Muḥammad, *Siḥr va Jādūgarī*, p. 100.
71. Banī Asadī, Ḥasan, *Barrasī-yi 'Avamil Mu'aththir Ijtimā'ī -Fardī dar Zawj-hā-yi Sāzigār va Nāsāzigār dar Shahr Kirmān,* M.A thesis, Tarbiat Modarres University, abstract.
72. Qur'ān 24:26.
73. Carlson, J., *Family Therapy*, p. 263.
74. Marasumi, Radmikako, "Human Rights and Violence against Women," in journal *Farzānih*, issue 8, p. 79.
75. Majlisī, *Biḥār al-Anwār*, vol. 7, p. 33.
76. Ibid., vol. 72, p. 264; Narāqī, Mullā Aḥmad, *Mi'rāj al-Sa'ādah*, p. 169.
77. Hājī Dih Ābādī, Muḥammad 'Alī , Proceedings of the International Scientific Applied Conference on the Various Aspects of Criminal Policies towards Narcotic Drugs, p. 139.
78. Ādharbāyjānī, Mas'ūd et al, Ravānshināsī-yi Ijtimā'ī ba Nigāhī bi Manābi' Islāmī, p. 253.
79. Mantiqī, Murtaḍā, Chikīdi-yi Tāzih-hā-yi Taḥqīq dar Dānishgāhha va Marākiz Taḥqīqātī-yi Iran, issue 28, p. 13.
80. Who (conduct) their affairs by mutual consultation, Qur'ān 42:38.
81. And consult them in affairs (of moment), Qur'ān 3:159.
82. Muḥammadī-Reyshahrī, *Mīzān al-Ḥikmah*, vol. 5, pp. 210, 211.
83. Majlisī, *Biḥār al-Anwār*, vol. 72, p. 98.
84. Ibid., vol. 75, p. 104, vol. 1, p. 160.
85. Qur'ān 39:17.
86. No mother shall be treated unfairly on account of her child, nor father on account of his child, Qur'ān 2:233.
87. And take mutual counsel together, Qur'ān 65:6.
88. "O my son! I see in a vision that I offer thee in sacrifice: now see what is thy view!" Qur'ān 37:102.
89. Al-Ḥurr al-'Āmilī, *Wasā'il al-Shī'a*, vol. 15, p. 195.
90. Ḥusaynī, 'Alī -Akbar, *Akhlāq dar Khānivādih*, pp. 440-443.
91. Majlisī, *Biḥār al-Anwār*, vol. 103, p. 253.
92. Farīd Tunikābunī, *Nahj al-Fasāḥa*, p. 2.
93. Ibn Shu'ba al-Harrānī, al-Ḥasan, Tuḥaf al-'Uqūl 'an Āl al-Rasūl, p. 238.
94. Nūrī, *Mustadrak al-Wasā'il*, vol. 14, p. 253.
95. Siemon, F. B., *Key Concepts and Theories in Family Therapy*, p. 209.
96. *Nahj al-Balāghah*, Aphorism 399.
97. Qur'ān 31:45.

98. Khānih Kūdak, *Ahkami ma va Kūdakan*, pp. 73-87.
99. Al-Ḥurr al-'Āmilī, *Wasā'il al-Shī'a*, vol. 14, p. 15.
100. Ibid., p. 22.
101. Ibid., p. 115, Ḥadīth 7.
102. Ibid., p. 18.
103. This was examined in Chapter 2 under Islamic narrations and arguments.
104. Qur'ān 4:35.
105. Qur'ān 4:34.
106. Qur'ān 4:128.
107. Tabresi, Faḍl ibn Ḥasan, *Majma' al-Bayān fī Tafsīr al-Qur'ān* , p. 69.
108. Isfahānī, Sayyid Abū al-Ḥasan, Wasīla al-Najāt ma'a Ta'āliqat al- Imām al-Khumeinī, p. 755; Najafī, *Jawāhir al-Kalām*, vol. 31, p. 201.
109. Therefore the righteous women are devoutly obedient, and guard in (the husband's) absence what Allāh would have them guard. As to those women on whose part ye fear disloyalty and ill-conduct, admonish them (first), (next) refuse to share their beds, (and last) beat them lightly; but if they return to obedience, seek not against them means (of annoyance): for Allāh is Most High, Great (above you all), Qur'ān 4:34.
110. Qā'imī, 'Alī , Nizām Ḥayāt Khānivādih dar Islām , p. 345.
111. Professor Muṭahharī also believes that such beating is not physical, but merely an expression of animosity (Mīrkhānī, 'Izzat al-Sādāt, Rūykardī Nuvīn dar Ravābit Khānivādih, p. 200).
112. Sadr, Sayyid Mūsā, Tanbīh Badanī-yi Zan dar Nigāhhā-yi Gūnāgūn,in Pazhūhish-ha-yi Qur'ānī, Daftar Tablīghāt Islāmī, vol. 7, issues 27-28, pp. 92-94.
113. Zuḥailī, *al-Tafsīr al-Munir*, vol. 5, p. 57.
114. Ibn Mājah, *Sunan*, vol. 1, p. 638.
115. Ibn Sa'd, *al-Tabaqāt al-Kubrā*, vol. 8, p. 165.
116. Nūrī, *Mustadrak al-Wasā'il*, vol. 14, p. 250, Ḥadīth 4.
117. Ibid., p. 250, Ḥadīth 3.
118. Mihrīzī, *Shakhsiyyat va Huqūq Zan* , p. 272.
119. It seems that this law is a right that God has given to men. Therefore, it is the man's choice whether to use this right or not (Hāshimī Rafsanjānī, Akbar et al, Tafsīr Rāhnamā, vol. 3, p. 369).
120. Studies show that men have in many cases abused the rights of women with violence (I'zāzī, Shahlā, *Khushūnat Khānivādigī*, pp. 100-160).
121. Qur'ān 4:128; Al-Ḥurr al-'Āmilī, *Wasā'il al-Shī'a*, vol. 15, pp. 90-91.
122. Majlisī, *Biḥār al-Anwār*, vol. 40, p. 113.
123. *Ibid.*, vol. 62, p. 300; Jazā'irī, Ghiyath al-Dīn, I'jāz-e Khurākihā , pp. 230-235.

124. Siemon, F.B., *Key Concepts and Theories in Family Therapy*, p. 25.
125. Faqīhī, 'Alī -Naqī, *Mushāvirih dar Āyeneh-yi 'Ilm va Dīn* , pp. 66-71.
126. And if ye fear a breach between them twain, appoint (two) arbiters, one from his family and the other from hers; if they wish for peace, Allāh will cause their reconciliation, Qur'ān 4:35.
127. Qā'imī, Alī , Nizām Ḥayāt Khānivādih dar Islām , p. 354.
128. Iḥsānbakhsh, Sādiq, *Naqsh Dīn dar Khānivādih* , vol. 2, p. 371.
129. Bihishtī, Aḥmad, *Khānivādih dar Qur'ān*, p. 106.
130. Al-Ḥurr al-'Āmilī, *Wasā'il al-Shī'a*, vol. 15, p. 267.
131. Ibid., p. 269.
132. Qur'ān 2:299.
133. Qur'ān 2:230.
134. For example, divorce is proper when there is no sexual intercourse between the spouses from the end of the last menstrual period to the time of divorce (Safā'ī, Sayyid Ḥusayn and Asadullāh Imāmī, Mukhtasar Huqūq Khānivādih, p. 223).
135. Ibid., p. 353.
136. Or separate with kindness, and Or set them free on equitable terms, Qur'ān 2:229 and 231.
137. Nor should ye treat them with harshness, that ye may take away part of the dower ye have given them, Qur'ān 4:19.
138. Farjād, Muḥammad Ḥusayn, Āsībshināsī -yi Ijtimā'ī-yi Sitīzihhāye Khānivādih va Talāq , p. 300.
139. Di Matteo, M., *Health Psychology*, vol. 2, p. 534.
140. Teyber, *Children of Divorce*, pp. 10-40.
141. Ibid., pp. 52-58.

CHAPTER 6

THE FAMILY SYSTEM IN ISLĀM

In addition to the recommendations regarding the relationships between family members and how to improve them, the teachings of Islām also provide recommendations regarding other aspects, such as money matters and rules within the family, both of which contribute to the efficiency of the family and protect it. In this chapter, we will deal with the family economy. Another part of this chapter consists of samples of successful family behaviour which might be a key to become like them. Then there are some examples of ineffectiveness, and key Islamic viewpoints regarding the family will be examined. At the end of this chapter, these viewpoints will be summed up in a step towards providing a comprehensive system of the family.

1. The Psychological Effects of the Economic Laws of Islām on the Family

The teachings of Islām have special economic rules for the family that not only manages and adjusts the economic system within the family, but plays an effective role in bringing balance and happiness to the family. In this section, we will examine three important economic issues concerning the family i.e. the marriage portion, living costs and inheritance, in order to discover their psychological effects.

1.1. The Marriage Portion or Dowry

The marriage portion is that which is given by the husband to the wife,[1] the amount of which they should agree upon.[2] After they are married, the woman becomes the owner of the marriage portion and can use it as she wishes. Before the time of the Prophet Muḥammad, the marriage portion was recognised, but it was modified by Islām and in certain cases annulled.[3] In the first place, the marriage portion is an important gift from a man to the woman who wants to live with him. The Qur'ān uses the word *sadaqah* for the marriage portion, which is of the same root as the word for "honesty" and conveys the meaning of honesty in belief. The word *niḥlah* has also been used, meaning "gift" or "offering."[4] This has a particular psychological effect on the wife. She will feel that the man loves her and has shown his love in practice and is ready to pay for it. The reason why the man should give such a gift is to do with the psychological differences between men and women and the way they express love. Doubtless, the apparent and psychological attraction of a man towards a woman is greater than that of the woman towards the man, and this is one reason why women are used in advertising nowadays. As a result, the man will be attracted to her. Her modesty and reticence further increases her attractiveness. The same situation is seen in the animal kingdom, where the male always persues the female.[5] In this respect, the man gives a gift to increase the woman's satisfaction with the marriage.

Another thing to consider is the value of the dowry for the woman. The biological and social conditions of women mean that throughout history they have always had a lower economic status than men,[6] since, instead of being gainfully employed, a considerable amount of a time is taken up when the woman is pregnant and nurturing a child. In addition, even today, she is responsible for running the house in most societies, all of which involves a lot of unpaid work. Therefore, the dowry is a relatively reliable economic support for her, and permits her to fulfil her family responsibilities with more assurance. There is evidence in Islamic texts of the economic importance of the marriage portion for women. In a certain sense, failing to give the marriage portion is a kind of theft,[7] and will make the sexual relationship between the man and his legal wife appears somewhat illegitimate.[8] It has even been mentioned in certain narrations as a sin that God will not forget.[9] It would not be talked of like this if the marriage portion was meant only for affective reasons and beginning a family life. The couple should both consent to the marriage portion[10] to make it legal, and it thenceforth becomes something which cannot be overlooked, even if it is a large amount.[11] Such aspects show how economically important it is.

The marriage portion also has a unique psychological effect on the man. He discovers that marriage is not an easy matter, for he has to invest in it from the very beginning. This causes him to approach marriage with deeper understanding. The marriage portion will also affect the marriage itself, since even quite generally, if we invest in something, we do not want to lose it easily, and the greater the investment, the more difficult it would be to close one's eyes to it. According to Festinger's cognitive dissonance theory, the more one pays for something, the more one will convince oneself of its acceptability.[12] And as for marriage, the man who has put great emotional and material investment in it will not give it up. Easily Hence, the marriage portion should not be a negligible amount.[13] A small amount is indeed acceptable according to marriage law, but because of the psychological effect, it is better if it is a sum that the individual would not easily ignore.

In general, it can be said that the marriage portion is a gift that strengthens the marriage bond and clears the way for the formation and expansion of a positive affective relationship. Even so, the love between the husband and wife is based on foundations that the marriage portion serves to strengthen rather than create. Therefore, a large marriage portion cannot generate love. It was said in the Prophet's Household:

> "Consider the marriage portion as a gift,[14] because if you overdo it, it will cause hostility between the man and the woman."[15]

It has also been said that the best Muslim women are the ones with the most beauty and the smallest marriage portion.[16]

After examining various sociological justifications for the marriage portion, some consider it more Islamic to regard it as a gift. The different terms by which it is known all indicate that it is given unconditionally, and there are ethical reasons stated in Islām teachings for having a small marriage portion, such as being open-minded in the calculation of its agreed value, considering certain spiritual equations, the woman's acceptance of it as a way for strengthening the family, consideration of the man's situation and its status as a gift. As for the woman receiving it as a gift, in addition to the points mentioned, she should be firmly committed to a shared life, accept various responsibilities, express gratitude and help consolidate the family.[17]

A notable aspect of contemporary Iranian culture is the proliferation of large marriage portions resulting in difficult marriages. Young Iranian women, despite being better educated, still look for a high marriage portion. After the victory of the Islamic Revolution there were, for a while, normal and balanced marriage portions, but after a few years, the trend went towards increasing the marriage portion.[18] As sociological reasons for high marriage portions, these have already been mentioned.[19]

As the marriage portion is a religious and legal liability for the husband, an excessive amount would put him under financial strain. In a successful marriage, the marriage portion is not usually demanded by the wife and rarely any problem emerges. However, if the marriage fails and results in divorce, the man will face a worse situation. Therefore, having a balanced look at the amount of the marriage portion and considering it more precisely as a definite debt can prevent subsequent problems to a certain extent. Otherwise, the marriage portion, which is supposed to consolidate the family bond, can cause hostility and other problems.

1.2. Living Costs

According to the teachings of Islām, the financial responsibilities of the family fall upon the man,[20] and include housing,[21] food, clothing[22] and education, and should be in accord with the expectations of the family and the conditions of the time. The wife has no responsibility towards the family finances, even if she has a high income. The basic responsibility of the wife is to collaborate in the stabilising effect of family life, and any failure in this will create responsibilities for her. In the family, the woman is responsible for establishing an appropriate relationship with her spouse and raising children. Her not being involved in earning the living costs of the family gives her the leisure that she needs to fulfil her responsibilities with more peace. An interesting point in family matters is that the living costs of a woman are more than those of a man. Most of the items in the house are used by the woman. The woman also cares more about clothing and decorative items. These require the woman's participation, and their lack or shortage will create problems for the woman in the first place. If the woman decides to provide them by herself, she will face a great deal of difficulty in fulfilling her duties as wife and mother. Attention to this rule and trying to implement it properly will provide the husband and wife with a special psychological space, so that the man will consider himself as the person responsible for providing the costs of the family and will handle the expenses of the family with a positive attitude. In this connection, the wife will only be expected to fulfil her family responsibilities. In this connection, the wife's activity and work at home will be her contribution to the running the household, while it is not a basic responsibility of hers. In order to provide for her expenses, she will not need to take a job, and will consequently consider herself indebted to the man and feel dependent upon him. As a result, she will carry out her spousal and maternal duties with love and dedication.

The woman is economically independent and in charge of her own property,[23] although she should not behave in a way that disturbs the family coherence. The financial administration of the family is the man's responsibility, and the woman should consent to this. This will help unite the family and its management, which is actually based on running the economy of the family and was referred to earlier with references from the Qur'ān.[24] Therefore, according to Islām, a wife is not required to engage in economic activities to earn an income for the family, although she may do so as long as it does not interfere with the family.

Another aspect of the living costs relates to children and one's parents in the case of need. The mutual rights of the children and parents require that, if one party is in need and the other party can provide, then they should do so. This financial ruling in Islām demonstrates how Islām does not consider the family limited to the framework of the nuclear family and includes those beyond the next of kin. This outlook entails a wide emotional and social network as mentioned in the discussions of family relationships.

1.3. Inheritance

Inheritance is another economic matter in Islām in which the properties of the deceased are shared out.[25] A given percentage depends on the family relationship, and close relatives have priority over others. The first level of inheritance relates to the children and parents of the deceased. If they are alive, no share of the inheritance is given to the next level, that of the siblings. In addition to being a kind of economic support for the family members, it also has a psychological effect on them that strengthens family relationships and unconsciously results in a continuing emotional relationship with the person's parents or children. The affective relations between family members should indeed go beyond the economic interests. However, sometimes the cognitive and affective foundations of the relationship are weak, and this economic incentive can help strengthen it. The inheritance law itself is further evidence of a wide family system.

2. Model Families in Islām

Each of the Islamic teachings referred to earlier, all of which derive from verses in the Qur'ān, the words of the Prophet or of the Imams, are further exemplified by the conduct of great figures in Islamic history, who always themselves abided by whatever advice they gave to others. Their behaviour in the family far surpassed that of others, and was something they sometimes spoke of as a model for others to follow.[26] Assimilating such behavioural models may be an easier way for people to improve their function and perform their duties, for the individual will put it into practice at the right time. This kind of learning is quite important,[27] for one of its factors is that the model is of high repute and strength of character, and is amenable to the learner. Moreover, such well-known models are effective and receive attention.[28]

The divine religious leaders consider the two principles of the importance of following a known personality and behavioural model,[29] and its credibility and image. According to this, they invite the people to follow appropriately. One such behavioural model according to the Qur'ān is the Prophet Abraham.[30] Moreover, God has said in the Qur'ān that the Prophet of Islām is a good model to be followed.[31] 'Alī , who was a close witness of the lifestyle of the Prophet, considered him the best model for everybody.[32] According to verses in the Qur'ān, the personality and behavioral characteristics of the Prophet[33] and his family are exemplary.[34] The Prophet's household consists of his daughter, Ḥaḍrat Fātima, her husband, Imām 'Alī , and their children, whom the Prophet took with him to the *mubāhala* ("mutual cursing"), which according to the Qur'ān was a matter of life and death.[35] There is much historical evidence to support the moral health and perfection of this family in both Sunni and Shi'ite sources.[36]

Imām 'Alī said:

> "Oh, people, look at your Prophet's household and follow their direction.They will never misguide you or lead you to meanness and destruction."[37]

Since these are all important ingredients of marriage and the family, we will give some examples from the lives of some of the great people in Islām.

2.1. Facing the Marriage

All the divine leaders of Islām considered marriage a good thing.[38] While being diligent in their spirituality, they never neglected worldly matters and always emphasised how marriage is not at odds with spirituality, but can even be a help. Imām Sādiq advised a woman to get married. Indeed, if renouncing the world and marriage were positive steps towards spirituality, then surely a person like Ḥaḍrat Fātima would have done so.[39]

These people paid little attention to materialistic matters or luxury and had a straightforward approach to marriage. They married without encumbrance[40] and advised their children to avoid luxury.[41]

The divine religious leaders paid attention to the selection of a spouse in matters of piety, reason and morality. The principle of similarity was kept in mind, as is clear in the marriage of Imām 'Alī and Ḥaḍrat Fātima.[42] According to the Prophet, there was no one other than Imām 'Alī who was like Ḥaḍrat Fātima.[43] A similar economic or social class wás not a criterion, there was no such a thing as a principle [44] and they they advised others not to pay attention to such things.[45]

The divine religious leaders allocated the marriage portion in a reasonable fashion. Fātima's marriage portion was 500 dirhams (or 2,000 grams of silver). The other daughters of the Prophet did not have a marriage portion in excess of this.[46] The marriage portion would be spent on things needed by the bride, and in the case of Fātima, only the necessary items were provided. The other Imams also gave their wives marriage portions in order to get whatever they needed for their lives. The Imams lived in their wives' houses, and responded to those who questioned this by saying that the wife had full control over how she spent the marriage portion.[47] The divine religious leaders also recommended that there be others present at marriage ceremony for celebration and the expression of happiness.[48]

2.2. The Prophet's Treatment of His Wives

An important moral and behavioural characteristic of the Prophet and the Imams was the way they treated their wives. The Prophet was the greatest model of all for men in the way they should treat women. Two verses in the Qur'ān indicate the Prophet's diligence in treating women well. In one of them, God addresses the Prophet, asking him why he does not permit for himself things which would please his wives, and which God has allowed him.[49] According to this verse, the Prophet cared about his wives' happiness so much that he would even give up his own happiness for them. In another verse,[50] God addresses the Prophet's wives, saying that if they unite against him, God will send Gabriel, the good believers and the angels to his help. This shows how forgiving the Prophet was towards his wives, so much so that God threatened his wives in order to defend him.

According to the Prophet's companions, whenever his wives asked him for something, he would agree with them, and he was very indulgent at home.[51] We are told that he Prophet himself said: "The best of you is the one who is kind to his wives, and I am the kindest to my wives."[52] An important characteristic of the Prophet's family life was his fair treatment of his wives, even under severe and exceptional conditions.[53] The Prophet's wives had different personalities,[54] and his kindness and forbearance created a peaceful atmosphere within the home. He would talk and laugh with his wives in such a way that at home he appeared as a normal husband, albeit one with exceptional values,[55] for he was consistently kind to his family and to the people, and would avoid any roughness or violence.[56] While accentuating his personal characteristics, the Qur'ān considers them a divine blessing, saying, "if thou hadst been stern and fierce of heart they would have dispersed from round about thee."[57]

2.3.The Prophet's Attitude Towards Children

Briefly stated, the Prophet's practice in the family was that of understanding, companionship,[58] humility, love[59] and forgiveness.[60] He did not search for faults in others or to blame them,[61] and he had the mildest of temperaments.[62] While respecting his family and others, from small children to adults, both male and female, he would establish a positive emotionally relationships with them.[63] In addition to doing his own work, he helped around the house by doing jobs such as cutting meat and milking the sheep.[64] He wore proper, suitable clothing and accessories when with his family and the people.[65] He treated his wives kindly like an ordinary person, in ways such as first giving them the perfume[66] and insisting on expanding his affective relationship with them in various aspects.[67] He was very sensitive to religious rules within the family,[68] and inattention to them would upset him. In certain verses, the Qur'ān addresses the Prophet's wives and the people in ways that demonstrate the Prophet's sensitivity in this respect.[69]

It is interesting to observe how the Prophet treated his children and all children in general, but especially girls at a time when they did not receive enough love and respect, and were even buried alive at birth.[70] In his nonverbal communication with them, he caressed and kissed his children,[71] and advised others to do likewise.[72] Sometimes he would play with the children.[73] Whilst at prayer, children would sometimes climb onto his shoulders, and he would accordingly extend the duration of his prostration.[74] He acted justly towards children and encouraged both sides in games and competitions.[75] Despite the greatness of his personality, he would let his children ride on his shoulders,[76] and would let the children of others do the same.[77] It happened many times that a child would urinate on his lap, but he would not allow the infant to be taken from his arms, drawing attention instead to the ill effect of stopping the child in the middle of his urine.[78] He treated girls very lovingly,[79] and this, to a large extent, helped to change the attitude of the people of that time towards their female offspring. He would talk respectfully to children[80] and greet them.[81]

2.4. The Way Imam 'Alī and Ḥaḍrat Fātima Lived

The Imams followed the example of the Prophet in the way they treated their children. Imām 'Alī was in charge of supplying water, firewood, sweeping and cleaning, and his wife, Ḥaḍrat Fātima, prepared flour and dough and baked bread.[82] In addition to this cooperative partnership, Imām 'Alī consulted Fātima on the affairs of the house and other important matters,[83] and she humbly concurred.[84] This couple, from whose family the great leaders of God were born, lived in a small house with simple items of the status of the poorer people of the time.[85]

The members of this family are Imām 'Alī, described in the Qur'ān as the Prophet's soul; Fātima, whom the Prophet called the best of women; Ḥasan and Ḥusayn, described as the Prophet's spiritual children in the Qur'ān[86] and, according to the Prophet, are the foremost youths of heaven; and Zeinab and Umm Kulthūm, who were the messengers of the epic of Karbala.[87] The Qur'ān has much praise for this family,[88] and it illustrates the finest model of general conduct.

Their emotional relationships were very strong. Fātima Zahrā told Salman of her love for 'Alī,[89] and she said to 'Alī himself:

> "I would lay down my life to protect you! I will always be with you for better or worse, no matter what."[90]

And 'Alī, who reciprocated her love, said upon her demise :

> "I have become restless, and grieve at night in anticipation of being with you in the next life."[91]

Throughout their lives together, they expressed affection for each other and often made merry.[92] The following words of Imām 'Alī show the depth of the healthy emotional relationship between them:

> "I swear to God! I have never made Fātima angry or forced her to do anything. Neither has she made me angry, and she has never denied my authority. Whenever I have looked upon her, worry and sadness have vanished from my heart."[93]

Fātima empathised with her husband in times of hardship and was patient and understanding, and would not make any unreasonable demands of him.[94]

The family was exemplary in the raising of their children. Fātima often sacrificed her own material needs for the sake of the children, and did her utmost to take care of them.[95] She showed them respect and would speak to them lovingly with such words as: "The sight of my eyes and the fruit of my heart."[96] She monitored all the moves and behaviour of the children and noted their absence.[97] Fātima and 'Alī took time to play with the children,[98] and despite all the social responsibilities, never failed to attend to the happiness and joy of their children. Not only did 'Alī play with his own children, but he would also play with the children[99] of others and with orphans, and would ensure fairness amongst them. This was while he ruled a great country.

The religious upbringing up the children, prayer and spirituality all received attention.[100] Altruism within the family and towards others was very important to them, so much that in surah *al-Insān* God rates it highly in this and the next world:

> *And feed the needy wretch, the orphan and the prisoner, for love of Him, (saying): We feed you, for the sake of Allāh only. We wish for no reward nor thanks from you.*[101]

Fātima Zahrā gave priority to others in her prayers and taught her children to do this as well.[102] For a woman, the most important night of her life is her wedding night, and the clothes and ornaments she wears for this are integral, but on the night of her wedding, she gave her new dress to a poor person who had come to her door and asked for old clothes.[103] In this she guides all women to spiritual joy and happiness.

2.5. The Family Practice of the Other Imams

The Imams are useful, exalted exemplars of family life. They regarded the personalities of their wives highly and gave them a great deal of credit.[104] In economic matters, they respect their independence,[105] and they helped them in spiritual matters.[106] The principle of tolerance towards the wife among the Imams was so great that the wives of some of them were provoked by opponents to assassinate them.[107] This shows that despite the incompatibility of their wives, they continued to treat them with tolerance. They paid attention to their ornaments and those of the family and the decoration of the house if requested by the family.[108] They would become intimate with, talk to, eat with and entertain those around them, both young and old.[109] They patiently endured the problems of life, and even in big issues, such as the death of a child due to the negligence of the other, showed so much patience that all would be surprised.[110] In treating their children, their principle was to show love and respect; they played with them, accepted them, gave them freedom and at the same time monitored them, ensured justice among them, avoided punishment and blame, and, in general, were gentle and tolerant with them.[111] The Imams, despite their sensitivity to religious matters, reformed the people, including their families, by their behaviour and attitudes,[112] while avoiding commands, direct prohibition or violent retribution in the case of mistakes by their family members.[113]

Great emphasis has been put in the verses of the Qur'ān and words of the Imams on the principle of respect for the father and mother and their important influence on the family, as already mentioned. The way the Prophet and his household (Ahl al-Bayt) treated their parents contains interesting lessons. The Prophet lost his parents while he was still a child. However, he showed the utmost respect to the children of his foster parents and put his clothes beneath their feet (so that they could sit on them).[114] Imām Sajjād avoided eating with his mother, out of fear that he might take a piece of the food that she may have wanted to take first, and thereby upset her.[115] When he saw someone who leaned on his father's arm while walking, without showing the necessary respect, he expressed dissatisfaction, and would not thenceforth talk to that person.[116]

3. The General Outline of the Family System in Islām

The discussions in this book show that the teachings of Islām regarding the family and all its psychological aspects contain both firm rules and good advice, since the teachings cover all aspects of the functions and relationships of individuals within the family and their rights and obligations. Therefore, one can infer from the teachings of Islām a comprehensive theory on the psychological aspects of the family. Here, we briefly provide some evidence of this.

3.1. The Comprehensiveness of Islām's View of the Family

This can be clarified from Islām's views of the basic issues regarding the family, as explained below.

The teachings of Islām consider that the nature of the family has a certain definition that consists of at least a man and a woman, but although the nuclear family is not considered the full domain of the family various definitions of the family are recognised. Islām allocates certain responsibilities to the first level of relatives of the family, from the grandparents to their grandchildren. Concerning the goals of the family, the teachings of Islām emphasise all aspects from the divine to the human which concern this world and the next. The principal values of the family are not limited to worldly life, for they include individual and social needs and relationship of the family members in respect of religious values.

The teachings of Islām have advice on family relationships and roles, verbal and nonverbal communication, and both emotional and sexual needs. There is much about the relationship of the husband and wife and of that between the parents and the children. Some of this has to do with the distribution of authority within the family, management, decision-making, and the various boundaries between family members. Also, Islām provides ideological, moral and behavioural guidelines for improving the efficiency of the family.

These teachings also contain a lot of guidance concerning the boundaries between the family members and others. The relationships with other relatives are more open that those with others. Islām emphasises the importance of relationships for the health and balance of the family, and disparages cutting them off or violating their boundaries. In this respect there are incentives, or occasionally corrective measures, to encourage people to protect these relationships.

The financial legislation of Islām allows for the material support of all members of the family, including the grandparents and grandchildren. This has a special effect on the family members and their relationships, as already mentioned.

The teachings of Islām also provide advice for the prevention of problems within the family, and for their solution, should they occur. Sometimes various steps are elucidated, and the legal rulings of Islām thereby provide effective solutions for families with severe problems, and provide for the health, balance and efficiency of the family as much as possible. In case of divorce, the negative emotional impact is reduced as much as possible.

3.2. The Most Important Health Strategies and the Appropriate Functioning of the Family in Islām

In order to have an effective family in which the entire family will fulfil the roles intended by Islām, certain characteristics and conditions should be taken into consideration. Considering the objectives of Islām in the formation of the family, including the development of religiosity and an understanding of the role of the divine prophets and their successors can help make the family more effective. Families that are not strong enough in these aspects will partly fail to realise the objectives Islām has defined for the family. Particular religious responsibilities relate to this dimension of values.

Justice is one of the vital concepts in the family system. In family therapy, the issue of justice, that is, the just distribution of fruits of happiness, is a central issue. Justice is realized through the expression of love, gratitude, respect for individual dignity, emotional security, and generally in all material and spiritual matters. For example, the parents, through their love and care, and their material and financial endeavours, help the children to develop. The children help by expressing their happiness, flourishing and establishing positive affections, and later by expressing gratitude, respect and perhaps financial help. Justice in human relationships through benevolent acts is a prerequisite for a balanced life. According to the idea of justice, one should acknowledge the views and feelings of all the family concerning their part in family life.[117] Justice is the foundation of all human systems,[118] and means putting everything in its proper place[119] to form a balanced equilibrium, but is not necessarily an equal investment. For how can one make up for the investment of the parents? As mentioned in the study of the duties of the children towards the parents, the work of the parents far outweighs anything the children can do for them. Indeed, Islām advocates a balanced approach that may be generalised as recognising the rights of family members and avoiding violating them. The teachings of Islām in fact focus on a finer interpretation of justice that emanates from clemency, which is far more effective.

Clemency, or compassion, involves the mild treatment of others, keeping good company and avoiding harsh or crude behaviour,[120] and contributes more than anything else to a good family. It is a kind of forbearance that expresses itself in mild and kindly behaviour.[121] The divine religious leaders have accentuated the concept of compassion between the husband and wife. The man is recommended to be compassionate towards his wife in all circumstances.[122] General examples have been given, such as the woman having been given in trust to the man,[123] that the happiness of the woman lies with the man,[124] and that the woman is in a weaker position and should receive special consideration.[125] In a Ḥadīth, the Prophet says:

> "I have been advised so much about women that I think perhaps divorcing a woman is not proper unless she commits a very bad thing publicly."[126]

This and similar hadiths from the Prophet's Household show that Islām has expects very much from the man in terms of his compassion towards and kind treatment of his wife. Clemency within the family requires that certain cognitive and affective grounds should exist, especially regarding the husband and wife. As these things have been covered throughout this study, particularly in Chapter 2, it will suffice to make here only a brief reference. Cognitively, it is important that the husband and wife attend to each other's psychological and gender differences, so that they know each other's characteristics and acknowledge them in the way they treat each other. They each come from different family backgrounds, with their own values and personality. By considering to their different histories and attempting to make them gradually compatible is another example of clemency. Also, comprehending the psychological differences of the parents and children is a part of the compassion between family members.Establishing positive affective relationships manifested by expressions of love, and an unconditional positive attentiveness to each other, are the foundations of compassion.

Compassion manifests as tolerance and patience if one's spouse is in a bad temper,[127] the overlooking of and forbearance of any unreasonable behaviour,[128] keeping good company,[129] kindness,[130] avoiding force and making someone angry,[131] upsetting one's wife,[132] helping one's wife to run the household affairs,[133] and collaborating with her in her interests and preferences.[134] It sometimes happens that, perhaps due to the man's treatment of his wife, she may not be able to deal with her husband properly, and as a result he may fail to pay attention to her. If this happens, forbearance and compassion are the best possible remedies, because if the man wants to fully restore his rights, he will often go too far and violate those of the wife.[135]

The wife is also advised to treat her husband as compassionately as possible, sometimes relinquishing minor rights[136] in order to maintain the family coherence and function properly. In Islamic texts, after fulfilling the divine religious duties, no higher responsibility has been defined for women than those they have towards their husbands.[137] Interestingly, fulfilling these responsibilities is regarded as equal to *jihād* for God.[138] Moreover, from the psychological point of view, a woman makes the most emotional investment in her husband, since he is the most important person for her.[139] An example of the wife's compassion is to fulfil her husband's affective needs at all times, even if he has failed to fulfil all her rights.[140] She has to try to function harmoniously with him and even have his consent in religious acts such as making religious vows, giving alms and fasting on recommended occasions.[141] She should serve her husband at home,[142] try to resolve disputes as soon as possible,[143] never annoy him, treat him mildly and simply,[144] and accept his excuses.[145] Flexibility within the family can be explained by the concept of compassion, and helps the family members to respond to each other through dialogue and interaction. On the other hand, a strict and inflexible family structure, which usually involves domination, subjugation and ensuing conflict, will only lead to problems and damage.[146]

Compassion between parents and children means that parents should treat their children mildly, without force,[147] and avoid violence.[148] Sometimes, they should pay more attention to some of the children[149] and treat them equitably, overlooking their mistakes.[150] Generally speaking, the parents should make efforts to ensure that their relationship with their children, and the relationships the children have with each other, do no result in harshness or separation.[151] Children should treat their parents respectfully,[152] and even if the parents have treated them unjustly, continue to behave properly towards them.[153] Respect for the parents is so important that the children should always avoid treating their parents harshly, and even if there is disagreement on important things such as religious matters, they should continue to treat them well without severing the relationships.[154]

3.3. A Final Word

From the discussions in this chapter, one can infer an outline of the ideal family. In the perfect family there is the proper observance of hierarchy, and the parents have authority over the children, and the children, even throughout adulthood, maintain a special respect for the parents. The husband and wife recognise the husband's authority, and in certain cases the woman accepts that the man has the final decision. Marital roles are performed well and there is friendship and love between the husband and wife. The parents are aware of their duties, which they diligently fulfil. According to what was said regarding the family, in an ideal family environment the requirements of ḥijāb, and the various relationship boundaries within the home and with others are observed. There is a commitment to piety and the avoidance of sins such as banned (*harām*) singing and music, drinking alcohol, gossip, slander, and moral vices such as vanity and jealousy. Indeed, errors may occur, but it is presupposed that piety should be observed. Justice should prevail so that the rights of each individual are considered.

As mentioned, the foremost Islamic principle for member of the family is compassion towards each other. One should be attentive to relatives, especially the parents of the husband and wife, while interaction and social support between the relatives is encouraged. An equality and similarity of the social levels of the husband and wife are an important foundation for the ideal family. There may be problems or differences in the ideal family, but boundaries are not violated in times of dispute, and after the emotions subside, the members of the family will try to reform and make up for weaknesses and inappropriate behaviour. Figure 3 below shows an outline of the ideal family.

Apparently, the ideal family has more value than an effective or healthy family. Based on such factors as problem-solving strategies, the emotional atmosphere of the family, adaptability to change in the various stages of family life, balance and distance in family relations, and effective inter-generation boundaries, family therapists make a distinction between the effective family and the disordered family.[155] In a parallel manner, all these attributes of the ideal family can be accordingly found in Islām. In addition, stable religious beliefs, justice-centeredness and compassion are three core concepts that apply to the ideal family according to Islām. It is evident that the formation of the family in Islām requires particular values and a special structure.

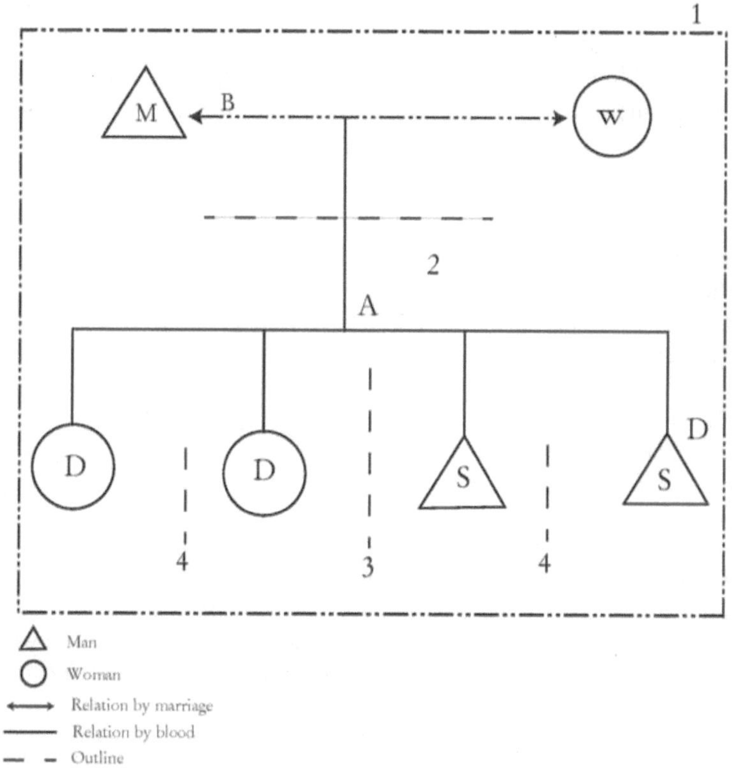

Boundaries within the family:

1. The entire family has a boundary which is neither completely open nor closed, but which monitors the entry of individuals into the family environment, particularly those who are not closely related.
2. There is a flexible boundary between the husband and wife, whereby they benefit from a special physical and mental space into which at certain times others need permission to enter.
3. The boundary between the male and female children, despite being

open, is subject to restrictions which include the need for special physical spaces in the house for girls and boys.
4. There is a boundary between two male or two female children, but which has fewer limitations than the boundary between the girls and the boys, and requires separate beds for each boy and girl.

Hierarchy within the family:

A. The husband and wife occupy the highest level of the family.
B. The man has more authority than the woman.
C. The children in the family, both male and female, are at the same level, although the elder male children have more authority in certain cases.

Notes

1. See jurisprudential books and verses of the Qur'ān, such as 4:4.
2. Al-Kulaynī, *Furū' Kāfī,* vol. 5, p. 378.
3. Muṭahharī, Murtaḍā, *Niẓām Huqūq Zan dar Islām*, p. 238.
4. Ibid., p. 235.
5. Ibid., pp. 232-234.
6. Al-Ḥurr al-'Āmilī, *Wasā'il al-Shī'a*, vol. 15, ch. 11, Ḥadīth 9.
7. Majlisī, *Biḥār al-Anwār*, vol. 103, p. 349.
8. Al-Ḥurr al-'Āmilī, *Wasā'il al-Shī'a*, vol. 15, p. 22.
9. Ibid.
10. Al-Kulaynī, *Furū' al-Kāfī,* vol. 5, p. 378.
11. Al-Ḥurr al-'Āmilī, *Wasā'il al-Shī'a*, vol. 15, p. 2.
12. Siddīq-Awra'ī, *Jāmi'i Shināsī-yi Masā'il Ijtimā'ī Javānān*, p. 111.
13. According to a narration, Imām 'Alī (as) said: "I do not want the dowry to be less than ten dirhams, as it will be similar to that paid for adultery" (Al-Ḥurr al-'Āmilī, *Wasā'il al-Shī'a*, vol. 15, p. 11).
14. Majlisī, *Biḥār al-Anwār*, vol. 100, p. 353.
15. Al-Ḥurr al-'Āmilī, *Wasā'il al-Shī'a*, vol. 15, p. 10.
16. Al-Kulaynī, *Furū' al-Kāfī,* vol. 5, p. 324.
17. Sharaf al-Dīn, Sayyid Ḥusayn, Tabyīn Jāmi'i Shinākhtī-yi Mahriyyeh, pp. 302-371.
18. Muḥsinī, Manūchihr, et al, *Izdivāj va Khānivādih dar Iran*, pp. 319, 322.
19. Sharaf al-Dīn, Sayyid Ḥusayn, Tabyīn Jāmi'i Shinākhtī-yi Mahriyyeh, pp. 68-318.
20. Al-Ḥurr al-'Āmilī, *Wasā'il al-Shī'a*, vol. 15, p. 237.
21. Lodge them where ye dwell, according to your wealth, Qur'ān 65:6.

22. Al-Ḥurr al- milī, *Wasā'il al-Shī'a*, vol. 15, p. 224, Ḥadīth 5.
23. To men is allotted what they earn, and to women what they earn, Qur'ān 4:32.
24. Nūrī, *Mustadrak al-Wasā'il*, ch. 62,Ḥadīth 3.
25. Qur'ān 4:11, 12, 176.
26. *Nahj al-Balāghah*, Letter 45.
27. Kadīvar, Parvīn, *Ravānshināsī-yi Tarbiyatī* , p. 128.
28. Hergenhahn, B. R., et al, *Introduction to the Theories of Learning*, p. 432.
29. *Nahj al-Balāghah*, Letter 45.
30. Qur'ān 60:4.
31. Ye have indeed in the Messenger of Allāh a beautiful pattern (of conduct) for anyone whose hope is in Allāh and the Final Day, and remembereth Allāh much, Qur'ān 33:21.
32. *Nahj al-Balāghah*, Sermon 160.
33. And lo! thou art of a tremendous nature, Qur'ān 68:4.
34. And Allāh only wishes to remove all abomination from you, ye Members of the Family, and to make you pure and spotless, Qur'ān 33:33; and Your companion is neither astray, nor is being misled, Nor doth he speak of (his own) desire, 53:2-3.
35. Say: "Come! let us gather together our sons and your sons, our women and your women, ourselves and yourselves: then let us earnestly pray and invoke the curse of Allāh on those who lie," Qur'ān 3:61.
36. Muḥammadī-Reyshahrī, Muḥammad, *Ahl al-Bayt dar Qur'ān va Ḥadīth.*
37. *Nahj al-Balāghah*, Sermons 97 & 160.
38. Al-Ḥurr al-'Āmilī, *Wasā'il al-Shī'a*, vol. 14, p. 3.
39. Ibid., p. 117.
40. Nūrī, *Mustadrak al-Wasā'il*, vol. 14, p. 187.
41. 'Abdūs, *Sīrih -yi Imāmān Shī'a*, pp. 26, 27.
42. Majlisī, *Biḥār al-Anwār*, vol. 43, p. 105.
43. Al-Kulaynī, *Kāfī*, vol. 1, p. 461.
44. The marriages of the Prophet, Imams 'Alī (as), Ḥasan, Ḥusayn and all their children confirm that they married women of different social and economic classes ('Abdūs, Sīrih -yi Imāmān Shī'a, pp. 6-17). Another example is the Prophet's marriage to Zeinab, the former wife of his adopted son, which, according to verses in the Qur'ān (33:37, 38), was done in order to facilitate marriage.
45. Jubīr's marriage is one such example, which was done upon the Prophet's advice. (Al-Kulaynī, *Kāfī*, vol. 5, p. 347).
46. Ma'rūf al-Ḥasanī, *Zindigī Davāzdah Imām*, pp. 83-84.

47. Al-Kulaynī, *Furū' Kāfī*, vol. 6, pp. 448, 476.
48. Majlisī, *Biḥār al-Anwār*, vol. 43, pp. 106, 115. Ma'rūf al-Ḥasanī, Zindigī Davāzdah Imām.
49. Qur'ān 66.1
50. Qur'ān 66.4.
51. Muslim ibn al-Hajjāj al-Qushayrī, *Saḥīḥ Muslim bi Sharḥ al-Nawawi*, vol. 4, p. 160.
52. Sadūq, *Man lā yahḍaruh al-Faqīh*, vol. 3, p. 425.
53. For example, on the occasion of *Hajjat al-Widā'*, he allocated each day and night to one of his wives (Tahdhīb, vol. 2, p. 89), and even during illness visited all his wives (ibid., vol. 3, p. 121).
54. 'Ulwān, 'Abdullāh Nāsiḥ, *Ta'addud al-Zawjāt fī al-Islām*, pp. 61, 75, 81, 82, 85. In addition, some verses of the Qur'ān also mention this matter, including 33:28-29 and 66.1-4.
55. Tabātabā'ī, Muḥammad-Ḥusayn, *Sunan al-Nabī*, p. 98; Majlisī, *Biḥār al-Anwār*, vol. 100, p. 353.
56. Dilshād Tehranī, Mustafā, *Sīrih-yi Nabavī*, pp. 15, 37.
57. Qur'ān 3:159.
58. It is part of the Mercy of Allāh thatthou dost deal gently with them. And had you been severe or harsh-hearted, they would have broken away from about you, Qur'ān 3:159.
59. Dilshād Tehranī, *Sīrih-yi Nabavī*, pp. 15-22.
60. But lower thy wings (in gentleness) to the believers, Qur'ān 15:88; Tabātabā'ī, *Tafsīr al-Mīzān*, vol. 15, p. 328.
61. Hold to forgiveness, comand what is right, but turn away from the ignorant [i.e. do not punish them], Qur'ān 7:199 is witness to this.
62. Muttaqī-Hindī, *Kanz al-'Ummāl*, vol. 3, p. 33.
63. Tabātabā'ī, *Sunan al-Nabī*, p. 35.
64. Ibid., p. 53.
65. Ibid., pp. 41, 73.
66. Ibid., pp. 48, 90-97.
67. Ibid., pp. 98-99.
68. Ibid., pp. 96, 146, 147.
69. Ibid., p. 150.
70. Qur'ān 7:27, 35, 53.
71. Majlisī, *Biḥār al-Anwār*, vol. 104, p. 99.
72. Ḥusaynīzādih, Sayyid 'Alī , Sīreh-yi Tarbiyatī-yi Payāmbar va Ahl al-Bayt, vol. 1, p. 79.
73. Ibid., p. 110.

74. Majlisī, *Biḥār al-Anwār*, vol. 42, p. 384.
75. Ḥusaynīzādih, Sīreh-yi *Tarbiyatī-yi Payāmbar va Ahl al-Bayt*, p. 109.
76. Majlisī, *Biḥār al-Anwār*, vol. 42, p. 384.
77. Ḥusaynīzādih, Sīreh-yi Tarbiyatī-yi Payāmbar va Ahl al-Bayt, p. 111.
78. Ibid., p. 105.
79. Al-Ḥurr al-'Āmilī, *Wasā'il al-Shī'a*, vol. 15, p. 100.
80. Majlisī, *Biḥār al-Anwār*, vol. 37, p. 71.
81. Tabātabā'ī, *Sunan al-Nabī*, p. 42.
82. Al-Ḥurr al-'Āmilī, *Wasā'il al-Shī'a*, vol. 14, ch. 124.
83. Dashtī, Muḥammad, *Nahj al-Ḥayāt*, p. 164-167.
84. For example, in an important matter Ḥaḍrat Fātima tells Imām 'Alī : "The house is your house and I am your wife. Do whatever you want." Majlisī, *Biḥār al-Anwār*, vol. 44, p. 70.
85. Ma'rūf al-Ḥasanī, Zindigī Davāzdah Imām, p. 85.
86. In Qur'ān 3:61, the word "*anfusanā*" is used in the sense of "our soul."
87. Sadūq, *Man lā yahḍaruh al-Faqīh*, vol. 4, p. 420.
88. The verse known as *tathīr* and the surahs *al-Kawthar*, *al-'Insān* and *al-'Aḥzāb*.
89. Dashtī, Muḥammad, *Nahj al-Ḥayāt*, p. 145.
90. Ibid., p. 147.
91. *Nahj al-Balāghah*, Sermon 202.
92. Nīlīpūr, Mehdī, *Farhang Fātimiyyah* , pp. 187 and 189.
93. Ibid., p. 186.
94. Dashtī, *Nahj al-Ḥayāt*, p. 22.
95. For example, it has frequently been said that Fātima often remained hungry in order to give her food to her children (Nīlīpūr, Mehdī, *Farhang Fātimiyyah* , pp. 157-158).
96. Ibid., p. 180.
97. Ansārī, 'Udhrā, *Jilvihā-yi Raftārī-yi Ḥaḍrat Zahrā* , p. 37.
98. Ibid.
99. Majlisī, *Biḥār al-Anwār*, vol. 41, p. 52.
100. Nīlīpūr, Mehdī, *Farhang Fātimiyyah* , pp. 76, 181-182.
101. Qur'ān 76:8-9.
102. Muḥammadī-Reyshahrī, *Ahl al-Bayt dar Qur'ān va Ḥadīth*, vol. 1, p. 398.
103. Nīlīpūr, Mehdī, *Farhang Fātimiyyah* , pp. 157-158.
104. 'Abdūs, Sīrih -yi Imāmān Shī'a, vol. 2, p. 8.
105. Al-Kulaynī, *Kāfī*, vol. 6, p. 480.
106. Ibid., vol. 2, p. 487.

107. Imām Ḥasan was poisoned by his wife, Ja'dah, and Imām Jawād by his wife, Umm-al-Faḍl (*The Life of the Twelve Imams*, vol. 1, p. 610, vol. 2, p. 467).
108. Al-Kulaynī, *Kāfī*, vol. 6, pp. 448, 475, 480.
109. Muḥammadī-Reyshahrī, *Ahl al-Bayt dar Qur'ān va Ḥadīth*, p. 459.
110. Evidence for this is Imām Sādiq's reaction to the sudden death of his child (*Ahl al-Bayt dar Qur'ān va Ḥadīth*, p. 456).
111. Ḥusaynīzādih, Sīreh-yi Tarbiyatī-yi Payāmbar va Ahl al-Bayt, vol. 1, pp. 77-137; Karīmīniyā, Muḥammad 'Alī , *Tarbiyat Ijtimā'ī, Raftārhā-yi Ijtimā'ī Pīshvāyān Islām* , pp. 93-118.
112. Karīmīniyā, *Tarbiyat Ijtimā'ī, Raftārhā-yi Ijtimā'ī Pīshvāyān Islām*, pp. 93-118.
113. In reply to those who asked him to guide his family on good and bad, Imām Reḍā said: "Violence is hidden beneath advice" (Ḥusaynīzādih, Sīreh-yi Tarbiyatī-yi Payāmbar va Ahl al-Bayt, vol. 1, p. 138).
114. Tabrisī, Faḍl ibn Ḥasan, *A'lām al-Warā*, p. 120.
115. Tabrisī, Abū-Nasr, *Makārim al-Akhlāq*, p. 221.
116. Al-Kulaynī, *Usūl Kāfī*, vol. 4, p. 50.
117. Siemon, *Key Concepts and Theories in Family Therapy*, p. 277.
118. Majlisī, *Biḥār al-Anwār*, vol. 78, p. 83.
119. *Nahj al-Balāghah*, Aphorism 437.
120. Majlisī, *Biḥār al-Anwār*, vol. 72, p. 438; vol. 84, p. 31.
121. Al-Ḥurr al-'Āmilī, *Wasā'il al-Shī'a*, vol. 14, p. 124.
122. Ibid., p. 111; Nūrī, *Mustadrak al-Wasā'il*, vol. 2, p. 551.
123. Imām 'Alī (as) said: "Inna hunn awwan 'indakum."
124. Al-Ḥurr al-'Āmilī, *Wasā'il al-Shī'a*, vol. 14, p. 122.
125. Ibid., p. 124.
126. Ibid., p. 121.
127. Ibid., p. 124.
128. Ibid., p. 121.
129. Ibid., p. 120.
130. Ibid., p. 122.
131. Nūrī, *Mustadrak al-Wasā'il*, vol. 15, p. 116.
132. Ibid., p. 250; Al-Ḥurr al-'Āmilī, *Wasā'il al-Shī'a*, vol. 15, p. 116.
133. Majlisī, *Biḥār al-Anwār*, vol. 101, p. 132.
134. Al-Ḥurr al-'Āmilī, *Wasā'il al-Shī'a*, vol. 15, p. 250.
135. This can be inferred from a Ḥadīth in Majlisī, *Biḥār al-Anwār*, vol. 71, p. 139.
136. This is supported by Qur'ān 4:128, which says: If a wife fears cruelty or desertion on her husband's part, there is no blame on them if they arrange an amicable settlement between themselves; and such settlement is best.

137. Al-Ḥurr al-'Āmilī, *Wasā'il al-Shī'a*, vol. 14, pp. 112, 126.
138. Ibid., p. 116.
139. Al-Kulaynī, *Furū' Kāfī*, vol. 5, p. 506.
140. Ibid., p. 112.
141. Al-Ḥurr al-'Āmilī, *Wasā'il al-Shī'a*, vol. 14, p. 112.
142. Ibid., p. 123.
143. Ibid., p. 116.
144. Ibid., p. 15.
145. Ibid., p. 111.
146. Mūsavī, Ashraf al-Sādāt, 'Amalkard Nizām Khānivādih va Bihdāsht Ravānī-yi A'zā-yi Khānivādih', in *Andīshih va Raftār Journal*, vol. 6, issues 2, 3, p. 92.
147. Farīd Tunikābunī, *al-Ḥadīth*, vol. 3, p. 110.
148. Al-Ḥurr al-'Āmilī, *Wasā'il al-Shī'a*, vol. 15, p. 200.
149. Farīd Tunikābunī, *al-Ḥadīth*, vol. 3, p. 67.
150. Al-Ḥurr al-'Āmilī, *Wasā'il al-Shī'a*, vol. 15, p. 200.
151. Ibid., p. 199.
152. Ibid., pp. 217 and 220.
153. Ibid., p. 217.
154. But if they strive with thee to make thee ascribe unto Me as partner that of which thou hast no knowledge, then obey them not. Consort with them in the world kindly, Qur'ān 31:15.
155. Siemon, F. B., *Key Concepts and Theories in Family Therapy*, p. 157.

BIBLIOGRAPHY

'Abdūs, Muḥammad Taqī and Muḥammad Muḥammadī Ishtihārdī, *Bīst Asl az Usūl Akhlāqī-yi Imāmān* (Qum: Daftar Tablīghāt Islāmī, 1377 A.H).

'Abdūs, Muḥammad Taqī, *Sīrih -yi Imāmān Shī'a*, 3rd impression (Qum: Daftar Tablīghāt Islāmī, 1375 A.H).

Ackner, R.A., *Selection of Russell's Thoughts, Psychology of Marital Relations*, translated by 'Abd al_Raḥīm Āgāhī (Tehran: Amīr Publications, 1370 A.H).

Adams, Paul et al, *Psychology of Fatherless Children* (*Ravānshināsī-yi* Kūdakān Mahrūm az pidar), translated by Khusru Bāqirī and Maḥmūd Attārān (Tehran: Tarbiyat Publications,1373 A.H).

Aḥmadī Abharī, 'Alī , 'Naqsh Imān va I'tiqād Madhabī dar Darmān Bīmārīhā', in *Andīshih va Raftār Quarterly*, vol. 3, Append. 9 and 10, (1376 A.H).

Aḥmadī, Dhikrullāh, *Nahād Āqilih dar Huqūq Kaifarī-yi Islām* (Tehran: Mīzān Publications, 1381 A.H).

Aḥmadī, Muḥammad Reḍā, 'Naqsh Silih-yi Rahim dar Bihdāsht Ravānī', *Ma'arifat*, Vol. 10, No. 46 (1381 A.H).

Aḥmadī, Sayyid Aḥmad, *Ravānshināsī-yi Nawjavānān va Javānān* (Isfahān: Termeh, Mash'al Publications, 1371 A.H).

'Akk, Khalid 'Abd al-Raḥmān, *Ādāb al-Ḥayāt al-Zawjiyyah fī Ḍaw' al-Kitāb wa al-Sunnah* (Beirut: Dār al- Ma'arifah, 1997).

________________ , *Binā' al-Usrah al- Muslima fī Ḍaw' al- Kitab wa al-Sunnah*, (Beirut:Dār al- Ma'rifah, 1998).

Al-Ansārī, al-Shaikh Murtaḍā, *Kitāb al-Makāsib* (Beirut: Mu'assasah al-Nu'mān, 1990).

'Arūsī al-Ḥuwaizī, 'Abd 'Alī ibn Jumu'a, *Nūr al-Thaqalain*, Edited by Sayyid Hāshim Rasūlī Maḥallātī (Qum: Ismā'īlīān Publications, 1370 A.H).

Fayḍ al-Kāshānī, Muḥsin, *al-Maḥajja al-Bayḍā' fī Tahdhīb al-'Iḥyā'* (Beirut: Nashr A'lamī li'l Maṭbū'āt, 1983).

Al-Ḥurr al-'Āmilī, Muḥammad ibn Ḥasan, *Wasā'il al-Shī'a*, edited by 'Abd al- Raḥīm Rabbānī Shīrāzī (Beirut: Dār 'Iḥyā' al-Turāth al-'Arabī, 1991).

Al-Kulaynī, Muḥammad ibn Ya'qūb, *Usūl al-Kāfī*, translated by Sayyid Javād Mustafavī (Tehran: Farhang Ahl Bayt Publications, n.d.).

______________, *Al-Kāfī* (Beirut: Dār al- Aḍwā', 1992 A.H).

Al-Tūsī, Muḥammad ibn Ḥasan, *Malādh al-Akhyār fī Fahm Tahdhīb al-Akhbār*, (Qum: Nashr Maktabah Ayatullāh al-Mar'ashī al- Najafī, 1406 A.H).

Al-Suyūtī, Jalāl al-Dīn, *al-Durr al-Manthūr* (Qum: Nashr Maktabah Ayatullāh al-Mar'ashī al- Najafī, 1404 A.H).

'Alwān, 'Abdullāh Nāsiḥ, *Ta'addud al-Zawjāt fī al-Islām* (Beirut: Dār al-Islām, 1988).

Amānī, Mehdī, *Jam'īyyat Shināsī-yi 'Umūmī Iran* (Tehran: Samt, 1380 A.H).

__________, *Mabānī-yi Jam'īyyat Shināsī* (Tehran: Samt, 1377 A.H).

Āmidī, 'Abd al-Vāhid, *Ghurar al-Ḥikam wa Durar al- Kalim* (Qum: Daftar Tablīghāt Islāmī, 1366A.H).

Amīnī, 'Abd al-Ḥusayn, *Al-Ghadīr fī al-Kitāb wa al-Sunna wa al-Adab* (Tehran: Dār al- Kutub al- Islāmīyyah, 1366 A.H).

Amīnī, Ibrāhīm, *Intikhāb Hamsar*, (Sāzemān Tablīghāt Islāmī, 1380A.H).

Ansārī, Murtaḍā, *Kitab al- Makāsib*, (Beirut: Mu'assasah al-Nu'mān, 1990).

Ansārī, 'Udhrā, *Jilvihāyi Raftārī-yi Ḥaḍrat Zahrā* (Qum: Daftar Tablīghāt Islāmī, 1372 A.H).

Ansāriān, Ḥusayn, *Niẓām Khānivādih dar Islām* (Qum: Umm Abīhā Publications, 1376 A.H).

A'rāfī, 'Alī -Reḍā, *Arā' Dānishmandān Musalmān dar T'alīm va Tarbiyat va Mabānī-yi Ān*, vol. 1 (Qum: Daftar Hamkārī Ḥawzah va Dānishgāh, 1377 A.H).

Argyle, Michael, *The Psychology of Happiness*, translated by Mas'ūd Gawharī et al (Isfahān: Jahād Dānishgāhī, 1382.A.H).

Askarī, Ḥusayn, *Naqsh Bihdāsht Ravān dar Izdivāj* (Tehran: Guftigū Publications, 1380 A.H).

Ayman, R. and Cemens, M. *Leadership: Theory and Research*, (Academe Press Inc. 1992)

āzād, Paimān, *Zīndigī bidūni Iḥsās Gunāh* (Tehran: Rawshanā'ī Publications, 1377 A.H).

Ādharbayjān, Mas'ūd et al, *Ravānshināsī-yi Ijtimā'ī ba Nigāhī be Manābi' Islāmī* (Qum: Pazhūhishkadih Ḥawzah va Dānishgāh and Samt, 1382 A.H)

Bābā Tāhir, *Du Baitīhā-yi Bābā Tāhir* (Tehran: Bāqirul 'Ulūm Publications, 1369 A.H).

Baḥrānī, Sayyid Hāshim, *al-Burhān fī Tafsīr al-Qur'ān*, vol.5 (Beirut: Mu'assasah al-A'lamī li al-Matbū'āt, 1999).

Banī Asadī, Ḥasan, *Barrasī-yi 'Avamil Mu'aththir Ijtemā'aī-Fardī dar Zawj-hā-yi Sāzigār va Nāsāzigār dar Shahr Kirmān*, M.A. Thesis, Tarbiat Mudarris University, 1375 A.H.

Banī-Hāshimī, Sayyid Muḥammad Ḥasan, *Tawziḥ al-Masā'il Marāji'* (Qum: Dater Intishārāt Islāmī, 1381 A.H).

Bānkīpūr Fard, Amīr Ḥusayn, 'Tahlīlī bar Ravābit Dukhtarān va Pisarān Dānishjū', in *Majmū'i-yi Maqālāt Hamandīshī-yi Barrasī-yi Masā'il va Mushkilāt Zanān* (Qum: Daftar Mutāli'at va Taḥqīqāt Zanān, 1380A.H).

Barker, Philip, *Basic Family Therapy* (Khānivādih Darmānī-yi Payih), translated by Muḥsin Dihqānī and Zuhrih Dihqānī (Tehran: Rushd Publications, 1375 A.H).

Baron, R. and Byrne, D. (1997) *Social Psychology*. Massachusetts: Viacom.

Bātinī, Muḥammad Reḍā, *Contemporary English-Farsi Dictionary* (Tehran: Farhang Mu'asir Publications, 1374 A.H).

Bayhaqī, Aḥmad ibn al-Ḥusayn, *al-Sunan al-Kubrā* (Beirut: Dar al-Ma'rifah, 1406 A.H).

Bernstein, F.C., *Methods of Treatment of Marital Problems* (Ravish-ha-yi Darmānī Mushkilāt Zanāshū'ī), translated by Ḥasan Tuzandihjānī and Nasrīn Kamālpūr (Mashhad: Marandīz Publications, 1380 A.H).

__________, *Marriage Therapy*, (Izdivāj Darmānī), translated by Ḥasan Pūrabedī Nā'īnī and Ghulām Reḍā Munshi'ī (Tehran: Rushd Publications, 1380 A.H).

Bīriyā, Nāsir, et al, *Rushd bā Nigarish bi Manābi' Islāmī*, vol. 2 (Tehran: Samt,1375A.H).

Bīshārat, Muḥammad 'Alī and Manīzhih Fīrūzī, 'Muqāyasah-yi Zanān va Mardān Nābārvar bar Ḥasab Sabk Delbastigī va Sāzish Ravānshinākhtī bā Bārdārī' in *Ravānshināsī va 'Ulūm Tarbiyatī Journal* (Tehran: University of Tehran, Vol. 33, No. 2, Fall & Winter 1382 A.H).

Bihishtī, Aḥmad, *Khānivādih dar Qur'ān* (Qum: Tarīqulquds Publications, 1361 A.H).

Carlson, J., *Family Therapy, Effective Guarantee*, (Khānivādih Darmānī, Tazmīn Kārāmad), translated by Shukūh Navvābīnizhād (Tehran: Anjuman Awliya' va Murabbiyān Jumhūrī Islāmī Iran, 1378 A.H).

Carlson N., *Physiology of Behavior*, (Massachusetts: Allyn and Bacon 1986).

Christensen, Arthur Emanuel, *Sassanid Persia* (Iran Dar Zamāne Sāsāniān), translated by Mujtabā Mīnavī (Tehran: Pazhūhishgāh 'Ulūm Insānī va Mutāli'āt Farhangī, 1370 A.H).

Dādsitān, Parīrukh and Maḥmūd, Mansūr, *Dīdgāh Piaget dar Gustarih-yi Taḥavvul Ravānī* (Tehran: Bi'that, 1374 A.H).

_______________, *Ravānshināsī-yi Genetic Vol. 2* (Tehran: Daryā Publications, 1372 A.H).

Daftar Hamkārī Ḥawzah va Dānishgāh, *Maktabhā-yi Ravānshināsī va Naqd ān,* vol. 1 (Tehran: Samt, 1369 A.H).

Dashtī, Muḥammad, *Nahj al-Ḥayāt, Farhang Sukhanān Fātima* (Qum: Amīr al-mu'minīn Research Institute Publications, 1372 A.H).

Deilamī, Aḥmad and Mas'ūd Āzarbāyjānī, *Akhlāqī Islāmī* (Qum: Ma'arif, 2000).

Dihkhudā, Alī Akbar, *Amthāl va Ḥikam* (Tehran: Sipihr, 1376 A.H).

___________ , *Lughatnāmih Dihkhudā* (Tehran: Tehran University Press, 1372 A.H).

Dilshād Tehranī, Mustafā, *Sīrih-yi Nabavī*, book 2 (Tehran: Ministry of Culture & Islamic Guidance Publications, 1372 A.H).

Di Matteo, M. Robin, *Health Psychology*, (Ravānshināsī Salāmat), translated by Sayyid Mehdī Mūsavī, et al (Tehran: Samt, 1378 A.H).

Dirāyatī, Mustafā, *Mu'jam Alfaẓ Ghurar al-Ḥikam wa Durar al-Kalim*, by Tamīmī āmidī (Qum: Daftar Tablīghāt Islāmī,1372 A.H).

Durant, William James, *The Story of Civilization: Rousseau and the Revolution*, (Tarikh Tamaddun, Rousou va Inqilab), translated by Ziā' al-Dīn 'Alāyi Tabātabā'ī, (Tehran: 'Ilmī va Farhangī Publications, 1370 A.H).

___________, *The Pleasures of Philosophy* (Lazzat Falsafi), translated by 'Abbās Zaryāb Khuyī, (Tehran: Franklin, 1354 A.H).

Durūdī Āhī, Nāhīd, 'Adam Tavāzun Nisbathā-yi Jinsī dar Izdivāj', in *Jam'īyyat Journal*, vol. 10, No. 41, Sāzmān Thabt Aḥvāl Kishvar, (1372 A.H).

Faqīhī, 'Alī Naqī, *Mushāvirih dar Āyiniyih 'Ilm va Dīn* (Qum: Daftar Intishārāt Islāmī, 1376 A.H).

Farhat, Karam Ḥilmī, *Ta'addud al-Zawjāt fī al-Adyān* (Cairo: Al- Afaq al-'Arabīyya, 2002).

Farīd Tunikābunī, Murtaḍā, *al-Ḥadīth, Rivāyāt Tarbiyatī az Maktab Ahl al-Bayt,* (Tehran: Daftar Nashr Farhang Islāmī, 1371 A.H).

______________ , *Nahj al-Fasāḥa* (Tehran: Daftar Nashr Farhang Islāmī, 1374 A.H).

Farjād, Muḥammad Ḥusayn, *Āsībshināsī-yi Ijtimā'ī-yi Sitīzihhā-yi Khānivādih va Talāq* (Tehran: Mansūrī Publications, 1372 A.H).

Fatḥī, Rasūl, *Relaxa Therapy* (Tehran: Umīd Inqilāb Publications, 1378 A.H).

Fattāl al-Nīshābūrī, Muḥammad ibn Aḥmad, *Rawḍa al-Wā'iẓīn* (Qum: Rāzī Publications, 1386 A.H).

Forsyth, D. R. *Our Social World*, 1st ed., (Brooks,/cole, 1995).

Ghazālī, Abū Ḥāmid, *Kīmiyā-yi Sa'ādat*, edited by Ḥusayn Khadīv Jam (Tehran: 'Ilmī va Farhangī Publications, 1386 A.H).

Ghubārī Bunāb, Bāqir, 'Bāvarhā-yi Madhhabī va Atharāt Ānhā dar Bihdāsht Ravān', *Andīshih va Raftār, Quarterly*, vol. 1, No. 4 (1374 A.H).

Goldenberg, I. and Goldenberg, H. *Family: An Overview.* (California: Wadsworth, Inc. Belmont, 1980).

Gush, Chianti 'Bad Omen Girls', (Dukhtarha-yi Bad Shugūn), translated by Ilhām Sādiqī, in *Kitāb Zanān*, No. 7 (1371 A.H).

Haiythamī, 'Alī ibn Abī Bakr, *Majma' al-Zawā'id wa Manba' al-Fawa'id* (Beirut: Dār al-Kutub al-'Ilmīyya, 1408 A.H).

Hājī-Dih Ābādī, Muḥammad 'Alī , *Proceedings of the International Scientific Applied Conference on the Various Aspects of Criminal Policies towards Narcotic Drugs* (Tehran: I.R. Iran Gazette, 1379 A.H).

Hakīmbāshī, Ḥasan, 'Ayah-yi Nushūz va ḍarb az Nigāhī Dīgar', in *Pazhūhish-ha-yi Qur'ānī*, vol. 7, Nos. 28-27 (Qum: Daftar Tablīghāt Islāmī, 1380 A.H).

Haqdūst, 'Alī Akbar et al, 'Barrasī-yi Dīdgāh Dānishjūyān 'Ulūm Pizishkī Pīrāmūn 'Avāmil Mu'aththir dar Izdivāj', in *Andīshih va Raftār, Quarterly*, vol. 2, No. 3 (1374 A.H).

Hāshimī Rafsanjānī, Akbar et al, *Tafsīr Rāhnamā* (Qum: Daftar Tablīghāt Islāmī, 1373 A.H).

Hay Lee. J. *Family Psychotherapy and Religion*, (Ravān Darmānī Khānivādih), translated by Bāqir Sanā'ī, (Tehran: Amīr Kabīr Publications, 1377 A.H).

Hergenhan, B. R. and Elson, Mathew. H., *An Introduction of Learning Theories*, translated by 'Alī Akbar Sayf (Tehran: Dānā Publications, 1374 A.H).

Hop Walker, L, 'Religion gives Meaning to Life', (Dīn bi Zindigī Ma'ana Mibakhshad) translated by A'azam Puyā, in *Naqd va Nazar Journal*, vol. 8, Nos. 1-2(1382 A.H).

Ḥusaynī, 'Alī Akbar, *Akhlāq dar Khānivādih* (Tehran: Islāmī Publications, 1369 A.H).

Ḥusaynī, Hājar and Sayyidah Fātima Muḥibbī, 'Gharb va Khānivādih-hā-yi Takvālidi', in *Kitāb Zanān*, vol. 6, No. 24 (Summer1383 A.H).

Ḥusaynī, K, "Nigāhī be Padīdi Fāl va Fālgīrī dar Iran", in *Irandukht*, No. 11 (1381 A.H).

Ḥusaynīzādih, Sayyid 'Alī , *Sīreh-yi Tarbiyatī Payāmbar va Ahl al-Bayt, vol. 1, Tarbiyat Farzand* (Qum: Pazhūhishkadih Howzeh va Dānishgāh, 1380 A.H).

I'zāzī, Shahlā, *Khānivādih va Tilivīziyun* (Mashhad: Marandīz Publications, 1373 A.H).

_____________ , *Khushūnat Khānivādigī "Zanān Kutak Khurdih"* (Tehran: Sāli Publications, 1380 A.H).

Ibn Abī al-Ḥadīd, *Sharḥ Nahj al-Balāghah*, edited by Muḥammad Abū'l Faḍl Ibrāhīm (Beirut: Dār al- 'Iḥyā' al-Turāth al- 'Arabī, 1385 A.H).

Ibn Mājah, Muḥammad ibn Yazīd, *Sunan* ibn *Māja*, Edited by Muḥammad Fu'ād 'Abd al-Bāqī (Beirut: Dar 'Iḥyā' al-Turath al-'Arabī, 1395 A.H).

Ibn Sa'd, *al-Ṭabaqāt al-Kubrā*, edited by Muḥammad 'Abd al-Qādir 'Aṭā (Beirut: Dār al- Kutub al- 'Ilmīyyah, 1410 A.H).

Ibn Shu'ba al-Ḥarrānī, al-Ḥasan ibn 'Alī, *Tuḥaf al-'Uqūl 'an Āl al-Rasūl* (Beirut: Mu'assasah al-A'lamī li al-Maṭbū 'āt, 1974).

Ibn Sīnā, Ḥusayn ibn 'Abdullāh, *Tadābīr al- Manāzil wa al-Sīyāsāt al-Ahlīyya*, (Baghdād: al-Fallāḥ Publications, 1929).

__________ , *al-Qānūn fī al-Tibb*, translated by 'Abd al-Raḥmān Sharafkandī, 6th impression (Tehran: Surūsh Publications, 1370A.H).

Iḥsānbakhsh, Sādiq, *Āthār al- Sādiqain* (Qum: Dar al-'Ilm, 1366 A.H).

__________ , *Naqsh Dīn dar Khānivādih (*Rasht: Jāvīd Publications, 1374 A.H).

Isfahānī, Muḥammad Mehdī, *Taghdhiyi bā Shīr Mādar va Mas'ale-yi Khīshāvandī* (Tehran: Dānishgāh 'Ulūm Pizishkī Iran, 1374 A.H).

Isfahānī, Sayyid Abī al-Ḥasan, *Wasīla al-Najāt ma'a Ta'āliq al-Imām al-Khumeinī*, (Tehran: Mu'assasah Tanzīm va Nashr Āthār Imām Khumeinī, 1380 A.H).

Ismā'īlī, 'Alī , *Javān, Angīzih va Raftār Jinsī* (Tehran: Liqā' al-nūr Publications, 1381 A.H).

Jamāl, Ibrāhīm Muḥammad, *Ta'addud al-Zawjāt fī al- Islām (*Cairo: Dār al-I'tisām, 1404 A.H).

Javān, Ja'far, *Jughrāfiyā-yi Jam'īyyat Iran* (Mashhad: Jahād Dānishgāhī Publications, 1380 A.H).

Jazā'irī, Ghiyath al-Dīn, *I'jāz Khurākihā* (Tehran: Parastoo Publications, 1375 A.H).

Jazā'irī, Sayyid 'Abdullāh, *al-Tuḥfa al-Saniyyah fī Sharḥ al-Nukhbah al-Muḥsiniyyah,* ([n.d., n.p.], 1353 A.H).

Jung, Carl Gustav, *Psychology and Religion*, (Ravānshināsī va Dīn), translated by Fu'ād Rawhānī (Tehran: Shirkat Nashr Kitāb-hā-yi Jibi, 1370 A.H).

Kadīvar, Parvīn, *Ravānshināsī Tarbiyatī* (Tehran: Samt, 1379 A.H).

Keiniyā, Mehdī, *'Avāmil Ijtimā'ī Talāq* (Qum: Matbū'āt Dīnī, 1373 A.H).

Kār, Mihrangīz, *Bachchehāye I'tiyād* (Tehran: Rawshangarān va Mutāli'āt Zanān Publications, 1375 A.H).

Karīmīniyā, Muḥammad 'Alī , *Tarbiyat Ijtimā'ī, Raftārhā-yi Ijtimā'ī Pīshvāyān Islām* (Qum: Pārsāyān Publications, 1377 A.H).

Kāzimīpūr, Shahlā, *Barrisī Dimographic Taghyīr Sinn Izdivāj*, Thesis, University of Tehran, 1351 A.H.

Khāwjawī, Muḥammad, *Tarjumih Asfār Mullā Sadrā* (Tehran: Mawlā Publications, 1376 A.H).

Khānih Kūdak, *Ahkām mā va Kūdakān* (Qum: al-Hādī Publications, 1376 A.H).

Khudāpanāhī, Muḥammad Karīm, *Ravānshināsī-yi Physiologic* (Tehran: Samt, 1380A.H).

Khudāraḥīmī, Siyāmak et al, *Ravānshināsī-yi Zanān* (Tehran: Khatam Publications, 1379 A.H).

Khumeinī, Sayyid Rūhullāh, *Taḥrīr al-Wasīla* (Qum: Dār al-ʻIlm, 1362 A.H).

Majlisī, Muḥammad Bāqir, *Biḥār al-Anwār*(Beirut: Mu'assasah al-Wafā', 1983).

______________, *Ḥilyat al-Muttaqīn* (Qum: Hijrat, 1380 A.H).

Makārim Shīrāzī, Nāsir, *Tafsīr Nimūnih*, vol. 1 (Tehran: Dār al-Kutub al-Islāmīyyih, 1368 A.H).

Mantiqī, Murtaḍā, *Chikīdi-yi Tāzih-hā-yi Taḥqīq dar Dānishgāhha va Marākiz Taḥqīqātī-yi Iran*, No. 28, (Ministry of Science, Research & Technology, 1381 A.H).

Marasumi, Radmikako, 'Human Rights and Violence Against Women', in *Farzānih Magazine*, No. 8, (Bānū Publications,1375 A.H).

Maʻrūf al-Ḥasanī, Hāshim, *Zindigī Davāzdah Imām*, translated by Muḥammad Rakhshandih (Tehran: Amīr Kabīr, 1373 A.H).

Maslow, Abraham, *Motivation and Personality*, (Angīzih va Shakhsiyyat), translated by Aḥmad Riḍvānī, (Mashhad: Āstān Quds Raḍavi Publications, 1367 A.H).

Mason, Paul Henry, *Child Development and Personality*, (Rushd va Shakhsiyyat Kūdak), translated by Mahshīd Yāsāyī (Tehran: Pāyā Publications, 1368 A.H).

Mazāhirī, Muḥammad 'Alī et al, 'Muqāyasah-yi Bihdāsht Ravānī dar Zawjhāyi Jashnhā-yi Izdivāj Dānishjū'ī va Zawjhā-yi 'Ādī', in *Anjuman Irani-yi Ravānshināsī Quarterly*, vol. 7, No. 1 (1382 A.H).

Michelle, Thomas, *Christian Theology*, (Kalami Masīḥī), translated by Ḥusayn Tawfīqī (Qum: Markaz Mutāliʻāt va Taḥqīqāt Adyān va Madhāhib, 1377 A.H).

Mihrīzī, Mehdī, *Shakhsiyyat va Huqūq Zan* (Tehran: 'Ilmī va Farhangī Publications, 1382 A.H).

Mīr-Aḥmadīzādih, 'Alī Reḍā, 'Reḍāmandī-yi Zanāshuyī in *Andīshih va Raftār journal*, vol. 8, No. 32(1382 A.H).

Mīrkhānī, 'Izzat al-Sādāt, *Rūykardī Nuvīn dar Ravābit Khānivādih* (Tehran: Safir Subh, 1380 A.H).

Ministry of Culture & Islamic Guidance, *Arzish-hā va Nigarish-hā-yi Iranian*, pp. 38-39.

Minuchin, Salvador, *Family and Family Therapy*, (Khānivādih va Khānivādih Darmānī), translated by Bāqir Sanā'ī, (Tehran: Amīr Kabīr Publications, 1375 A.H).

Minuchin, S. and H.C. Fishmand, *Family Therapy Techniques*, (Harvard College, 1981).

Muḥammadī Reyshahrī, Muḥammad, *Ahl al-Bayt dar Qur'ān va Ḥadīth*, translated by Ḥamīd Reḍā Shaikhī, Ḥamīd Reḍā Āzhīr (Qum: Dār al-Ḥadīth, 1379 A.H).

_______________ , *Mīzān al-Ḥikmah*, translated by Ḥamīd Reḍā Shaikhī (Qum: Dar al- Ḥadīth, 1379 A.H).

Muḥibbī, Sayyidah Fātima , "The West and the Phenomenon of Single-Parent Families," translated by Hājar Ḥusaynī, Fātima Bakhtiārī, *Women*, issue 24.

Muḥsinī, Manūchihr and Pūr Reḍā Anvar, Abulqāsim, *Izdivāj va Khānivādih dar Iran* (Tehran: Arvan Publications, 1382 A.H).

Mūsavī, Ashraf al-Sādāt, 'Amalkard Nizām Khānivādih va Bihdāsht Ravānī A'zā-yi Khānivādih', in *Andīshih va Raftār Journal*, Nos. 22-23.

Mūsilī, Aḥmad ibn 'Alī , *Musnad Abī Ya'lā* (Beirut: Dār al- Kutub al-'Ilmīyyah, 1418 A.H).

Muslim ibn al-Hajjāj al-Qushayrī, *Saḥīḥ Muslim bi Sharḥ al-Nawawī* (Beirut: Dār al-Kitāb al- 'Arabī, 1987).

Mustafavī, Sayyid Javād, *Bihisht Khānivādih*, Quds Publications (Qum: Dār al-Fikr, 1372 A.H).

Muṭahharī, Murtaḍā, *Akhlāq Jinsī dar Islām va Jahān Gharb* (Qum: Daftar Intishārāt Islāmī, 1359 A.H).

____________, *Ta'līm va Tarbiyat az Naẓar Islām* (Qum: Sadrā Publications, 1372 A.H).

____________, *Mas'alih-yi Ḥijāb* (Qum: Sadrā Publications, 1368 A.H).

____________, *Niẓām Huqūq Zan dar Islām* (Qum: Sadrā Publications, 1371 A.H).

Muttaqī Hindī, 'Alā' al-Dīn, *al- Murshid ila Kanz al-'Ummāl fī Sunan al-Aqwāl wa'l Af'āl* (Beirut: Mu'assasah al- Risālah, 1409 A.H).

Najafī, Muḥammad Ḥasan, *Jawahir al-Kalām fī Sharḥ Sharā'i' al-Islām* (Tehran: Dār al-Kutub al-Islāmīyyah, 1362 A.H).

Narāqī, Mullā Aḥmad, *Mi'rāj al-Sa'ādah* (Tehran: Jāvidān Publications, n.d).

Narāqī, Mullā Mahdī, *Jāmi' al-Sa'ādāt* (Najaf: Matba'ah al-Najaf al-Ashraf, 1963).

Nīlīpūr, Mehdī, *Farhang Fātimiyyah* (Isfahān: Markaz Farhangī Shahīd Mudarris, 1380 A.H).

Nīshābūrī, Muḥammad ibn Ḥusayn, *Misbāḥ al-Sharī'a* (Qum: Imām Sādiq Publications, 1416 A.H).

Nīsī, 'Abd al-Kāzim et al, 'Muqāyasah-yi 'Amalkard Taḥsīlī, Salāmat Ravānī va Jismānī-yi Dānishāmūzān Pisar Fāqid Pidar va Vājid Pidar'in *'Ulūm Tarbiyatī va Ravānshināsī Journal of Shahīd Chamrān University*, vol. 8, Nos. 3-4(1380 A.H).

Nūrī-Tabarsī, Ḥusayn, *Mustadrak al-Wasā'il va Mustanbat al-Masā'il* (Beirut: Nashr Mu'assisah ahlulbayt li Iḥyā' al-Turāth, 1988).

Perin, Lawrence. A, *Personality Psychology, Theory and Research* (Ravānshināsī-yi Shakhsiyyat, Nazariyah va Taḥqīq), translated by Muḥammad Ja'far Javādi and Parvīn Kadīvar (Tehran: Mu'assisah Khadamātī Farhangī Rasā, 1372 A.H).vol.2, pp. 221-223.

Qā'imī, 'Alī , *Niẓām Ḥayāt Khānivādih dar Islām* (Tehran: Anjuman Awliya' va Murabbiyān Jumhūrī Islāmī Iran, 1368 A.H).

Qarā'atī, Muḥsin, *Tafsīr Nūr*, vol. 7 (Qum: Markaz Farhangī Darshāyī az Qur'ān, 1380 A.H).

Qurayshī, 'Alī -Akbar, *Qāmūs Qur'ān* (Tehran: Dār al-Kutub al-Islāmīyyah, 1375 A.H).

Qumī, Sheikh 'Abbās, *Safīnat al-Biḥār wa Madīnah al-Ḥikam wa'l Āthār* (Qum: Dār al- Uswah, 1422 A.H).

_____________ , *Mafātīḥ al-Jinān*, translated by Ilāhī Qumshi'ī (Qum: Masjid Jamkaran Publications, 1381 A.H).

_______________ , *Muntahā al-Āmāl* (Tehran: Hijrat Publications, 1370 A.H).

Ra'ūf, Hiba, *Mushārikat Siyāsī-yi Zan*, translated by Muḥsin Ārmīn (Tehran: Qatrih Publications, 1377 A.H).

Rashīd Reḍā, Muḥammad, *Al-Minār fī Tafsīr al-Qur'ān* (Beirut: Dār al-Fikr, 1303 A.H).

Rāstī, Zahrā and Akram Ismā'īlī, *Inḥilāl Nikāḥ bi Vāsitih-yi 'Ayb*, (Articles 1121-1125, Iranian Civil Code) (Tehran: Safir Subh, 1380 A.H).

Report of the United Nations, Special Repot *Violence Women* (1995).
Rusenbaom, Heidi, *Family as a Structure Against Society* (Tehran: Markaz Nashr Dānishgāhī, 1367 A.H).

Sadr, Sayyid Mūsā, 'Tanbīh Badanī-yi Zan dar Nigāhhā-yi Gūnāgūn' in *Pazhūhish-ha-yi Qur'ānī*, Daftar Tablīghāt Islāmī, Vol. 7, Nos. 27-28 (1380 A.H).

Sadūq, Muḥammad ibn 'Alī , *al-Amālī* (Qum: Mu'assisah al-Bi'thah, 1417 A.H).

____________, *Al-Khisāl* (Qum: Intishārat Islāmī, 1362 A.H).

_____________, *Man lā Yahḍuruh al-Faqīh* (Beirut: Dār al-Aḍwā', 1413 A.H).

Saif, Sūsan, *Te'urī-yi Rushd Khānivādih* (Tehran: Al-Zahrā University Press, 1368 A.H).

Sajjādī, Sayyid Ibrāhīm, 'Qur'ān va Mushārikat Ijtimā'ī Zanān', in *Pazhūhishhāyi Qur'ānī*, Daftar Tablīghāt Islāmī, vol. 7, Nos. 27-28 (1380 A.H).

Safā'ī, Sayyid Ḥusayn and Asadullāh Imāmī, *Mukhtasar Huqūq Khānivādih* (Tehran: Dādgustar Publications, 1376 A.H).

Sālārī, Muḥammad, *Siḥr va Jādūgarī* (Qum: Mashhūr Publications, 1380 A.H).

Sālārīfar, Muḥammad Reḍā, 'Marzhā dar Khānivādih az Dīdgāh Islām va Maktab Sākhtnigar', in *Ḥawzah va Dānishgāh Quarterly*, (1381 A.H).

______________, *Muqāyasah-yi Khānivādih Darmānī-yi Minuchin ba Dīdgāh Islām dar Khānivādih*, M.A. Thesis, Pazhūhishkadih Ḥawzah va Dānishgāh, 1379 A.H.

______________, Hamsarguzīnī dar Andīshih-yi Dīnī, *Kitāb Zanān*, No. 25 (1383 A.H).

Sārūkhānī, Bāqir, *Muqaddamih-yi bar Jāmi'i Shināsī-yi Khānivādih* (Tehran: Surūsh, 1370 A.H).

Satir, Jane, *Making a Man in Family Psychology*, (Ādam Sāzī Dar Ravānshināsī-yi Khānivādih), translated by Bihrūz Bīrashk, (Tehran: Rushd Publications, 1370 A.H).

Sayyid Mīrzā'ī, Sayyid Muḥammad, *Jam'īyyat Shināsī-yi 'Umūmī* (Tehran: Shahīd Bihishtī University, 1381 A.H).

Siddīq-Awra'ī, Ghulām-Reḍā, Jāmi'i Shināsī-yi Masā'il Ijtimā'ī Javānān (Mashhad: Jahād Danishgāhī Publications, 1374 A.H).

Sharaf al-Dīn, Sayyid Ḥusayn, *Tabyīn Jāmi'i Shinākhtī-yī Mahriyyih* (Qum: Imām Khumainī Educational & Research Institute, 1380 A.H).

Shafī'ī Māzandarānī, Sayyid Muḥammad, *Rāz Khushbakhtī* (Qum: Mashhūr Publications, 1377 A.H).

Sharīf Raḍī, *Nahj al- Balāghah,* translated by Muḥammad Ja'far Imāmī and Muḥammad Reḍā Āshtiānī (Qum: Amīr al-mu'minīn School, 1375 A.H).

Shukrkun, Ḥusayn et al, *Makātib Ravānshināsī*, vol. 2 (Tehran: Daftar Hamkārī Ḥawzah va Dānishgāh & Samt, 1372 A.H).

Siemon, F. B., *Key Concepts and Theories in Family Therapy*, translated and Compiled by: Sa'īd Pīrmurādī (Tehran: Humām Publications, 1379 A.H).

Subhānī, Ja'far, *Nizām al-Nikāḥ fī'l Sharī'a al-Islāmiyya al-Gharrā* (Qum: Imām Sādiq Publications, 1417 A.H).

Tabātabā'ī, Sayyid Muḥammad Ḥusayn, *Tafsīr al-Mīzān*, translated by Sayyid Muḥammad Bāqir Mūsavī Hamadānī (Qum: Jāmi'ah Mudarrisīn Publications, 1374 A.H).

____________, *Sunan al-Nabī*, translated by Muḥammad Hādī Fiqhī (Qum: Islāmiyyah Publications, 1375 A.H).

____________, *Shī'a dar Islām* (Qum: Daftar Intishārāt Islāmī, 1373 A.H).

Tabātabā'ī Yazdī, Muḥammad Kāzim, *al-'Urwa al-Wuthqā* (Beirut: Mu'assasah al-A'lamī lil-Maṭbū'āt, 1409 A.H).

Tabrisī, Abū Nasr Ḥasan ibn Faḍl, *Makārim al-Akhlāq* (Qum: Manshūrāt al-Raḍī, 1972).

Tabrisī, Faḍl ibn Ḥasan, *A'lām al-Warā bi A'lām al-Hudā* (Qum: Dār al-Kutub al-Islāmīyyah, [n.d.]).

_______________, *Majma' al-Bayān fī Tafsīr al-Qur'ān* (Beirut: Dār al-Ma'rifah, 1988).

Tannen, Deborah, *Speech Differences in Women and Men*, (Tafavuthā-yi Kalāmi Dar Zan va Mard), translated by Qarāchidāghī, Zuhrih Futūhī (Tehran: Awḥadī Publications, 1375 A.H).

Tirmidhī, Muḥammad ibn 'Isā, *al-Jāmi' al-Saḥīḥ(huwa Sunan al-Tirmidhī),* edited and commented on by Aḥmad Muḥammad Shākir (Beirut: Dār 'Iḥyā' al-Turāth al-'Arabī, n.d.).

Tūsī, Khawajah Nasīr al-Dīn , *Akhlāq Nāsirī*, edited and annoted by Mujtabā Mīnavī and 'Alī Reḍā Haidarī (Tehran: Khārazmī Publications, 1360 A.H).

Tyber, Edward, *Children of Divorce*, (Bachchi-ha-yi Talāq), translated by Tūrāndukht Tamaddun (Tehran: Chikāmih Publications, 1372 A.H).

'Ulwān ,'Abdullāh Nāsiḥ, *Ta'addud al-Zawjāt fī al-Islām*(Beirut: Dār al-Islām,1988).

'Uthmān Nijāti, Muḥammad, *Qur'ān and Psychology*, (*Qur'ān* va Ravānshināsī), translated by 'Abbās 'Arab, (Mashhad: Āstān Quds Raḍavi Publications, 1376 A.H).

Vakīlī, Mahnāz, *Nikāḥ Muvaqqat az Kitāb Zubda al-Bayān*, M.A. Thesis, Islamic Azād University Central (Tehran: 1375 A.H).

Wahhābī, Zahrā, *Naqshi TV dar Bizihkārī Atfāl va Nawjavānān*, M.A. Thesis, Islamic Azād University, Narāq Branch (Tehran: 1379 A.H).

Zamakhsharī, Maḥmūd ibn 'Umar, *Al-Kashshāf 'an al-Ḥaqā'īq al-Ghawāmiḍ al-Tanzīl* (Beirut: Dār al-Kitāb al-Qurā, 1407 A.H).

Zamīrī, Muḥammad-Reḍā, "Mashrūb Khārī Jurmī 'Alayhi Zanān va Khānivādih," in *Kitab Zanān*, issue 20.

Zeiger, Johnnie, 'Superiority of the Male Child', (Bartarī Farzand Pisar), translated by Zuhrih Dihqānī in *Zanān Journal*, No. 50.

Zuḥailī, Wahba Mustafā, *al-Tafsīr al-Munīr fī'l 'Aqīda wa'l Sharī'a wa'l Manhaj*, (Beirut: Dār al-Fikr al-Mu'āṣir, 1411 A.H).

INDEX

A

'Abdūs, 102, 181, 183
'Arūsī-Ḥuwaizī, 102
'Askarī, Ḥusayn, 154, 155
'Ātif Wahīd, Muḥammad Kāzim,
A'rāfī, 3, 35
Abraham, 35, 111, 123, 145, 168
Ackner, R. A, 66
Ādāb al-Ḥayāt al-Zawjiyyah, 66
Adams, Paul, 69
afterlife, 16, 27, 29, 47, 55, 82, 98, 110, 111, 112, 114
Ahl al-Bayt dar Qur'ān va Ḥadīth, 184
Aḥmadī, Muḥammad Reḍā, 69, 70
Aḥmadī, Sayyid Aḥmad, 37
Aḥmadī-Abharī, 'Alī, 124
Akhlāq Nāsirī, 35
Akhlāq dar Khānivādih, 129, 157
Akhlāq Jinsī dar Islām va Jahān Gharb, 35, 66
Akk, Khālid 'Abd al-Raḥmān, 66
al-Mustafa International Research Institute (M.I.R.I.), IX
al-Burhān fī Tafsīr al-Qur'ān, 101
al -Durr al-Manthūr, 38, 127
al-Ghadīr, 70
al-Ḥadīth, 39, 99, 100, 101, 128, 185
al-Haythamī, 'Alī ibn Abī Bakr, 66
al-Ḥurr al-'Āmilī, Muḥammad ibn Ḥasan, 35, 36, 37, 38, 39, 40, 41, 65, 66, 67, 68, 69, 70, 98, 99, 100, 101, 102, 103, 104, 124, 126, 127, 128, 129, 155, 157, 158, 159, 180, 181, 183, 184, 185
al-Jāmi' al-Saḥīḥ (Sunan al-Tirmidhī), 102
al-Maḥajja al-Bayḍā' fī Tahdhīb al-'Iḥyā', 35, 102
al-Sunan al-Kubrā, 99
al-Suyūtī, Jalāl al-Dīn, 38, 127
Amānī, Mehdī, 36, 37
Āmidī, 'Abd al-Vāhid, 126, 128, 129, 155, 156
Amīnī,'Abd al-Ḥusayn, 70
Ansārī, 'Udhrā, 156, 183
Ārā'i Dānishmandān Musalmān dar T'alīm va Tarbiyat va Mabānī-yi Ān, 35, 189

INDEX

Argyle, 68
Arzish-hā va Nigarish-hā-yi Iranian, 38, 196
Āzād, Paimān, 36
Ādharbāyjānī, Mas'ūd, 37, 38, 39

B

Baḥrānī, Sayyid Hāshim, 101, 125, 129
Banī-Hāshimī,Sayyid Muḥammad Ḥasan, 36
Bānkīpūr Fard, Amīr Ḥusayn, 98
Barker, Phillip, 70, 103
Baron, R. A, 104
Barrisī Dimographic Taghyīr Sinn Izdivāj, 37
Basic Family Therapy, 70, 103
behaviour, 2, 11, 12, 16, 19, 20, 22, 25, 27, 33, 34, 46, 49, 54, 55, 56, 59, 64, 76, 79, 80, 93, 95, 98, 103, 107, 110, 112, 113, 115, 118, 119, 120, 123, 134, 135, 136, 137, 138, 139, 140, 141, 143, 147, 148, 152, 163, 168, 172, 173, 176, 177, 178
Beihaqī, Aḥmad ibn al-Ḥusayn, 99
belief in God, 27, 107
belief in the afterlife, 110
Bernstein, 127
Bīshārat, Muḥammad 'Alī, 68
Biḥār al-Anwār, 8, 35, 36, 37, 38, 39, 40, 41, 65, 66, 67, 69, 70, 71, 98, 99, 100, 101, 102, 103, 104, 125, 126, 127, 128, 129, 155, 156, 157, 158, 180, 181, 182, 183, 184
Bihishtī, Aḥmad, 159
Bīriyā, 99, 101, 125
blood relations, 13, 14
Buré, Jean, 143

C

Carlson, J, 154, 157
Carlson, N. R, 98
Catholics, 26
chastity, 11, 27, 47, 52, 79, 96, 98
Child Development and Personality, 195
child's development, 54, 79
Children of Divorce, 69, 159
children, , 1, 2, 8, 9, 11, 12, 14, 15, 16, 17, 22, 27, 31, 33, 34, 35, 45, 51, 53, 54, 55, 62, 63, 64, 78, 79, 80, 81, 82, 83, 84, 85, 88, 90, 91, 92, 94, 95, 102, 110, 113, 117, 118, 119, 120, 122, 123, 133, 135, 137, 138, 139, 145, 146, 153, 154, 166, 167, 168, 169, 170, 171, 172, 173, 174, 175, 176, 177, 178, 179, 180, 181, 183
Christian Theology, 36
contentment, 114
cross, 26, 60, 111
cultural taboo, 45

D

Daftar Hamkārī Ḥawzah va Dānishgāh, 65
Dashtī, Muḥammad, 183
day of judgment, 110
definition of the f'y, 14
Dihkhudā, 'Alī Akbar, 129
Dilshād Tehranī, 182
Di Matteo, M, 125, 126, 159
Dirāyatī, Mustafā, 126
divine mission, 109

E

economic factors, 137
economic rules of Islām, 14
education, 16, 21, 25, 29, 33, 45, 82, 136, 143, 166
employment, 9, 25, 29, 33, 138, 142
ethics, 2, 7, 107

F

Fayḍ al-Kāshānī, 11, 188

faith, 9, 19, 24, 28, 29, 30, 32, 33, 52, 59, 77, 93, 95, 107, 113, 115, 122, 124, 141, 143
familial relationships, 8
Families and Family Therapy, 35, 98, 99, 100, 103
families in Islām, 168
family, 1, 14, 69, 86, 89, 98, 101, 102, 107, 112, 122, 143, 147, 155, 157, 163, 173, 174, 181, 184
family and society, 94
family disputes, 141
family economy, 2, 62, 150, 163
family hierarchy, 13, 146
family in Islām, 15, 47, 78, 98, 175, 179
family life, 2, 7, 9, 11, 13, 28, 30, 34, 51, 56, 57, 107, 110, 113, 114, 135, 145, 148, 164, 166, 170, 173, 175, 178
family members, 13, 16, 17, 31, 32, 75, 90, 91, 92, 94, 108, 112, 113, 114, 115, 116, 117, 120, 122, 123, 133, 137, 138, 146, 150, 163, 167, 173, 174, 175, 176, 177
family models, 2
family problems, 1, 2, 56, 78, 91, 115, 133, 142, 143, 145, 150, 152
Family Psychotherapy, 102
family relations, 8, 55, 56, 57, 59, 62, 63, 151, 178
family relationships, 16, 45, 50, 55, 56, 59, 60, 61, 62, 63, 64, 76, 98, 117, 136, 167, 174
family system, 1, 55, 76, 84, 86, 90, 95, 135, 167, 175
family ties, 60, 61 62, 85
Faqīhī, 'Alī -Naqī, 159
Farhang Fātimiyyah, 183
Farīd Tunikābunī , 39, 65, 99, 100, 101, 128, 157, 185
Farjād, Muḥammad Ḥusayn, 154, 155, 156, 159
Fatḥī Āshtiānī, 3
Fatḥī, Rasūl, 67
Fātima Zahrā, 28, 35, 84, 123, 168, 169, 171, 172, 183
Fattāl al-Nīshābūrī, Muḥammad ibn Aḥmad, 72
first-level family, 15
Fīrūzī, Manīzhih, 68
Forsyth, D. R, 35
France, 143
Freud, 45, 46
friendship, 12, 18, 21, 31, 54, 85, 95, 117, 120, 150, 178
Furū' Kāfī, 39, 180, 185

G

generosity, 116
Gharavī, Sayyid Muḥammad, 2
Ghazālī, Abū-Hāmid, 9, 35
Ghurar al-Ḥikam wa Durar al-Kalim, 126, 128, 129, 155, 156
God's love, 19
Goldenberg, H, 35
Goldenberg, I, 35
grandparents, 14, 15, 62, 98, 174, 175
guardianship, 15, 88, 89, 94

H

hadiths, 8, 95, 176
Hājī Dih Ābādī, Muḥammad 'Alī, 157
Ḥaqdūst, 'Alī -Akbar, 39
Hay-Lee, J, 86, 102
Health Psychology, 68, 124, 125, 126, 159
heaven, 7, 60, 62, 80
hell, 16, 19, 95, 111, 149
ḥijāb (the Islamic veil), 63, 96, 178
honesty, 112

Hope Walker, L, 125
household (*Ahl al-Bayt*), 1, 2, 8, 25, 27, 75, 87, 92, 95, 167, 168, 173, 177
human community, 1, 12, 19
human relationships, 138, 175
humanities, IX, 7
Ḥusaynīzādih, 69, 157, 182, 183, 184
Ḥusaynī, 'Alī Akbar, 129
husband and wife, 2, 8, 9, 11, 12, 13, 17, 18, 23, 27, 28, 30, 31, 45, 49, 50, 51, 52, 53, 56, 57, 58, 59, 75, 76, 77, 78, 79, 91, 92, 93, 95, 96, 107, 112, 117, 119, 120, 134, 135, 136, 137, 139, 140, 141, 142, 144, 146, 147, 151, 152, 153, 166, 174, 176, 178

I

Ibn Abī al-Ḥadīd, 125, 129
Ibn Sīnā, Ḥusayn ibn 'Abdullāh (Avicenna), 8, 9, 35, 67
Iḥsānbakhsh, Sādiq, 128, 159
Imām 'Alī, 28, 61, 64, 87, 100, 126, 150, 168, 169, 171, 172, 180, 183, 184
Imām Bāqir, 29, 123
Imām Ḥasan, 184
Imām Ḥusayn, 102
Imām Jawād, 32, 184
Imām Kāẓim, 122
Imām Reḍā, 32, 184
Imām Sādiq, 71, 128, 169, 184
Imamate, 109
Imāmī Asadullāh, 102, 199
inheritance, 60, 167
Inḥilāl Nikāḥ bi Vāsitih-yi 'Ayb, 66
intimate, 51, 95, 96, 113, 127, 173
Iran , 1, 20, 22, 24, 25, 135, 136, 137, 138, 157, 180
Iranian civil code, 87
Iranian culture, 165
Iranian family, 150
Iranian TV, 137
Isfahānī, Sayyid Abū al-Ḥasan, 158
Islamic Revolution, 165
Islamic teachings, 2, 19, 24, 27, 49, 56, 60, 75, 92, 139, 150, 151, 168
Islamic texts, 2, 7, 18, 19, 30, 46, 51, 54, 77, 114, 134, 135, 137, 140, 164, 177
Ismā'īlī, Javān, 65
I'zāzī, Shahlā, 155, 158
Izdivāj va Khānivādih dar Iran, 37

J

Jamāl, Ibrāhīm-Muḥammad, 35
Jāmi'i Shināsī-yi Masā'il Ijtimā'ī Javānān, 37, 180
Javān, Angīzih va Raftār Jinsī, 65
Javān, Ja'far, 37
Jawāhir al-Kalām, 36, 39, 158
Jilvihāyi Raftārī-yi Ḥaḍrat Zahrā, 183
Jesus Christ, 52
Jews, 26
jihād, 47, 57, 78, 79, 177
Jughrāfiyā-yi Jam'īyyat Iran, 194
Judgment Day, 111
Jung, Carl Gustav, 125

K

Kāfī, 36, 37, 38, 39, 65, 69, 70, 71, 72, 99, 100, 101, 104, 124, 125, 126, 127, 128, 129, 155, 156, 180, 181, 182, 183, 184
Kanz al-'Ummāl, 40, 124, 126, 156, 182
Kār, Mihrangīz, 156
Kashshāf, 67
Kāzimīpūr, Shahlā, 37
Kīmiyā-yi Sa'ādat, 35
Kerman, 141
Key Concepts and Theories in Family Therapy,

35, 67, 69, 98, 102, 157, 159, 184, 185
Khājavī, Muḥammad, 65
Khānivādih dar Qur'ān, 159
Khānivādih va Tilivīziyun, 155
Khudāraḥīmī, Siyāmak, 100
Khumeinī, Sayyid Rūhullāh, 36, 66, 158
Khudāpanāhī, Muḥammad Karīm, 98
Kulaynī, Muḥammad ibn Ya'qūb, 36, 37, 38, 39, 65, 69, 70, 71, 72, 99, 100, 101, 104, 124, 125, 126, 127, 128, 129, 155, 156, 180, 181, 182, 183, 184, 185

L

love, 8, 9, 12, 13, 27, 31, 46, 50, 53, 65, 78, 81, 95, 108, 117, 118, 119, 120, 145, 148, 152, 156, 164, 165, 167, 170, 171, 172, 173, 175, 176, 178

M

Ma'rūf al-Ḥasanī, 181, 182, 183
ma'rūf, 76
Mabānī-yi Jam'īyyat Shināsī, 37
Mafātīḥ al-Janān, 72
Majlisī, 35, 36, 37, 38, 39, 40, 41, 65, 66, 67, 69, 70, 71, 98, 99, 100, 101, 102, 103, 104, 125, 126, 127, 128, 129, 155, 156, 157, 158, 180, 181, 182, 183, 184
Majma' al-Bayān, 66, 68, 158
Majma' al-Zawā'id, 66
Makārim al-Akhlāq, 38
Makārim Shīrāzī, Nāsir, 68, 123
Making Humans in Psychology of the Family, 65, 125, 126, 128, 154
Maktabhā-yi Ravānshināsī va Naqd ān, 65
Man lā yaḥḍaruh al-Faqīh, 129, 156, 182, 183
Mansūr, Maḥmūd, 68, 69, 101
Mantiqī, Murtaḍā, 157
marriage, 2, 7, 8, 9, 10, 11, 12, 14, 16, 17, 18, 19, 20, 21, 22, 23, 24, 25, 29, 30, 31, 32, 33, 34, 45, 46, 47, 48, 49, 50, 51, 52, 53, 54, 55, 58, 63, 69, 75, 76, 78, 85, 95, 96, 98, 109, 122, 134, 135, 138, 141, 149, 151, 152, 163, 164, 165, 166, 168, 169, 181
marriage ceremony, 8, 18, 19, 20, 169
Marriage Therapy, 127
marriageable age, 8
Mas'alih-yi Ḥijāb, 104
Maslow, Abraham, 40
Masnad ibn Ya'lā, 66
Mason, Paul Henry, 37
Mazāhirī, Muḥammad 'Alī , 3, 68
members, 2, 8, 14, 24, 58, 86, 89, 92, 107, 111, 117, 118, 119, 143, 171, 174, 175, 178
Mi'rāj al-Sa'ādah, 128, 157
Michel, Muḥammad, 36
Ministry of Culture & Islamic Guidance, 38
Minuchin, Salvador, 35, 86, 89, 98, 99, 100, 101, 103
Mīr-Aḥmadīzādih, 'Alī Reḍā, 154
Mīzān al-Ḥikmah, 39, 71, 100, 125, 128, 155, 156, 157
modern life, 1, 136
modern society, 150
moral, 2, 28, 52, 61, 94, 112, 113, 114, 115, 122, 138, 139, 143, 168, 169, 174, 178
morality, 1, 22, 28, 52, 54, 98, 169
Motivation and Personality, 40
mubāhala, 168
mubāshirat, 46
Muqaddamih-yi bar Jāmi'i Shināsī-yi Khānivādih, 35, 36, 37, 38
Muḥibbī, Sayyidah Fātima, 69
Muḥsinī, Manūchihr, 37, 180
Muḥammad Ḥanafiyyah, 102
Muḥammadī-Reyshahrī, 39, 71, 100, 125,

128, 155, 156, 157, 181, 183, 184
Muntahā al-Āmāl, 40, 99
Muṭahharī, Murtaḍā, 12, 35, 53, 66, 68, 103, 104, 158, 180
Mūsavī, Ashraf al-Sādāt, 185
Mushāvirih dar Āyiniyih 'Ilm va Dīn, 159
Mūsilī, Aḥmad ibn 'Alī, 66
Mustadrak al-Wasā'il, 37, 38, 40, 41, 66, 67, 68, 70, 99, 100, 101, 102, 126, 127, 128, 157, 158, 181, 184
Mustafavī, Sayyid Javād, 127, 128
Muttaqī Hindī, 'Alā' al-Dīn, 40, 124, 126, 156, 182
Mutual respect, 9

N

Nahj al-Balāghah, 37, 72, 104, 126, 127, 129, 155, 157, 181, 183, 184
Nahj al-Fasāḥa, 65, 99, 154, 157
Nahj al-Ḥayāt, 183
Najafī, Muḥammad-Ḥasan, 36, 36, 39, 158
Narāqī, Mullā Aḥmad, 37, 128, 158
Narāqī, Mullā Mahdī, 197
niḥlah, 164
Nīlīpūr, Mehdī, 183
non-family members, 94
Nonverbal Communication, 118
nuclear family, 55, 136, 137, 150, 167, 174
Nūr al-Thaqalain, 102
Nūrī-Tabarsī, Ḥusayn, 37, 38, 40, 41, 66, 67, 68, 70, 99, 100, 101, 102, 126, 127, 128, 157, 158, 181, 184

O

optimism, 113, 114
Organization for Researching and Composing University textbooks in the Humanities (S.A.M.T), IX
Our Precepts and the Children, 102
Our Social World, 35

P

Paradise, 61, 81, 111, 115, 121, 135
parents, 2, 7, 9, 12, 13, 14, 16, 18, 23, 24, 31, 34, 51, 54, 56, 57, 58, 59, 62, 63, 78, 79, 80, 81, 82, 83, 84, 85, 86, 87, 88, 90, 92, 93, 94, 95, 102, 109, 117, 118, 119, 120, 122, 133, 137, 139, 144, 146, 153, 154, 167, 173, 174, 175, 176, 177, 178
patience, 115, 116
peace, 8, 11, 18, 48, 49, 50, 51, 52, 54, 85, 88, 107, 111, 116, 120, 143, 150, 159, 166
peace of mind, 8, 50, 59, 107
Perin, Lawrence. A, 101
Personality Psychology, Theory and Research, 101
Physiology of Behavior, 98
piety, 27, 28, 30, 33, 47, 77, 129, 151, 169, 178
pray, 19, 54, 84, 123, 181
pregnant, 22, 79, 153, 164
Prophet Muḥammad, 1, 2, 7, 8, 16, 32, 35, 46, 53, 56, 61, 64, 72, 77, 79, 80, 81, 83, 84, 87, 92, 93, 95, 96, 97, 104, 109, 119, 120, 121, 123, 144, 148, 149, 152, 156, 163, 165, 168, 169, 170, 171, 173, 176, 181
Protestants, 26
psychological attributes, 27
Psychology and Religion, 125
Psychology of Fatherless Children, 69
Psychology of Women, 100, 103
puberty, 94
public morality, 98
Pure Family, 2

Q

Qā'imī, 'Alī, 104, 155, 158, 159
Qāmūs Qur'ān, 67
Qumī, Sheikh 'Abbās, 40, 72, 99

Qur'ān, 1, 8, 15, 16, 18, 19, 23, 28, 29, 32, 34, 35, 36, 37, 38, 39, 40, 41, 46, 48, 49, 50, 51, 53, 54, 55, 56, 60, 61, 62, 63, 64, 65, 66, 67, 68, 69, 70, 71, 72, 76, 78, 82, 83, 84, 87, 88, 92, 93, 94, 96, 97, 98, 99, 100, 101, 102, 103, 104, 107, 110, 112, 116, 117, 118, 119, 120, 123, 124, 125, 126, 127, 128, 129, 140, 142, 144, 147, 148, 149, 151, 155, 156, 157, 158, 159, 164, 167, 168, 169, 170, 171, 173, 180, 181, 182, 183, 184, 185
Qur'ānic principle, 154
Qur'ānic verse, 12, 29, 78
Qurayshī, 'Alī -Akbar, 101

R

rafath, 46
Ramaḍān, 48
Rashīd Reḍā, 36, 67, 68, 98, 102
Rāstī, Zahrā, 66
Ravānshināsī Nawjavānān va Javānān, 37
Ravānshināsī-yi Genetic, 101
Ravānshināsī-yi Ijtimāʿī ba Nigāhī bi Manābiʿ Islāmī, 37, 38, 39, 67, 68, 103, 104, 157
Ravānshināsī-yi Physiologic, 98
rayḥāna, 75
relationships, 1, 2, 8, 11, 13, 14, 16, 18, 20, 21, 46, 54, 55, 57, 58, 60, 62, 63, 76, 85, 90, 91, 96, 107, 108, 110, 113, 114, 116, 117, 118, 119, 120, 133, 136, 139, 140, 143, 145, 150, 163, 167, 170, 171, 174, 175, 176, 177
Relax Therapy, 67
religion, 7, 10, 19, 23, 25, 26, 28, 56, 64, 76, 79, 82, 85, 109, 113, 141, 143, 152
religious belief, 2, 25, 28, 29, 107, 109, 110, 115, 123, 140, 141, 179
religious ceremonies, 143
religious denomination, 25
religious duties, 19, 47, 77, 79, 122, 123, 139, 177
religious education, 109, 143
religious factors, 139
religious insight, 107
religious leaders, 8, 19, 20, 21, 27, 29, 30, 31, 32, 34, 36, 46, 47, 49, 52, 54, 55, 56, 57, 59, 60, 61, 62, 64, 75, 76, 77, 80, 83, 86, 87, 109, 110, 112, 113, 114, 115, 116, 118, 120, 121, 123, 129, 143, 144, 145, 148, 149, 150, 152, 156, 168, 169, 176
religious principles, 143, 144
religious texts, 1, 23, 47, 59, 84, 123
Research Institute of Ḥawzah and University (R.I.H.U), IX
resurrection, 60, 62, 63, 110, 111, 112, 143
reverence, 9
Rushd bā Nigarish bi Manābiʿ Islāmī, 99, 101
Rusenbaum, Heidi, 154

S

sadaqah, 164
Sadūq, Muḥammad ibn 'Alī, 125, 129, 156, 182, 183
Safāʾī, Sayyid Ḥusayn, 102, 159
Saif, Sūsan, 36
Sālārī, Muḥammad, 157
Sārūkhānī, 35, 36, 37, 38, 41
Satir, 65, 125, 126, 128, 154
second-level family, 15
Siddīq-Awraʿī, 37
Selection of Russell's Thoughts, Psychology of Marital Relations, 66
sexual act, 27, 48, 49, 50, 95, 140
sexual activity, 95
sexual corruption, 23, 52
sexual crimes, 46

sexual desires, 20, 21, 22, 23, 30, 45, 46, 47, 48, 49, 52, 53, 148
sexual deviation, 98
sexual disinclination, 102, 148, 149
sexual emotions, 134
sexual exchange, 48
sexual harassment, 96
sexual intercourse, 47, 48, 96, 159
sexual liaisons, 95
sexual matters, 10, 11, 45
sexual motivations, 24
sexual nature, 12, 95
sexual needs, 8, 22, 47, 50, 78, 96, 135, 174
sexual problems, 51, 147, 154
sexual relations, 66, 99, 147
sexual relationship, 20, 46, 47, 48, 49, 50, 53, 65, 95, 135, 139, 150, 164
sexual satisfaction, 18, 47, 66
sexual urges, 22
sexuality, 45, 46, 47, 48, 50, 53, 96
Sharaf al-Dīn, Sayyid Ḥusayn, 180
Sharḥ Nahj al-Balāghah, 125
Sharī'a, 20, 22, 77, 88
Shī'a dar Islām, 125
Siemon, F, B, 35, 67, 68, 69, 102, 157, 159, 184, 185
Siḥr va Jādūgarī, 157
sins, 30, 61, 62, 79, 95, 111, 114, 121, 178
Sīrih-yi Nabavī, 182
social life, 12, 133
Social Psychology, 104
social relationships, 18, 45, 55, 136, 137
society, 7, 9, 13, 14, 18, 21, 22, 32, 37, 53, 56, 63, 76, 78, 86, 95, 120, 135, 151
sociology of the family, 25, 31
states: Every people has a marriage, 36

T

Ta'addud al-Zawjāt fī al-Islām, 182
Ta'līm va Tarbiyat az Nazar Islām, 35, 68
Tabātabā'ī, Sayyid Muḥammad Ḥusayn, 11, 35, 39, 67, 68, 69, 70, 98, 103, 125, 129, 182, 183
Tabrisī, Faḍl ibn Ḥasan, 37, 38, 66, 68, 184
Tadābīr al-Manāzil, 35
Tafsīr al-Mīzān, 11, 35, 36, 39, 67, 68, 98, 102, 103, 129, 182
Tafsīr al-Minār, 36, 67, 68, 98, 102
Tafsīr Nimūnih, 68, 123
Taghdhiyi bā Shīr Mādar va Mas'ale-yi Khīshāvandī, 100
Taḥrīr al-Wasīla, 36
Tarbiyat Ijtimā'ī, Raftārhā-yi Ijtimā'ī Pīshvāyān Islām, 184
Tarjumih Asfār, 65
Tawḍīḥ al-Masā'il Marāji',36, 37, 38, 39
teachings of Islām, 8, 14, 16, 18, 19, 20, 22, 23, 27, 29, 31, 32, 33, 46, 47, 48, 49, 52, 55, 56, 57, 61, 62, 63, 64, 77, 79, 81, 85, 86, 87, 92, 93, 94, 96, 98, 114, 116, 117, 118, 119, 121, 137, 140, 141, 142, 143, 146, 150, 151, 153, 163, 166, 173, 174, 175, 176
Tirmidhī, Muḥammad ibn 'Isā, 102
Teyber, Edward, 69, 159
The Family as a Structure against Society, 129, 154
The Psychology of Happiness, 68
the United States, 143
third-level family, 15
Tūsī, Nasīr al-Dīn, 10, 11, 35

U

'Ulwān, 'Abdullāh Nāsiḥ, 182
'Urwah al-Wuthqā, 67, 69, 70

V
verbal communication, 117
Virgin Mary, 52

W
Wahhābī, Zahrā, 155
Wasā'il al-Shī'a, 8, 35, 36, 37, 38, 39, 40, 41, 65, 66, 67, 68, 69, 70, 98, 99, 100, 101, 102, 103, 104, 124, 126, 127, 128, 129, 155, 157, 158, 159, 180, 181, 183, 184, 185
wife's rights, 149, 150

Y
Yaḥyā 52
Yūsuf (Joseph), 97

Z
zakāt, 56
Zamakhsharī, Maḥmūd ibn 'Umar, 67
Zīndigī bidūni Iḥsās Gunāh, 36
Zuḥailī, 158

www.ingramcontent.com/pod-product-compliance
Lightning Source LLC
Chambersburg PA
CBHW021435080526
44588CB00009B/526
9781911361329